Challenging Anthropocene Ontology

Challenging Anthropocene Ontology

Modernity, Ecology and Indigenous Complexities

Elisa Randazzo and

Hannah Richter

BLOOMSBURY ACADEMIC
LONDON • NEW YORK • OXFORD • NEW DELHI • SYDNEY

BLOOMSBURY ACADEMIC
Bloomsbury Publishing Plc, 50 Bedford Square, London, WC1B 3DP, UK
Bloomsbury Publishing Inc, 1359 Broadway, New York, NY 10018, USA
Bloomsbury Publishing Ireland, 29 Earlsfort Terrace, Dublin 2, D02 AY28, Ireland

BLOOMSBURY, BLOOMSBURY ACADEMIC and the Diana logo are trademarks of
Bloomsbury Publishing Plc

First published in Great Britain 2024
Paperback edition published 2026

Cover design: Adriana Brioso
Cover image © *Ethnography*, 1939, © David Alfaro Siqueiros/SOMAAP/DACS 2023. The
Museum of Modern Art (MoMA), New York/Scala, Florence.

A catalogue record for this book is available from the British Library.

Library of Congress Cataloging-in-Publication Data

ISBN: HB: 978-0-7556-3467-5
PB: 978-0-7556-3471-2
ePDF: 978-0-7556-3469-9
eBook: 978-0-7556-3468-2

Typeset by Deanta Global Publishing Services, Chennai, India

For product safety related questions contact productsafety@bloomsbury.com.

To find out more about our authors and books visit www.bloomsbury.com and sign up for
our newsletters.

To Sascha, Eraj and Maya

Transparency no longer seems like the bottom of the mirror in which Western humanity reflected the world in its own image. There is opacity now at the bottom of the mirror, a whole alluvium deposited by populations, silt that is fertile but, in actual fact, indistinct and unexplored even today, denied or insulted more often than not, and with an insistent presence that we are incapable of not experiencing.

Édouard Glissant, *Poetics of Relation*

Contents

Acknowledgements

This book is the result of a creative co-authorship and friendship several years in the making. It is grounded in the authors' shared passion for radical critical interrogation beyond disciplinary boundaries and our desire to, in a play on Sara Ahmed's figure of the feminist killjoy, remain uncomfortable. Remaining uncomfortable is here taken to mean for our respective disciplines, as readers and commentators on the theories and scholarship we engage with, but also in the sense of our own willingness to ask and stay with uncomfortable questions rather than enjoying the comfort of scholarly certainties, in this case those surrounding the Anthropocene and its relationship to nonmodern 'others'. While this endeavour was both intellectually exciting and academically productive, the arguments, debates and insights at the core of this project proved challenging, transformative and profoundly political for both authors. For the personal support and intellectual inspiration that helped us in and through moments of challenge and vulnerability, we are grateful to each other first. But we would also like to extend our gratitude to colleagues, friends and family who all contributed to giving this speculative and, we hope, indeed uncomfortable intervention, which started as nothing more than an interesting idea spun out on a flight from Sofia to London, its tangible reality of black ink on white pages.

We would first like to thank our colleagues at the Critical Humanities and International Politics research group, Francesca Batzella, Ben Nutt, Ignasi Torrent, Ivor Sokolić, Pierre Parrouffe and Siobhan Bygate. Their collegiate aid and care eased our daily struggle of balancing the demands of the neoliberal university with those of this unwieldy book. Without them, this project would have neither been started nor completed. We are grateful to Ignasi Torrent, Adam Barker, David Chandler, Pol Bargués, Sara Raimondi and Valerie Waldow for engaging with the ideas and arguments of this book on various occasions and providing constructive and invaluable feedback, even when it was at times difficult to hear. Elisa Randazzo would like to thank the organizers of the 2019 EISA Annual Conference for the opportunity to host a panel that inspired our ideas. And UCL's STEaPP for support in the latter stages of this manuscript's production. Hannah Richter is extremely grateful for being invited to share and develop the draft for this book on two occasions. She thanks Tom Lundborg and Regan Burles for organizing the fascinating and intellectually stimulating workshop 'Geopolitics and Planetary Boundaries Workshop' in Sigtuna, Sweden, and all participants for their sharp and thoughtful engagement. She also extends her gratitude to Małgorzata Litwinowicz-Droździel for the opportunity to expose the book's fledgling draft to the interdisciplinary audience of the 'Time as a Category of Measurement, Transfer and Experience in 19th and early 20th century Europe' conference in Warsaw, Poland, and all participants for their valuable comments. In due recognition of their financial support for a workshop at the University of Hertfordshire, UK, in 2018 that laid the ground for the author's collaboration, we thank UACES. Chapter 2 was developed from the journal article 'The Politics of the Anthropocene: Temporality, Ecology, and Indigeneity' published in *International Political Sociology*. For the permission to use it for this book we would like to thank the journal as well as the publisher *Oxford University Press*.

In the years that lie between that fateful 2019 Sofia-London flight and the publication of this book, the authors encountered not only the challenges that come with thinking and writing a book together, but also those of a global pandemic, uncertain employment in a difficult academic job market and expanding families. Facing all of them at once would not have been possible without a never-ending stream of support and encouragement from friends and family. We are grateful to Waltraud, Peter, Dee, Barış and Tom, and to Maria Nivea, Davide, Paolo, the Rostaqis, the Tellaies, Cristina, Jessica, Elisabetta and Livia for those words of encouragement (and the occasional, necessary nagging), which have left their mark on these pages. Most importantly, to our closest, Sascha, Eraj and Maya, who suffered through (and rejoiced at) every turn of this with us. The invisible support net that they weave enables and safeguards our, occasionally treacherous, intellectual labour of love.

Introduction

Wither the Anthropocene

In 1999, geoscientist Paul Crutzen, who won the Nobel Prize in Chemistry for his research on the ozone layer, allegedly uttered the following words at a conference on Earth system science: 'Stop using the word Holocene . . . We're not in the Holocene anymore. We're in the [. . .] the [. . .] the Anthropocene!' (quoted in Davies 2018: 42). Following Crutzen's declaration, the concept of the Anthropocene was quickly adopted by geo- and environmental sciences to describe human-made changes in the ecological constitution of planet Earth so fundamental that they warrant classification as a new geological epoch. But mapping the Anthropocene's no longer brave new world did not remain a prerogative of the sciences. Over the past two decades, a vast and increasingly diverse body of social theory and empirical social research has been assembled under the conceptual umbrella of the Anthropocene. As Moore notes in the introduction to *Anthropocene or Capitalocene?*, 'the Anthropocene has become a buzzword that can mean all things to all people' (2016: 3). Viewed from a distance, Anthropocene accounts are unified by their shared interest in the ongoing environmental degradation caused by Anthropos as a geological force, its effects on resource attainment and redistribution, and its hastening impact on poverty and socio-economic development (Zalasiewicz et al. 2011; Moore 2016a; 2016b; Davies 2018; Dawson 2016; Hird 2017).

At the core of this Anthropocene discourse lies a shared concern for understanding what exactly has brought human societies face to face with ecological changes so profound that they warrant classification as a new Earth age. Against this background, the concept of the Anthropocene has breathed new life into sharp critiques of the extractive tendencies of capitalism, the insufficiency of techno-scientific solutions to climate change and the uneven spread of its effects on human and nonhuman communities alike. These critical perspectives are the central focus of this book. It will begin its exploration through a closer look at the existing Anthropocene literature in order to reveal the ontological presumptions and political implications at work here. Despite existing attempts at structuring overviews (Johnson and Morehouse 2014; Davies 2018; Wakefield 2018), the internal diversity of the literature makes it increasingly difficult to discern what exactly is at stake in the theoretical diagnosis of the Anthropocene. The concept initially promised an analytical framework to draw out the social, economic and political patterns that enabled human activities to leave a mark on Earth history. It increasingly also operates as a theoretical device that interrogates human-centrism as modernity's driving principle that underpins human advancement at the expense of the planet. More recently, a third dimension has been added to the complex body of Anthropocene scholarship: that of post-colonial critique (Povinelli 2016; 2021; Yusoff 2019; Danowski and Viveiros de Castro 2017). The compelling scholarship advancing the former offers sobering accounts of inequality, exploitation and rampant consumerist expansion, and has done much to highlight the socio-economic and political dimensions of climate change. It draws out how the same, marginalized communities facing the most severe effects of climate change today were also at the centre of structures of exploitation that served the political and economic expansion of European Empires that gave rise to the Anthropocene climate emergency.

This new, critical Anthropocene scholarship challenges its predecessors to rid themselves of the modern-Western presumption that the climate catastrophe constitutes an unprecedented challenge in the face of which the fight for survival has just begun for human communities. It opens Anthropocene theory to the radically different experiences of those who have been on the receiving end of existential threats much longer than modern societies have. In doing so, these perspectives bring to the fore the violence experienced by non-Western, colonized societies. But they also draw attention to the systems of governance that have enabled said societies to survive against the permanent threat of erasure, of which extreme climate events are but one expression. The experiences of marginalized communities have broken up the Anthropocene into what Kathryn Yusoff has termed 'a billion Black Anthropocenes' (2019). For a multiplicity of Anthropocenes, solutions can only ever be context-specific and contingent. Western attempts at mitigating ecological changes and their effects with the modern-liberal tools of planning, steering, managing and directing are not to interfere with non-Western communities that possess and exercise self-sustaining protocols that have long enabled them to cope, survive, and even thrive, in the face of extinction. Western societies can, at best, attempt to create their own versions of a relational, context-specific sustainability and resilient governance that has long been practised outside the West.

The new, critical Anthropocene theory realizes self-consciously that it is itself not value-free. Its origins in Western, Eurocentric social and political theory raise important questions about the suitability of employing its conceptual tools to engage with alternative ontologies. The encounter between the Anthropocene and its non-Western others has raised important questions about what happens not only to the ontological frameworks but also to the political claims and struggles of different political communities when they are forced under the conceptual umbrella of the Anthropocene, with its specific problem diagnosis and governmental solutions. In recent years, critical theoretical approaches to the Anthropocene have generated a host of interventions aimed at designing affirmative theories of action that highlight and support the particular political claims of marginalized communities in the Anthropocene, such as those over land, cultural- or ecological relations. In particular, this has taken the form of engagement with Indigenous communities (Gibson-Graham and Roelvnik 2009; Rival 2009; Haraway 2015, 2016; Danowski and Viveiros de Castro 2018). Indigenous cosmologies and political agendas often centre issues of ecological relations to land and other nonhumans, and Indigenous communities have long been existentially threatened by the encroachment of human-made climate change. Western climate activism has sought to open up to Indigenous experiences in order to broaden its perspectives on the effects and potential mitigation of climate change, but also with the expressed aim of finding governmental solutions to environmental issues that can work for an uneven planet. As the youth-led environmental movement Fridays4Future tweeted with reference to a speech by Angela Davis in 2022, 'if you say climate justice, you cannot ignore anti-colonialism'.[1] Though there are substantial differences between critical Anthropocene theory and Western environmental activism in the twenty-first century, they share the desire to reach out to substantial alterity to unhinge the interrogation of climate change from modern-liberal, capitalist actors, their ontological frameworks and their political tools. This desire is what compels Anthropocene environmentalism to look to Indigenous world views to unlock other ways of thinking, living and governing in the end times.

What does this shift add to conceptualizing a politics of action in the Anthropocene present of unprecedented planetary changes? The engagement with non-Western world views reveals not so much a desire to save humankind from the effects of climate change. It rather expresses the wish to learn how to live with the certainty and irreversibility of an unfolding, existential disaster. Anthropocene literature and Anthropocene environmental politics that embrace non-Western alterity seek to dispense with the hubris that marks techno-scientific responses to climate change. Learning with (rather than learning from) marginalized Indigenous communities opens up avenues to come to terms with the limits and, at times, futility of human agency under radically uncertain planetary conditions. Anthropocene critiques, and Indigenous thought and scholarship, similarly stress the need to be mindful of manipulation by the epistemic and political forces of hegemonic liberalism. They reject simplification and resist both the generalization of what are complex and specific world views and governance systems and any white saviour complex that might emerge in the encounter. After all, a power-conscious turn to the Indigenous requires a humbling of environmental movements and ecological theory alike to permit a critical interrogation of the modernist legacies of the Global North's climate politics, and to shine a light on radically diverse experiences with nature, extinction and living in the drawn-out end of times.

There certainly appear to be strong affinities between the ontological relationality and the resilient, nonmodern governance that prominently mark Anthropocene environmentalism on the one hand, and Indigenous thought, scholarship and political activism on the other hand. While these affinities can potentially open novel theoretical and political avenues for Anthropocene theory, this book is not concerned with sourcing new opportunities for the Western Anthropocene, but instead with its existing workings and limitations. In this book, we undertake a critical examination of the ontopolitics of the Anthropocene driven by, but not limited to, those parts of the Anthropocene literature that have recently turned to liberal modernity's 'ecological others'.

With William Connolly (2004), we understand ontopolitics as a method of theoretical investigation that reveals how ontological assumptions about what the world is like ground, structure and limit the horizon of what is politically possible, right or necessary. This book unpacks where, and to what effect, ontopolitics is at work in the propositions of Anthropocene theory. We posit that not only science-adjacent parts of the literature but importantly also critical, posthuman and post-liberal approaches to the Anthropocene are marked by an ontopolitics that is path-dependent on the foundational presumptions of liberal modernity. It is particularly in the engagement with non-Western, Indigenous alternatives, we argue, that the liberal-modern theoretical legacy of Anthropocene ontology comes to the fore, and that the political presumptions and limitations it imposes can therefore be unpacked and interrogated.

An obvious stumbling block for thinking a nonmodern governance of environmental changes and challenges through Indigenous thought and scholarship is the danger that such a turn to the Indigenous might feed into modernity's colonial legacies. A number of both Western and Indigenous critiques have drawn out how aiming to learn from Indigenous communities in a global context where the divisions of power and wealth, between those who own land and have the right to form a sovereign state and those who do not, are still those of settler colonialism, is simply another form of colonial expropriation, this time in the register of ideas (Todd 2015; Watts 2013; see also Chandler and Reid 2018, 2019). Indeed, these critiques form an important backdrop and motivator for the arguments developed in this book. The authors agree that sensitivity to the power relations that contextualise any engagement with Indigenous thought is acutely necessary, and that such sensitivity is often not adequately displayed in prominent examples of the Anthropocene turn to 'the Indigenous'. However, while this starting point is crucial in establishing at least one incongruence in Anthropocene theory's treatment of Indigenous agency, the ontopolitics that this book aims to draw out and problematize go beyond the inadequately acknowledged continuity of colonial extraction in the politics and ideas of the anthropocenic end of times. In part, this is the case because these critiques have been so eloquently and fully developed that there would be little to add for us.

In part, it follows from the fact that the object of this book's critical investigation is not the politics and ethics of Anthropocene theory's engagement with alterity, but rather the underpinnings, presumptions and logic at work in the ontology of the (Western) Anthropocene itself, and the way these condition and constrain what is rendered politically visible, and viable. In the following, we will engage with Indigenous cosmologies, Indigenous scholarship and stories from Indigenous environmental activism not with a view to depicting an 'Indigenous ecology' in itself that is ontologically and/or politically distinct from Western environmentalism in the Anthropocene. Rather, Indigenous ecology will be assembled as a critical mirror, designed to call into question the foundational assumptions and necessities that the following chapters will draw out as marking Anthropocene theory and Anthropocene environmental activism alike, most chiefly the binary distinction between liberal modernity and its non-Western others, the need for a relational ontology to be total, and the latent primacy of ontology over politics. Anthropocene ontology, as we will show in Chapter 1, draws heavily on new materialist and posthuman theories that unpack the world as composed of interrelated networks connecting multiple humans and nonhumans (see for example Morton 2013). Within these relational entanglements, all entities enjoy ontological equality insofar as neither is assumed to hold a pre-given primacy or asymmetrical significance within the process of making or maintaining a particular world. Indigenous ecologies, on the contrary, as we will show in the following, neither presume the ontological equality of all planetary entities nor do they shy away from insisting on foundationally distinct roles, responsibilities and values that certain humans, certain nonhumans and certain ecological relations hold.

Indigenous ecologies, we will show, do not fit, and thus challenge the ontopolitical mould which Anthropocene theory offers us as internally plural but universal. Here, relationality, ontopolitical linkages and nonmodernity play out in multiple ways. Indigenous ecologies blur and subvert the boundaries of foundational primacy and dependency, stability and contingency, internality and otherness, generality and specificity that structure Anthropocene ontopolitics. The past years have certainly seen a proliferation not only of Anthropocene engagements with Indigeneity but also of critical interventions in the former. This book goes beyond these works insofar as it is neither designed as a contribution to the debate on the Anthropocene's Indigenous turn nor does it aim to merely draw out the Anthropocene's ontological modernity and coloniality through the contrast with Indigenous alterity (as, for instance, convincingly achieved by Povinelli 2016, 2021). Rather, the book interrogates and reveals how this ontological modernity plays out in, and limits, the political presumptions and propositions of Anthropocene theory and Anthropocene environmentalism. This is achieved by creating novel encounters on various political and theoretical sites, among others between Indigenous planning, Extinction Rebellion activism, Indigenous resurgence and the rights of nature, which are thereby highlighted as potential spaces for theoretical and political production beyond the arguments developed in this book.

The critical mirror of Indigenous ecology

What we have so far referred to as the 'critical mirror' that this book holds up to Anthropocene ecology is, importantly, a theoretical tool constructed for a methodological purpose. As a methodological device of critique, the critical mirror is collated from a multiplicity of mediated Indigenous cosmological frameworks,[2] Indigenous scholarly works and stories of sustainable Indigenous practices and Indigenous environmental activism. The ideas, arguments and events that make up the mirror are real and embodied in Indigenous settings. While mediated through the act of recounting, analysing and meaning-making, the authors of this book hope to do justice to them in the way that they engage them. However, our mirror of Indigenous ecology is not intended to serve as the truthful and complete representation of the ontology and politics of a particular Indigenous community, or of something like a shared, abstractable Indigeneity itself. Collated from different geographical regions and times, and featuring different sections of Indigenous communities, including scholars, politicians and grassroots activists, the critical mirror is invariably highly selective, incomplete and unbalanced in the way it features different communities. The Indigenous ecology it sets up is not a Kantian thing-in-itself, or a thing at all. If a descriptor is necessary, Deleuze and Guattari's assemblage seems most suitable.

Although a formal methodology to guide the theorization of assemblages was not developed by Deleuze and Guattari in their work, the notion has been employed flexibly in post-foundational social theory, particularly with a view of capturing non-representable multiplicity instead of reducing it to unitary descriptors (Nail 2017). Beyond being a mere methodological tool, the assemblage is a disruptive episteme that can fundamentally question the basis of qualitative enquiry (Adams St. Pierre 2017). Deleuze and Guattari's assemblage has no essential ontological reality that can be captured in representation, but instead highlights how the ontological realm always exceeds any particular figure or structure used to render it intelligible. Utilized as a theoretical-methodological tool, Deleuze and Guattari's assemblage demands a 'metaphysical commitment to immanence' (Kleinherenbrink 2015: 153). It does not reveal aspects of reality that were previously hidden, are absolutely external to or clearly different from a particular ontology in order to expand and improve on the former. Rather, the assemblage can only reveal the conditionedness, limitedness and particularity of all ontological forms and the pathways for political actualization they offer. In the words of Deleuze and Guattari, its 'relation to an outside is not another "model"' but rather 'makes thought itself nomadic' (1987: 24) – unhinged from the determinacy of ontological claims.

This book's critical mirror of Indigenous ecology represents an assemblage that 'has neither object nor subject; it is made of variously formed matters, and very different dates and speeds' (Deleuze and Guattari 1987: 4). For the critical mirror, one should 'never ask what [it] means' bur rather 'what it functions with' (Deleuze and Guattari 1987: 5); it is 'a little machine', a 'literary machine' that links directly to other machines of theoretical and social production, to the 'war machine, love machine, revolutionary machine' (Deleuze and Guattari 1987: 5). The critical mirror of Indigenous ecology hence does, in itself, neither destroy, produce or transform, instead, it is used to weave ideas and stories with the aim of rendering visible the hidden path-dependencies of the Western Anthropocene. It allows us to show where different routes are possible but remain untreaded on the inside of the Anthropocene's conceptual and political reservoir. Importantly, we do not claim to be able to tell the stories of Indigenous communities better or more truthfully than others. We merely seek to highlight that these stories *can* be told in a way that calls into question the core presumptions of Anthropocene theory, and to draw out the alternative pathways for thought and action that become visible for Anthropocene environmentalism if we take these alternatives seriously. Thus, when we speak of Indigenous ecology in the following, this is not to invoke the distinct ecological beliefs, values and attitudes that a particular, let alone all, Indigenous communities hold. Rather, it is to employ exemplary stories from the realm of Indigenous environmental thought and politics to render visible the excess of ontological forms and political pathways that by far transcends the determinisms of Anthropocene ontopolitics.

However, the weaving together of Indigenous experiences in the critical mirror raises important questions about whether, and under what conditions, it is possible and even legitimate to speak of 'Indigenous' as a collectivizing singular that spans and connects more than a specific community. This issue has been extensively and controversially discussed by Critical Indigenous Studies (CIS) scholars; these debates demand careful attention on the part of the authors of this book as they situate not only the terminology of our critical mirror, but the ethics and politics of assembling the former. The richness and diversity of viewpoints on what constitutes the essence of 'Indigeneity' is telling of the diversity of lived experiences among Indigenous communities worldwide, despite the prevalence of accounts from North America and Australia. These important debates shed light on the context-specific dynamics that affect the cosmology of each Indigenous community and shape claims, struggles, origin stories, as well as the relationship with the modern state system and settler-colonial structures more broadly (Simpson 2011; Alfred 1999; Coulthard 2014; Tuhiwai-Smith 1999; Moreton-Robinson 2015).

Indigenous experiences are singular, specific and produce political claims and governance regimes that reflect a diversity of cosmological frameworks, social histories and marks left on the former by settler colonialism. Though this diversity is acknowledged by both Indigenous and non-Indigenous scholars and commentators alike, theoretical accounts engaging with Indigenous analytics, as well as practical, practitioner-based exchanges with marginalized communities, often deploy the term 'Indigenous' as a unified category of analysis, representative of a particular experience with marginalization and structural violence that places these communities on common ground. Since 'the imposition of labels and definitions of identity on Indigenous people has been a central feature of the colonization process from the start' (Alfred 1999:

84), the issue of definitions must be approached with considerable caution. Similarly, scholars have pointed to the political nature of defining the limits of Indigeneity from the outside-in. Not only is this problematic because it forcefully collectivizes 'many distinct populations whose experiences under imperialism have been vastly different' (Tuhiwai-Smith 1999: 6), but also because it prevents distinctions between Indigenous self-identification and those processes of identification operating (and rooted in) the very state system whose interests are served by delegitimizing Indigenous self-determination struggles.

The question of definitions thus not only delineates 'who *is* Indigenous' but is also pertinent to the political question of claims and rights to land (Corntassel 2003). Against this background, a number of Indigenous commentators have stressed that, to some extent, a common-ground definition of Indigeneity that is dynamic and accounts for the specificities and material differences across groups but also communicates solidarity in their shared anti-colonial struggles can exist (Corntassel 2003; Aikau, Goodyea-Ka'opua and Silva 2016). They suggest that 'part of being Indigenous in the 21st century is that regardless of where or how we have grown up, we've all been bathed in a vat of [. . .] imperialism' (Simpson 2011: 32). The effects of forced assimilation, resource extraction, exploitation and destruction, experienced under continuous colonization is here understood as a grounding 'consistency across Indigenous contexts' on the basis of which 'a generalizable Indigenous ontology and taxonomy' (Hokowhitu 2016: 85) can be, and in some cases has been, created. Similarities across Indigenous communities further 'may serve a unifying function, particularly in efforts to explain the cultural basis of [a] movement's goals to non-Indigenous people' (Alfred 1999: 88).

However, importantly, assembling an Indigenous common ground vis-à-vis the colonial West does not mean that Indigenous experiences are here forcefully merged and flattened to facilitate the creation of a 'unifying vocabulary and basis for collective action' (Alfred 1999: 88). While a generalizable Indigenous ontology featuring 'essentialised pillars, including land, language, and culture' (Hokowhitu 2016: 85) has been deployed by some to reclaim a degree of agency and to enable a common language to be developed in order to talk about decolonization across Indigenous groups, it is important to note that place-based specificity grounds 'broader networks of relationship' (Justice 2016: 20) in the local realities of Indigenous communities. This grounding is necessary to 'position' any trans- or pan-Indigenous movement, as 'place always matters' (Justice 2016: 21); place allows reflection on what is at stake when multiple Indigenous histories, distinct traditions and cultures, are brought to interact on an 'equal basis' (Allen 2012: xii).

Committed to an analytic of transformation beyond the discursive hegemonies and simplified narratives that position Indigenous communities vis-à-vis the knowledge relations and moral codes of the settler state, CIS scholars emphasize the complex nature of the relationships that characterize Indigenous communities, and stress that acknowledging the earlier implies abandoning the hubris of knowing, and embracing unlearning. For CIS, we have to be comfortable with the unknown and the unintelligible rather than seek to own, control and exploit knowledge. For Daniel Heath Justice, this means continuing 'to connect across and through [...] differences' (2016: 23), but to do so in ways that honour difference, intelligibility, untranslatability. This fluid approach, that emphasises relationships over essences, has implications for how we understand definitional boundaries. As Taiaiake Alfred suggests, manifesting 'localised Native nationalism' (1999: 88) together with the effort to bring together 'words, ideas, and symbols from different Indigenous cultures' (1999: 88) is then not incompatible with, but rather allows for mounting a successful challenge to the wider structural violence of colonialism while at the same time being locally resonant, respectful of the integrity of the political traditions of individual communities, and open to the 'moments of inexplicability or uncertainty' (Justice 2016: 23.) that seep through alterity.

While not all Indigenous scholars would endorse it, the earlier debate appears to settle on the tentative compromise that using the term Indigenous to link different cosmological principles and experiences is possible if it is made clear that any such Indigenous collectivity is always non-unitary and constructed with a distinct political edge and aim. This book's critical mirror of Indigenous ecology is assembled in exactly this spirit. The book does not seek to offer an outside-in definition to establish or reinforce a particular determination of who is Indigenous. In resisting to endow our critical mirror with an ontological essence, we retain distance from conceptual definitions that seek to 'speak on behalf of' or seek to represent Indigeneity. Substantial collective definitions of Indigeneity that may facilitate emphasis on shared experiences, common-ground, or even trans- and pan- Indigeneity, we maintain, would need to come from within the collective memory and experiences of imperialism, which are not accessible to the authors of this book.

A word on positionality

This book does not aim to speak on behalf of Indigenous communities, to represent them or to conduct Indigenous analytics. We agree with Aileen Moreton-Robinson that such representation would be a misguided objective for non-Indigenous scholarship, which 'can engage with Indigenous analytics but not produce them' (2016: 4). Western scholarly efforts that attempt the earlier are always acutely at risk of continuing an epistemological hierarchy where it is on the side of the colonizers that ideas and knowledge about Indigeneity are produced (Tuhiwai-Smith 1999: 1–2). Many Indigenous scholars consider such attempts at representation as necessarily problematic even when researchers seek to engage with Indigenous communities to 'serve the greater good' or 'a specific emancipatory goal for an oppressed community' (Tuhiwai-Smith 1999: 2). They reinscribe the West's '"positional superiority" over the known, and yet to become known, world' (Tuhiwai-Smith 1999: 63) and obfuscate the contribution that Indigenous methodologies and analyses can make to what we consider knowledge (Tuhiwai-Smith 1999: 63).

This book engages with Indigenous ecologies, stories of Indigenous environmental action and the reflection of both in the CIS tradition not in order to represent (any or all) Indigenous experiences, but in order to interrogate and disrupt Anthropocene theory's core assumptions and ontopolitical workings. We are precisely not suggesting that the burden of investigating the achievements and shortcomings of Western Anthropocene theory should fall on CIS or Indigenous thought and scholarship, but are rather embarking on this quest as scholars of the modern West. However, we want to highlight that reading CIS scholarship has importantly helped the project of this book because it has opened up space to critically explore the '*kinds* of knowledge' (Andersen 2016: 57; emphasis in original) Anthropocene theory produces, not least by 'denaturalizing the whiteness' (Andersen 2016: 58) of the Anthropocene's epistemological dynamics and of its ontological principles, chiefly the fact that it operates (primarily) through foundationally firm ontological principles. CIS challenges the tendency of Western critical theories to abstract and ontologise ideas and actions in a way that underpins and reinforces anti-colonial agency (Tallbear 2016: 74).

The authors certainly do not seek to exempt their critical mirror of Indigenous ecology from the political situatedness of knowledge production. We do not claim to be 'able to observe without being implicated in the scene' (Tuhiwai-Smith 1999: 138), which would detach and absolve our academic research from the political and economic violence of modernity. Our relationship to our research is at the core of the critical and reflective endeavour espoused by this book, and inherently linked to the problematizing of an Anthropocene that operates through binaries and necessities, not only in its ontological presumptions, but more importantly in the implications it generates for governing Anthropocene societies within and beyond the West. We position ourselves neither as the outside observers of an objective Indigenous knowledge nor as inside knowledge-holders but as politically grounded outsiders. As such, we are externally situated, critically engaged explorers of the complexities of Indigenous cosmologies and scholarship who aim to retain and, where necessary, recover the interwovenness of Indigenous knowledge and Indigenous politics in the thicket of the 'multiple ways of being either an insider and an outsider' (Tuhiwai-Smith 1999: 138).

Since the academic production of knowledge remains an essentially political endeavour involved in legitimizing and delegitimizing ways of knowing and being in the world, acknowledging positionality in this sense is a key step in 'transforming institutional practices and research frameworks' (Tuhiwai-Smith 1999: 140) beyond the default of an implied, never acknowledged, standpoint, analytical register and political toolbox. However, we acknowledge that our own critical situatedness and the political sensitivity with which, we hope, we approach Indigenous thought and scholarship does not automatically prevent or absolve us from the charge of 'exercising intellectual arrogance' (Tuhiwai-Smith 1999: 180) of the Western-modern kind. After all, we remain two scholars who read and write about Indigenous ecology from the comfortable armchair position of academia in the Global North. We are necessarily distant from, because unaffected by, the political struggles that Indigenous communities face. For this reason, some Indigenous scholars, like some Western academics, will consider our engagement with Indigenous thought and scholarship as fundamentally illegitimate (see, for instance, Chandler and Reid 2018). The authors of this book believe that they cannot, and indeed should not, conclusively resolve critical questions regarding the position from which, and the legitimacy with which, we write this book on and with Indigenous thought and scholarship. We can only make a claim for the value of the arguments developed in this book, and position it against the background of an Indigenous debate where Western engagement and allyship are not universally rejected but controversially discussed.

For the Western scholarship that rejects any engagement with Indigeneity *a priori*, we ask whether such blanket rejections might not be too simple, and too comfortable, of an answer because they risk freezing Indigenous communities in an ontological and political status of alterity. The authors of this book will instead stay with and within the uncomfortable tensions and challenges that mark the theoretical space of engaging with Indigeneity. We point to the politically transformative impetus of a project that does not seek to interrogate, dissect or expropriate Indigenous thought but whose critical gaze remains firmly directed to the Western Anthropocene itself. In laying open the epistemological and ontological limitations behind some of the necessities that underpin contemporary Western thinking and acting on the Anthropocene's ecological catastrophe, this book's critical intervention is decidedly political. Where Anthropocene theory ambiguates directed and planned political action, we highlight the compatibility of (Indigenous) posthuman ontologies with pursuing alternative realties through concrete, dynamic, and complex projects of enacted, grounded agency. This has immediate consequences for how we assess, prioritize and give legitimacy to projects of Anthropocene governance not only in the West but, importantly also, at the still colonised margins.

Chapter overview

The groundwork for this book's critical intervention is laid by a structured overview of the landscape of Anthropocene theory. The first chapter divides the existing scholarship into a catastrophic strand focused on how humanity can politically respond to the climate crisis and an ontological strand that seeks to utilize the Anthropocene as an opening in the way we approach *being in the world* to reconceptualize Anthropos, the Earth and their relationship. The chapter shows how the theorists of the Anthropocene catastrophe continue the trajectory of Western modernism by advocating for the pooling of rational human inventiveness to counteract and survive the Anthropocene catastrophe. The liberal subject has created the Anthropocene mess – but a different kind of human subject can get us out. The ontological strand of Anthropocene theory, on the contrary, dismantles the modernist hope underpinning this line of argumentation. Acting on the Anthropocene here requires, first and foremost, de-centering our understanding of being to the planetary and rethinking human communities as produced, shaped and limited by their many nonhuman entanglements.

We argue that the arguments that each strand develops in its respective register are not cancelled out by the points and criticisms developed by the other strand. Both strands offer in themselves complex, logical and well-justified but incongruent accounts of the Anthropocene that ultimately do not speak to each other, meaning that one strand cannot readily be identified as 'winning' the contest of theorizing the Anthropocene. The ontological strand of Anthropocene theory has effectively shown that the urgent call to collective action in the face of the climate catastrophe cannot belie, and does not do away with, the fact that such action, without a fundamental ontological reconfiguration of modern thought, must make use of political tools that are at best ill-equipped for their task, at worst worsen rather than improve, the repercussions of human intervention into a poorly understood planetary ecology. However, on the other hand, prioritizing ontological reconfiguration over political action on ecological changes places ontological Anthropocene theory at risk of cementing a tendency towards depoliticization into the foundation of its theoretical architecture.

Chapter 2 looks at what we termed the ontological strand of Anthropocene theory's engagement with alterity hinged on the perceived parallel with Indigenous communities' relational ontologies. We suggest that this selective and superficial parallel is however blown up to an Anthropocene totality that conceals divergent ontological and political projects. The chapter begins by drawing out how Anthropocene ontology parallels Indigenous ecologies insofar as it recognizes the agency of nonhumans, is grounded in a relational conception of being and finds political expression in practices of resilience. While Anthropocene theorists increasingly put this parallelism to work to support their claims, they however bracket those dimensions that stand in tension with Western Anthropocene ontology, especially Indigenous endorsements of rational planning and political steering, and the interwovenness of sustainability and Indigenous political claims. Rather than acknowledging these tensions, the chapter shows that perspectives consistent with the ontological strand of Anthropocene theory are marked by a tendency to marginalize and render them invisible through introversive enfolding in an Anthropocene that is posited to be able to accommodate all multiplicity. While the former position themselves against the *a prioris* and universals of liberal modernity, they develop an Anthropocene concept that functions exactly in the mode of a modern universal.

Calling into question whether stark political tensions and power struggles can really be accommodated within a totalizing Anthropocene ontology, Chapter 3 renders problematic the relationship between ontology and political practice within Western environmentalism. The chapter explores the Extinction Rebellion as a prominent case of contemporary Western environmental activism to unpack its ontological presumptions and their link to political action, before rendering visible the distinct logic of its operativity in the critical mirror of Indigenous ecology. The chapter aligns with critiques of the movement as white, elitist and Western-modern, but situates this critical reading in an in-depth analysis of the underlying logic of Extinction Rebellion activism that is absent from these critiques. First, we argue that Indigenous ecologies are marked by a genuinely relational engagement with human and nonhuman causes that treats them as indivisible, which is markedly different from the Extinction Rebellion's call to prioritize saving nonhuman nature over human social concerns. The chapter, second, contrasts the Extinction Rebellion's introversive, norm-building functionality with an Indigenous environmental activism that flexibly employs its established ontological-cultural foundations to drive action towards concrete political aims. Finally, the chapter highlights how Extinction Rebellion rejects any engagement with political institutions and structures in its desire to transgress political boundaries but thereby leaves existing power structures and inequalities unchallenged. Indigenous ecological activism, on the contrary, is flexible in its political strategies because it prioritises political outcomes.

Chapter 4 then interrogates a different mode of environmental political action in the Anthropocene in the critical mirror of Indigenous ecology: granting legal standing to nonhuman subjects. Where the rights of nature are legally implemented, for instance in the constitutions of Ecuador and Bolivia, or in legislation to protect specific ecosystems in Australia and New Zealand, they are formulated and justified with reference to the cosmologies and value systems of the country's Indigenous communities. Perspectives from the ontological strand of Anthropocene theory, the chapter shows, can only reject the rights of nature as a political pathway because of its anthropocentric underpinnings, and the modern-liberal logic of individual rights into which Indigenous principles are here shoehorned. Indigenous engagements with rights of nature legislation complicate any such simple assessment. Whether the rights of nature are to be discarded or endorsed here depends on the particular logic of rights enacted, and on how they affect the political forcefield they are situated in. The chapter shows how anthropocentric guardianship models as well as rights- and property-based understandings of ecosystems are not diametrically opposed or even completely absent from Indigenous cosmologies as distinct as Australian Aboriginal ecologies and the practices of Saami reindeer farmers in Norway. Examining Ecuador's and New Zealand's landmark rights of nature legislation, the chapter shows that it is their effect on the advancement of local Indigenous interests, and not the accuracy with which they represent Indigenous cosmologies, that has shaped Indigenous engagements with the legal protection of nonhumans and sealed the political fate of the legislation.

Finally, in Chapter 5, we make the case that Indigenous agency, in its cosmological basis and its political expression, dynamically shifts between and flexibly combines elements from the political and the ontological register of Anthropocene theory. Indigenous thought and political activism aim to resist the modern-Western colonial State not only as a political institution but also as a mechanism of worldmaking. Where critical perspectives, in highlighting Indigenous agency, emphasize resistance and resilience as its primary expressions, within both Indigenous scholarship and Indigenous political practice the latter are beaconed by political actions aimed to transform, produce, improve or govern. These expressions of directed Indigenous agency closely resemble, and at times directly draw on, a mode of acting that the ontological strand of Anthropocene theory urges us to discard as irrevocably liberal-modern. While Indigenous ecologies cannot and should not be utilized to decide on a path at the crossroads of Anthropocene theory, they can show the former that multiple ways forward exist, which do not have to involve a decision in the mode of clear-cut binaries.

The contemporary scholarship on the Anthropocene is marked by the obsession with finding an ontological solution to the ecological mess that modern Anthropos has left us in, and absolution for the guilt of colonial modernity. Against the background of our engagement with ideas, arguments and stories from Indigenous scholarship and activism, our argument cautions against both related impulses. Because the relationship between ontology and politics is indeterminate, unstable and locally specific, we suggest that a better ontology does not guarantee us a better environmental politics, and that the more we prioritize the quest for *the right* Anthropocene ontology, the more we entangle ourselves in the ontological thicket of liberal modernity. We conclude that the way forward for ecological politics in the Anthropocene is possibly not so different from that associated with the Holocene after all. Maybe, the difference must lie in actually fulfilling it this time: tackling the power relations that direct human and nonhuman relations.

The rise of Anthropocene theory

Politics, ontology and the feedback loop of Western humanism

In order to launch this book's critical intervention into contemporary scholarship on the Anthropocene, it is first necessary to map the theoretical field it targets. The first chapter is dedicated to the task of surveying the vast and increasingly uneven landscape of what we, in the following, will term 'Anthropocene theory'. At a superficial level, the idea of the Anthropocene is rather straight forward. For the Earth system scientists that coined the term (Crutzen 2002; Steffen et al. 2011), the extent and speed of anthropogenic changes to the planet are so vast that they must be captured at the scale of Earth ages. In the Anthropocene, whose starting point is tentatively located in the sweeping industrialization of the nineteenth century, humanity has become the most impactful geological force (Waters et al. 2016). 'The Anthropocene', as Steffen et al. write, thus 'provides an independent measure of the scale and tempo of human-caused change – biodiversity loss, changes to the chemistry of atmosphere and ocean, urbanization, globalization – and places them in the . . . context of Earth history' (2011: 756–7).

The Anthropocene concept offers a theoretical umbrella for measuring and describing climate change. Located at the level of Earth history, it lends gravity and urgency to the environmental degradation observed. Anthropocene scholarship from the geosciences, the social sciences and the arts and humanities converges on the insight that, in one way or another, climate change forces a re-evaluation of humanity's ecologically blind striving for continuous human advancement and modernization. For Anthropos, at least for the Anthropos of the industrialized West, the Anthropocene means the end of business as usual. On this shared basis, the existing Anthropocene literature however contains a multiplicity of ontological, political and ethical claims for how we should think the changed Earth, or rather change our thinking of an Earth that never was the inert matter that modern humanists imagined it to be. Brought to life to signpost just how badly humanity has failed in its quest to rule the planet, the story of the Anthropocene, as a concept, is yet one of remarkable success.

Our starting point for retracing and mapping the theoretical proliferation of the Anthropocene in contemporary scholarship that aims to engage with, and respond to, climate change is a certain divide noted in previous attempts at generating an overview of the existing literature. Stephanie Wakefield frames this distinction temporally as that between thinking the Anthropocene either as 'front loop' or as 'back loop' (2018: 5), while Sverre Raffnsøe distinguishes between the Anthropocene's 'human turn' and its 'posthuman turn' (2016: xvii; see also Latour 2017). The Anthropocene's human branch, the argument goes, is composed of those scholars who remain close to the geosciences and retain a focus on diagnosing and seeking to mitigate recent ecological changes from the perspective of a human species *still seeking to move forward*. On the contrary, the posthuman branch of Anthropocene scholarship is not interested in how the existing tools of science, philosophy and politics can mitigate the effects of climate change, but instead *looks back* to disrupt the anthropocentric image of modern-liberal thought that has underpinned the violent exploitation of the Earth.

Here, an adequate response to recent ecological challenges must be grounded in a fundamental ontological shift away from the modern-liberal subject and towards a materially entangled understanding of the human condition. It is the latter perspective that, at this point, by far dominates the field of contemporary Anthropocene theory in the humanities and social sciences, which is the subject of this chapter's interrogation. Somewhat paradoxically, the story of the Anthropocene is thus one of progress after all – of *theoretical progress* beyond the idea of human progress at the expense of the Earth; of progress beyond the beyond the human exceptionalism of a modern 'politics and metaphysics carved in steel and brick' (Wakefield 2018: 5). This chapter's map of Anthropocene theory will on the one hand reiterate and flesh out the divide between these two distinct strands of the scholarship. But on the other hand, it will interrogate the presumption of theoretical-ontological progress underpinning the second strand.

While the existing scholarship on the Anthropocene can certainly be categorized and grouped in different ways, we suggest that a productive way of grasping the divide noted by several commentators is to distinguish between those approaches that focus on the Anthropocene as a *catastrophic rupture* that calls humanity to action and those that identify the former primarily as an *opportunity to think* the human, and their place on Earth, differently.[1] At a first glance, distinguishing between a catastrophic perspective on the Anthropocene and one that embraces its new ecological condition as a prompt to think differently appears as nothing but a slight variation of the human/ posthuman divide. However, only the former problematizes the narrative of a smoothly progressing Anthropocene theory that has realized its full potential as it has managed to strip itself from its humanist baggage. Thinking the Anthropocene as catastrophe and as opportunity, we argue, takes place in two distinct registers of argumentation, the political and the ontological. Both strands of scholarship develop the issue at hand *in their respective register* to a degree of complexity and intricacy that the other side cannot meet. But at the same time, their particular contribution to thinking the 'Anthropocene problem' does not cancel out the issues their counterpart has raised in the other register. There is no doubt that the dissolution of human exceptionalism performed by those thinkers that open up a new perspective on being in and through the Anthropocene resolves some of the untenable presumptions of liberal modernity that remain unaddressed by those scholars who focus on mapping the ecological catastrophe we find ourselves in as political challenge. But it is equally the case, we will suggest, that developing better ontological tools to grasp nonhuman shaping power does not automatically absolve Western societies from the manifest necessity or even responsibility to act on the effects of climate change.[2]

Leaving the flawed ontological presumptions of climate science and climate politics unexamined not only reduces their effectiveness but also places them at risk of perpetuating the epistemic underpinnings of modernity's exploitative tendencies. However, at the same time, rendering collective human action secondary to, and conditional on, the 'right' ontology in an absolute sense is a luxury not all Anthropocene subjects can afford, and implicitly inscribes in the very way we think the Anthropocene a remoteness and shieldedness from its worst effects. As we will argue as follows, the 'ontology first' logic of conceptually speculative Anthropocene theory places even critical, radical scholarship in danger of faithfully applying and thereby ultimately reproducing the modern philosophical parameters it seeks to escape. As it stands, Anthropocene theory thus has to contend with being caught in the feedback loop of modern humanism, which comes to the fore in the posthuman ecologies it has inspired just like it does in the calls for mobilizing human ingenuity in the face of the Anthropocene catastrophe – only differently.

To draw out the distinction between an Anthropocene theory focused on the political response to a catastrophic present and an alternative branch of scholarship that instead uses the Anthropocene as a starting point to free Western ontology from its modern-human confines, we will zoom in on their distinct uses of a shared hinge: deep time. Deep time serves as a temporal marker for how profoundly different the Anthropocene condition is from what came before – regardless of whether this before is envisioned as the Holocene, modernity or pre-capitalist production. Linked to the research of the eighteenth-century geologist James Hutton, the concept of deep time slightly predates the recent turn to the Anthropocene but is widely used in the Anthropocene literature to draw attention to the insignificance and contingency of human life on Earth and its scales of measurement in the face of the 'longue durée of life' (Hird 2017: 258) and the planet. At the heart of the concept lies an understanding of time that is 'dislocated . . . into a spatial register' (Heringman 2014: 56) and thus must be understood as dynamically co-constituted with a particular geological condition. It allows us to understand anthropocenic changes as both shaped by and shaping our understanding of time. Nevertheless, deep time is not primarily deep, but long.

It performs a zooming out to a geological timescale where even rapid changes take place over thousands of years, making it possible to consider 'the present in terms of the deep past' (Zalasiewicz et al. 2011: 840). This highlights the significance of the human-made ecological changes that mark the Earth age of the Anthropocene.

The Anthropocene offers us a framework for confronting the carbon signature of the human species, but it also puts us in dialogue with the archaeological and geological signatures of ancestral species and geological processes themselves. However uncomfortably, the Anthropocene situates the history of the species in deep time, and in that respect it takes up a challenge much older than the Enlightenment and modernity. (Heringman 2014: 79)

In the Anthropocene, (human) time is out of joint. As Dipesh Chakrabarty argues in *The Climate of History in a Planetary Age*, the Anthropocene's deep time ends 'the experienced time of mutuality between the Earth and humans' (2021: 183), with the former being nothing but constant background to the actions of the latter. The Earth's temporality frees itself from the confines of human time, and breaks into the latter by force, reminding humanity that its deep time has existed before, and independently of, the short lifetime of Anthropos (2021: 202–4).

Planetary catastrophe and the Anthropocene as a political challenge

For the first branch of Anthropocene scholarship, zooming out from the comparatively short-lived temporality of human history to the deep time of the Earth reveals just how profound the human imprint on the global environment is (Steffen et al. 2011). 'If it is not the end of the world', as Christophe Bonneuil and Jean-Baptiste Fressoz write in their outline of the Anthropocene 'shock', 'it is certainly the end of an epoch' (2013: 22). What constitutes a significant and comparatively rapid change within the timeline of the Earth is nothing short of a speedily unfolding catastrophe if brought back to the scale and time of human species life. While the geological time of the Holocene constituted a 'slow and apparently timeless backdrop for human actions', in the Anthropocene it transforms itself 'with a speed that can only spell disaster for human beings' (Chakrabarty 2009: 205).

The thinkers and works we group together here as the first strand of Anthropocene theory all base their arguments on the lethal threat that the catastrophic rupture of climate change constitutes for all of humanity. Chakrabarty, not usually known for addressing the human species in its entirety, in this sense refers to the Anthropocene's ecological changes as the 'shared catastrophe that we have all fallen into' (2009, 2017). The long-term perspective of deep time brings into view just how profoundly humanity has broken with the Holocene – by breaking the Earth itself, as we knew it: 'in order to understand the current environmental crisis you have to think about very long ago' (Davies 2018: 20; see also: Zalasiewicz et al. 2011). The Anthropocene's planetary discontinuity brings into view the scale of the climate catastrophe humanity is facing. It highlights the urgency with which it needs to be politically addressed in order to secure the fragile planetary conditions that allow for human survival. In the catastrophic perspective on the Anthropocene, the planetary reality of climate change grounds a political call to action. We use the term 'political' in the broad sense of Hannah Arendt's philosophy here. Politics, for Arendt, marks a collective activity unfolding the power to shape not only a social community in its structures and dynamics, but the human condition itself in its relation to the world (1958: 198–201). Understood in this sense, an anthropocenic call to political action means that in the face of the climate catastrophe, humanity must mobilize its scientific, governmental and economic tools in order to avert the fate of extinction, but also to mitigate the drastic, and globally unequally distributed, costs that climate change is already producing.

A first body of scholarship where a comprehensive assessment of the Anthropocene's unfolding catastrophe grounds a plea for humanity to act are the writings of those geoscientists who named and first mapped the Anthropocene, especially its conceptual father Paul Crutzen (2002) and the scientists of the Anthropocene Working Group (Waters et al. 2016; Steffen et al. 2011; Zalasiewicz et al. 2011; Zalasiewicz 2015). Surveying the state of the anthropogenically altered planet, scientists map which environmental changes have only just begun to come into effect, such as global warming and the rise of sea levels, and where human activity has already profoundly transformed the Earth, such as large-scale agriculture and urbanization that has reduced biodiversity in a manner 'abrupt on geological time scales' (Waters et al. 2016: 140). Zalasiewicz, who supports a formalization of the Anthropocene as a distinct Earth age with a 'golden spike' of accelerated ecological changes around 1950, suggests that the particular value of the concept lies in 'giving us a perspective, against the very largest canvas, of the scale and the nature of the human enterprise, and of how it [. . .] "intertwines" [. . .] with the other processes of the Earth system' (2015: 12). Even in its geoscientific use, the Anthropocene is thus primarily 'a story', albeit 'a rather remarkable one, of Earth history' (2015: 12). It renders intelligible the scale of human planetary intervention and of the fallout it has created for all life on Earth.

The alarming story of the Anthropocene leads geoscientists to call for the use of all tools available to humanity, particularly those of science and technology, to mitigate the fallout that will result from its vast environmental changes. As Crutzen writes in his Anthropocene outline 'Geology of Mankind', a 'daunting task lies ahead for scientists and engineers to guide society towards environmentally sustainable management during the era of the Anthropocene. This will require appropriate human behaviour at all scales, and may well involve internationally accepted, large-scale geo-engineering projects' (2002: 23). Steffen et al. similarly conclude that their findings 'reinforce the urgency for effective Earth System stewardship to maintain a global environment within which humanity can continue to develop in a humane and respectful fashion' (2011: 756). Largely absent from these science-led discussions are reflections on whether the ontological presumptions and conceptual and methodological apparatuses of modern science have been called into question by the very anthropocenic changes mapped here.

However, framing the Anthropocene as a catastrophe for the planet and its human inhabitants that demands urgent collective action is not necessarily coupled with scientific naivety and disregard for the ontological and epistemological underpinnings of the diagnostic tools employed. The Anthropocene catastrophe also functions as analytical hinge for a number of theories acutely aware of humanity's material entanglements – even if this does not lead all authors to adopt a posthuman theoretical stance. The shared political driving force of these diverse approaches is their explicitly critical stance towards Western liberalism, which is here identified as the systemic culprit behind anthropocenic changes. Meaningful political action in and on the Anthropocene must therefore tackle and transform the root of liberal politics and economics. A first important contribution to this 'onto-epistemologically conscious' literature on the Anthropocene catastrophe is Andreas Malm and Alf Hornborg's critical intervention in the discursive proliferation of the Anthropocene concept, which they set up against their 'paradoxical and disturbing' observation that 'the growing acknowledgement of the impact of societal forces on the biosphere should be couched in terms of a narrative so completely dominated by natural science' (2014: 63).

Malm and Hornborg take issue with the fact that Anthropocene geoscience – and the wider scholarship informed by its findings – hold an artificially unified humanity responsible for ecological changes that were caused by a small number of industrialized Western nations. The Anthropocene concept, they suggest, 'is an ideology more by default than by design' (Malm and Hornborg 2014: 67) because it naturalizes climate change as the inevitable product of collective human advancement when it is in fact the contingent product of a global capitalism that feeds off inequality and requires the exploitation of human and nonhuman life. In his more recent *Corona, Climate, Chronic Emergency: War Communism in the Twenty-First Century* (2020), Malm discusses the anti-capitalist emergency measures, from state-controlled production to limited consumption, that were enacted during the Covid-19 pandemic as suitable means to tackle the underlying, actual crisis of climate change, of which the pandemic was merely a taste and symptom.

Following a similar line of argumentation, Jason Moore proposes to replace the concept of the Anthropocene with that of the Capitalocene (for whose creation he credits Malm, at the time a PhD student at Lund University) rooted in Marx's philosophy. For Moore, the Capitalocene offers a better analytical grasp of the economic and onto-epistemic system that created both the ruthless exploitation of nature and its modern-liberal externalization from human society that gave rise to the Anthropocene catastrophe (2016a: 3–4). Following Moore, capitalism 'put nature to work' (2016a: 3) by ideologically framing it as a lifeless resource with no purpose beyond the fuelling of economic production and industrial modernization. The othering of humans and nonhumans keeps the capitalist machine in motion, supplying it with cheap labour and 'Cheap Nature' (Moore 2016b). While the Anthropocene, even if it often is with a critical view, accepts the nature/society binary of liberal modernity as a given, the Capitalocene aims to shed light on the socio-epistemic conditions under which nature became society's 'other'. Like Malm and Hornborg, Moore strongly objects to the idea that climate change is a catastrophe faced by humanity as an undifferentiated whole.

This objection is not only grounded in the recognition that most of humanity – 'Indigenous peoples, enslaved Africans, nearly all women, and even many white-skinned men (Slavs, Jews, the Irish)' (Moore 2016b: 79) – were victims rather than perpetrators of the exploitative violence that altered the Earth irreparably, but maybe more importantly problematizes how the

Anthropocene perpetuates the capitalist communitization of costs without doing anything to challenge the highly selective distribution of profits (Moore 2016b 82). Because capitalism is kept in motion through the exploitation of labour and externalized nature, following Moore, actual change must become operational on both levels and achieve 'a different ontology of nature' (Moore 2016b 114) at the same time as it redistributes wealth, Moore's Capitalocene hence offers a political action plan where the first step lies in breaking open the idea of a uniform human collective frozen in an Anthropocene shock that was the inevitable result of its continuous progress.

In his very own take on the Anthropocene as a political challenge, Bernard Stiegler starts from the observation that in 'the second decade of the twenty-first century, we . . . find ourselves trying to live within a state of emergency that is permanent, universal and unpredictable, and that seems bound to become unliveable' (2018: 204). Responsible for the Anthropocene emergency is here again a globalized capitalism which, aided first by mass media and then by digital technology, has automated not only all processes of production and consumption, but with it all social and psychological processes that make up human existence. For Stiegler, the Anthropocene is an 'Enthropocene' (2018: 51) characterized by the fast-paced, automated production of relational entropy. Capitalism places in front of us the objects, achievements and values we are meant to desire, and offers conveniently automated pathways for actualization that do not require any steering, thinking or acting input from humans (Stiegler 2014: 20–50, 2018: 45–50). As a consequence, individuals have lost what Stiegler, with reference to Gilbert Simondon's technological philosophy, calls their capacity for individuation – their capacity to independently create and shape social relations.

The Anthropocene as Enthropocene conditions a present that has no future because humanity is caught in the feedback loop of automated capitalism that continuously extends its present into the future (Stiegler 2018: 37–9, 56). Human communities rendered passive by self-directed flows of capital and information speed towards the climate catastrophe without notable resistance. Capitalist 'standardization seems to be leading the contemporary Anthropocene to the possibility of the destruction of life qua the [. . .] destruction of biodiversity, cultural diversity and the singularity of both psychic individuations and collective individuations' (Stiegler 2018: 41). In one of his interviews, Stiegler suggests that he 'can no longer sleep during the night [. . .] because of worries that [his] children will no longer have any future' (2015; own translation). The political task that the Anthropocene catastrophe poses for Stiegler is 'to govern in time' (2018: 116) in a way that ruptures capitalist automation, resurrects human inventiveness and renders the future indeterminate again. His turn towards the ancient Greek city states as ideal types for the kind of collective creativity Stiegler seeks to recover reveals more than a modicum of nostalgic humanism at the heart of his writing (Stiegler 2014: 56–7, 72). However, Stiegler's humanism is not only politically and economically post-liberal, but also grounded in an idea of the subject as ontologically marked by and secondary to its technological entanglements. For Stiegler, the Anthropos that outlives the Anthropocene is yet to be made through technological relations no longer automated by the capitalist machine (Stiegler 2018: 85).

Chakrabarty finally offers a very different framing of the catastrophic Anthropocene that is much more explicitly based on a posthuman reconfiguration of ontology. His initial thoughts on the topic, published as 'The Climate of History: Four Theses' (2009), were met with overwhelming criticism that targeted especially Chakrabarty's framing of climate change as a shared catastrophe that affects, and thus must be responded to by, humanity as a whole (Malm and Hornborg, 2014; Davies 2018). This collectivization of the Anthropocene call to action is illustrated pointedly by Chakrabarty's much-quoted observation that in the Anthropocene 'there are no lifeboats here for the rich and the privileged' (2007: 221). In his subsequent writings, Chakrabarty reiterates but clarifies his stance; while the experience of and power to mitigate anthropocenic changes might be radically unequal, Chakrabarty insists that this does not take away from the fact that the climate catastrophe is unfolding at a planetary level, placing all of humanity at its receiving end (2021: 45–56). In *The Climate of History in a Planetary Age*, he offers a historian's take on how deep time de-centres temporality away from the past and future of humanity, which are contingent and short-lived if measured in the timescale of Earth itself. The planetary perspective Chakrabarty adopts is directly informed by posthuman scholarship on the Anthropocene. For Chakrabarty, 'Latour's – and some other scholars' – attempt to open up vistas of aesthetic, philosophical and ethical thought help us to develop points of view that seek to place the current constellation of environmental crises in the larger context of the deeper history of natural reproductive life on this planet' (2021: 152).

Exploring the history of humanity's planetary shaping power brings into view how agency, as Chakrabarty draws from Latour, has never been the prerogative of the human subject. However, Chakrabarty's Anthropocene history is interested in the ontological reconfiguration of shaping power only to the extent that they help humanity in forming an effective political response to climate change. Posthumanism, he argues, 'by itself cannot address the political. Any theory of politics adequate to the planetary crisis humans face today would have to begin from the same old premise of securing human life' (2021: 91). For Chakrabarty, the Anthropocene does not undo Anthropos but doubles it – to the rational subject of modern liberalism it adds the ecologically entangled human who is existentially threatened by climate change. However, and this is Chakrabarty's important divergence from the posthuman project, the Anthropocene catastrophe undoes neither the rational agency nor the particular ethical value of the human subject. While Chakrabarty's Anthropocene theory bears little resemblance to his post-colonial writings, it is at this point that he formulates a post-colonial defence not only of humanism, but of technological modernity:

> But where are the anticolonial, late-modern, and the late-modernizing leaders of Asia and Africa the Nehrus, the Nassers, the Sukarnos, the Nyereres, the Senghors, the Frantz Fanons – in this story? Latour's argument in *We Have Never Been Modern* and elsewhere remains founded on a face-off between 'we moderns from the Western world' or 'the Westerners [and] the Whites (whatever nickname one might wish to give them)' on the one hand and the Indigenous peoples of America on the other [. . .]. Are we to assume that anticolonial leaders desiring to 'catch up' with the West – a desire that still propels the politics of India and China (remember Deng Xiaoping's 'four modernizations' campaign?) – were simply advocating pale, unoriginal copies of their forerunners in the West – mimic, derivative desires condemned by history to repeat the West's folly? (Chakrabarty 2021: 113)

For Chakrabarty, the Anthropocene debate, even as it criticizes 'the selfish interests of "the West"' (Chakrabarty 2012), remains thoroughly steeped in the narratives of the former. It incorporates non-Western perspectives and experiences only in the context of, and as so far as they support, the case they are building against liberal modernity. But what is bracketed here are the ideas, political projects and ethical weight of non-Western subjects and peoples who seek to make independent use of modernity's economic, technological and political tools in order to free themselves from the dependent position that colonial exploitation and the systemic global inequality it set up had placed them in. The uncomfortable question that Chakrabarty poses for Anthropocene theory, and one that will stay with us throughout this book, is what the posthuman shift in register to the planetary level does to the legitimacy of their interests, claims and projects.

The thinker maybe most often associated with a call to action in the face of the climate catastrophe – but one that does neither include the fall of global capitalism nor the recognition of a posthuman planetary ontology among its chief demands – is Clive Hamilton. Hamilton's arguments are hinged on the profound rupture that the Anthropocene means not only for humans, but for all life on Earth. Precisely because humanity is, in myriad ways, entangled with the existence of nonhumans, Hamilton argues, not unlike Chakrabarty, that it would be misguided to assume that the Anthropocene is a catastrophe only if viewed from the perspective of human survival, while the Earth remains indifferent (Hamilton 2017: 14). Our 'disturbance of the Earth System has rendered it more unstable and unpredictable' (Hamilton 2017: 22); relative long-term continuity in the Earth's creative processes have given way to a complex Earth system that is subject to fast-paced shifts and unpredictable ruptures. The radical discontinuity of anthropocenic changes causes Hamilton to distance himself from approaches that, like the Capitalocene scholarship, retrace the present threat to the underlying continuity of capitalism. 'To draw an analogy', Hamilton suggests, 'in the insurrectionary year 1848 Karl Marx would not have argued that one should look to the lessons of peasant revolts for an understanding of the situation or a political response' (2017: 24).

Introducing a distinction between anthropocentrism as a 'scientific fact – humans are the dominant creature, so dominant that we have shifted the geological arc of the planet – and anthropocentrism as a normative claim: that it is right and proper that humans should be masters of the Earth' (2017: 18), Hamilton sides with the former. Humanity, for him, can neither deny nor escape its profound planetary shaping power and therefore has a responsibility to act on the ecological catastrophe it caused (2017: 37). Responding to critics who read his *Earthmasters* (2013) as enthusiastically advocating for geoengineering to protect the sociopolitical status quo of an ecologically exploitative humanity, Hamilton emphasizes that drastic ecological intervention – of the same scale as the environmental destruction that gave birth to the Anthropocene – can, if at all, only be a 'regrettable measure' (Hamilton 2013: 208; see also: 2017: 30) of last resort. If undertaken at all, the guiding logic behind such ecological intervention must be different from the Promethean drive that has led to the depletion of natural resources in the name of human advancement.

Appropriate action on climate change must instead be guided by a 'new anthropocentrism' (2017: 37), which Hamilton refers to as Soterianism in reference to Sotera, the Greek goddess for safety, preservation and deliverance from harm (2017: 18). Hamilton's 'new anthropocentrism' implies that the newly geologically powerful humanity must understand its shaping power as ecologically embedded in a life-word 'built by us out of nature but constrained by it' (2017: 44). While the Anthropocene catastrophe reveals the failure of modern humanism, this failure is here not a consequence of the misguided overestimation of human power but rather effect and thus proof of the former. Humanity, following Hamilton, is exceptional in its geological shaping power and must therefore use this power to create a better ecological ethics, science and politics. To save the Earth, the modern fantasy of mastering it must be relinquished – but not the inventiveness of a rational-liberal subject, which we now need more than ever. Following Hamilton, 'surviving in the Anthropocene will depend on science, even if it depends more on politics' (2017: 47).

The theories we have grouped together here into a first strand of Anthropocene thought are held together by a certain positivist catastrophism. The undeniable reality of anthropogenic ecological changes renders the Anthropocene, regardless of whether or not scholars accept or contest the term, and regardless of whether or not they accept its classification as a new Earth age, an unprecedented catastrophe for life on Earth that transcends all ontological and political contestations. Deep time anchors the reality and scale of the Anthropocene catastrophe, and grounds the urgent need for collective political action. Only part of the catastrophic Anthropocene scholarship, the part associated with the geosciences, actually turns a blind eye to the fact that the Anthropocene, as a state of affairs that is real to and recognized by (parts of) humanity, reflects a particular ontology that is productively intertwined with global power structures. Thinkers like Stiegler, Chakrabarty or Malm and Hornborg are well-aware of, and explicitly dissect, what the latter refer to as the ideological situatedness and functioning of the Anthropocene. But importantly, and, as we will see, different from the second strand of Anthropocene theory, they nevertheless insist that there is *something catastrophic* behind the Anthropocene curtain. In the face of the ecological catastrophe, which is unequally distributed but without escape for all of humanity, genealogical analysis and ontological speculation must ultimately take the backseat.

The catastrophic perspective on the Anthropocene does not suggest that political, economic and scientific responses to climate change should and could take place within modern-liberal paradigms operating according to 'business as usual'. The shared Anthropocene catastrophe is the effect of the modern drive to conquer and master the Earth. Ecological destruction finds its roots in the twin projects of Western imperialism and global capitalism, coupled with the fatal error of misclassifying human agency as autonomous from nonhuman nature. However, Anthropocene catastrophism does not call into question the exceptionalism of human agency, because now, the argument goes, we can afford to do so less than ever. In the Anthropocene present, brought about by the misuse of humanity's powerful tools of reason, inventiveness and coordinated planning and steering, it is imperative to re-direct the former to allow humans and nonhumans to survive the climate catastrophe.

Ontological openings in the end times

While the climate catastrophe is still present as a distinct marker of Anthropocene scholarship, it has been superseded by a flood of publications that approach recent ecological changes in a different fashion. While not all thinkers that shape this second strand of Anthropocene theory subscribe to the labels new materialist, posthumanist or posthuman, they share the assumption that responding to the Anthropocene does not require a human 'techno-fix' (Hamilton 2013: 164). Rather, it necessitates a fundamental rethinking of the ontological status and shaping power of humanity vis-à-vis the nonhuman Earth. This second strand of Anthropocene theory opposes the diagnostic positivism and political pragmatism of the first strand in favour of understanding, and proposing to utilize, the Anthropocene as an ontological opening through which the world can be remade as relationally entangled. The entangled Earth is populated by a multiplicity of humans and nonhumans that continuously shape and re-shape the former together. Here, deep time is employed to draw out how the Anthropocene is driven and characterized by processes that emerged not only long before the 1950s spike of accelerated human geophysical activity, but long before Anthropos as a species appeared on the face of the Earth.

Zooming out to the scale of planetary time relativizes the status of humanity and reveals the contingency of its future as 'the Anthropocene sweeps humankind into the turbulent flow of geohistory' (Davies 2018: 10). As Latour notes, the Anthropocene marks a radical discontinuity only if viewed from the perspective of humanity and measured with the scale of human history. In itself, 'the passage of time does nothing to the world. There is no history' (Latour 2017: 171). For the Earth, humanity's rise is recent, and its survival or extinction, just like the fate of any other species, is a radically contingent event. What the deep time of Earth ages reveals is thus not the Earth's 'vibrancy or its agency so much as its tendency to remain indifferent' (Colebrook 2017b: 3). The ontological strand of Anthropocene theory consciously resists catastrophist narratives and imageries not because there is no urgent ecological threat to be addressed, but because identifying the Anthropocene – definitely and universally – as unprecedented challenge for the Earth is underpinned by the same modern-liberal anthropocentrism that caused its ecological ruptures and that blinded human societies towards them. Subscribing to the Anthropocene catastrophe here means upholding faith in human reason as a materially unencumbered capacity that can diagnose and conceptualize the former accurately and has the capacity to devise strategies to effectively manage and mitigate its effects. The Anthropocene catastrophe therefore falls short of providing understanding for what is actually at stake in the Anthropocene: a seismic shift in thinking and being, a fundamental ontological turn comparable to that of the Copernican Revolution, and indeed complementary to the former. Not only is humanity not the centre of the universe, but we are also not essential to the planet we inhabit. In the Anthropocene, the modern dualism between creative rationality and passive-receptive matter, between culture and nature, can finally no longer be upheld (Latour 2017: 13–19).

The most prominent, albeit not the most radical version of an Anthropocene theory where the former is ontological opportunity rather than, or at least even more so than, lethal threat, can be found in Bruno Latour's Gaia writings. Latour's work is marked by a continuous concern for drawing out how all the inventions and achievements modern societies have been displaying so proudly have only been possible through, and because of, the active collaboration of a multiplicity of nonhumans, and therefore 'never been modern' (1993). However, only Latour's more recent writings explicitly engage with the conditions of human life in the face of climate change. Latour certainly cannot be accused of disregarding the urgency of addressing the rapid ecological changes that mark the former. After all, it is this urgency that inspired his infamous proclamation that critique 'has run out of steam' and must be replaced with an engaged mode of doing social theory that productively addresses rather deconstructs ecological and other 'matters of concern' (2004: 248). Some of Latour's writings point to pathways for governing (in) the Anthropocene, such as a European politics that actively engages in nonhuman diplomatic negotiations (2017: 100–6). However, his primary concern clearly lies with addressing the climate crisis through an ontological reconfiguration of the human condition.

In *After Lockdown*, Latour references Hamilton in stressing that the Anthropocene lesson cannot lie in simply decentring climate change away from the human position to embrace the consequences of anthropogenic climate change (2021: 250–61). For Latour, such a disengaged posthumanism would mirror the neoliberal abdicating of all individual responsibility glorified by Ayn Rand – 'Atlas shrugged all over again' (2021: 262). However, Latour's call for turning towards, not away from, the profound ecological changes and challenges of the Anthropocene condition does not take away from the fact that, for him, they must be addressed, first and foremost, on an ontological level. The fundamental Anthropocene shift is one that still has to be achieved – a different account of human life, agency and inventiveness that recognizes the 'imperative' (Latour 2021: 51) role nonhumans play in constituting and maintaining all of the achievements conventionally ascribed to Anthropos.

For Latour, Anthropocene deep time forces into view the extent to which modern science and philosophy have mistaken their anthropocentric imageries for the dynamics of Earth itself. Deep time not only precedes and extends beyond human life on Earth, but also disperses the linearity of temporal order and the universal applicability of a singular timeline. In the face of a deep time that moves in circles, loops, along multiple lines and at different speeds, there 'is nothing that authorizes us to re-use the old markers such as [. . .] "future" and "past"' (Latour 2018: 32–3; see also: Latour 2017: 137). 'The Anthropos of the Anthropocene? It is Babel after the fall of the huge tower.

Finally, humans are not universifiable. Finally, they are not off the ground! Finally, they are not outside of terrestrial history!' (Latour 2017: 121–2). Deep time ruptures modern teleology, progress and finitude – and opens up space for the recognition that humans have always lived entangled with a nonhuman Earth that is powerful and threatening.

Understood in this sense, the Anthropocene brings with it a catastrophic collapse only for the modern-liberal mode of reasoning, which was long overdue because of its unsustainability, in more than one sense. On the level of social theory, the Anthropocene constitutes an opening towards a less rigid, more multi-faceted and more materially grounded understanding of the way life on Earth is produced by networks spanned between its different inhabitants. 'As soon as one translates "the time of the end" by "the end of the times," one finds oneself on the brink of a dizzying metamorphosis – and an irresistible temptation to shift to eternity while abandoning the time of finitude and mortality' (Latour 2017: 197). It is in this sense that Latour, in *After Lockdown*, inverts Kafka's *Metamorphosis*; Gregor Samsa's transformation into a beetle renders him not a monstrous outcast but the only human adapted to survive in a posthuman world (Latour 2021: 111).

In Latour, the anthropocenic human condition is one of 'unconfined interiority' (Latour 2021: 54). There is no environment, only a multitude of connective relations that render all life on Earth fundamentally engendered (Latour 2021: 76). While modernity is built and oriented on limits, binaries, borders and camps – with the Anthropocene, understood as a distinct geohistorical age being one of them (Latour 2021: 81–3) – the transformed posthumans of the Anthropocene accept that they are always, absolutely and limitlessly entangled. Only the universe surrounding the Earth can be researched, analysed and understood clearly because it lies on the outside of these Earthly entanglements (Latour 2021: 81–3). Any part of the former can only be approached and analysed from the inside of its connections. The consequence is, importantly, not an Anthropocene relativism – meaningful knowledge of the Anthropocene condition can and should be assembled. However, the Anthropocene can only be known in a way that is local, partial and tentative (Latour 2017: 136, 2021: 100–4). The pathway towards living in the Anthropocene should thus not lead us towards a new mastery of the Earth that would allow humanity to escape the climate catastrophe. Rather, 'to get out, we need to get out of the idea of getting out' (Latour 2021: 146).

Isabelle Stengers places the act of 'characterizing' the Anthropocene closer to writing science fiction than to a positivist scientific knowledge production aimed at 'unveiling' an objective, pre-existent truth (2015: 34). Such certainty, for Stengers, would only repeat the liberal-modern 'story of progress, including the one that enables us to see the truth of what we are facing' (2015: 67). Like Latour, Stengers employs the concept of Gaia as an umbrella for all acts pertaining to this project of characterizing. Gaia, 'she who intrudes, asks nothing of us, not even a response to the question she imposes' (2015: 46). In Stengers' writing, the distinct temporality of Gaia is an extended present without exteriority. Again, there is no way out – not out of the manifest ecological changes societies are experiencing, but more importantly also not out of the ontological impasse they have created for the modern-liberal order of being; 'she who intrudes, signifies that there is no afterwards' (Stengers 2015: 57). Stengers' Anthropocene first and foremost challenges humans to think – to develop new ontological tools to capture and organize the world they inhabit. 'Naming Gaia is accepting to think with this fact: *there is no choice*' (Stengers 2015: 58; emphasis in original) but to ditch the modern-liberal compass that locates truth, value and good life, because it has proven to offer no orientation.

Placing Stengers on the side of an ontological response to the Anthropocene that we distinguish from those theories focused on manifest action on the climate catastrophe should by no means suggest that her intervention in the Anthropocene debate is not explicitly political (Stengers 2013b: 176–7). What we seek to highlight is merely that for Stengers, as for Latour, any appropriate political response to the Anthropocene cannot utilize the existing governmental tools available to (modern) states but requires that we first assemble a new analytical and political tool box where planetary interconnectedness and the chaotic force of Gaia occupy a central place, but from which causal necessity, linear progress and economic growth have been discarded. For Stengers, the 'State cannot be trusted in the face of Gaia' (2015: 75), and neither can science. Both are caught up in the logic of necessity without alternative that has always kept liberal modernity in motion despite its evidently destructive effects on humans and nature (Stengers 2015: 49–50; see also: Da Silva 2022). Because Anthropocene politics, for Stengers, cannot happen without having characterized Gaia first, 'the intrusion of Gaia upsets the order of temporalities' (Stengers 2015: 104) in a way that places an atemporal thinking, understanding and mapping of the human condition before the immediate political reaction to whatever the particular environmental challenge of the day might be. In the Anthropocene, 'the time of struggle cannot postpone the time of creation. It cannot delay until "after," when there is no longer any danger' (Stengers 2015: 104).

Radicalizing Stengers' conceptualization of politics as a sphere that the Anthropocene must radically transform, a number of scholars employ the concept of resilience to emphasize how a non-linear ecological relationality necessitates shifting political action to a logic of flexible, *ad hoc* adaption (O'Brien 2017; Wakefield 2017; Chandler 2013). Resilience does not so much describe a new mode of effectively steering governance. It is rather presented as a tool to generate the epistemological self-reflexivity that allows political communities to orient themselves under the conditions of an ecological shaping power that brings a certain end to the modernist politics characterized by private/public or subject/object distinctions. Following Wakefield, Grove and Chandler, resilience must be thought as a problem-space that undoes and exceeds

> modernist practices of security, such as problems of non-linear ecosystem change and collapse. It offers a critique of modernist planning practices oriented around logics of centralisation, control and prediction as causing those environmental problems centralised planning sought to prevent in the first place, and instead offers a variety of governmental reforms designed to reconfigure social and environmental governance around principles of reflexivity, adaptive management and institutional change [. . .] as a means of living with and developing through emergent disruptions. (2020: 4)

Resilience is the mode of political governance still possible after ontological Anthropocene theory has stripped the former of its humanist, anthropocentric component parts. Chandler emphasizes that the 'ontopolitical' (2018) approaches, tools and techniques assembled under the umbrella of resilience are political in the particular sense that they ontologically order ontic experiences in the Anthropocene in a way that is alternative to that of modern liberalism. Building an 'oystertecture' of mile-long oyster banks off Staten Island, Wakefield and Braun suggest (2018), offers a way to mitigate the impact of flooding on the human community of New York while relinquishing modernist political planning and control; the extent and effectiveness of protection is here shaped by and thus dependent on the agency of the assembled oysters. The inherent vagueness of resilience, which scholars working on and with the concept continuously have to defend against charges of limited practical applicability is, we suggest, rooted in its peculiar status as the political proposal of an Anthropocene scholarship that has renounced governance as we know it. For the ontological strand of Anthropocene theory, politics is a matter to be taken up again only once we have succeeded in 'getting out' of our modernist aspirations of 'getting out' of the Anthropocene. As we are only making the first, tentative ontological advances on our long path to this escape, we cannot yet see clearly the contours of a nonmodern Anthropocene politics and hence cannot yet put the former into practice.

While Stengers, the resilience scholarship and even Latour maintain that the question of politics remains urgent, but for now demands engagement on the level of ontology until we have definitively disabled the recuperative pull of modern-liberal politics, other thinkers more radically suggest that politics itself is a symptom of humanity's aspirations to rule and steer, and must end in the Anthropocene. In this view, resilience is a flawed pathway for putting the Anthropocene's ontological openings into practice because it still embodies the modernist idea of effective collective management (Evans and Reid 2013; Chandler 2018). Critiques of resilience as still 'all too modern' call for an explicitly affirmative understanding of anthropocenic changes. Even if these potentially imply the end of human life on Earth, they allow for a transformation in the way we understand political subjectivity and agency profound enough to escape liberal-modern recuperation. Evans and Reid, in this sense, describe politics for the Anthropocene as a process of 'learning to die [. . .] which celebrates the end of the possible as a condition for the beginning of the new. Beyond the possible, it posits the question of absolute freedom' (2013: 178). As long as we view the Anthropocene as a call to collective action in the hope of achieving a possible end, regardless of whether the participants and parameters of political action have been reconfigured, we will not escape the modernist pitfall of ultimately recuperating the exceptional agency of Anthropos.

Claire Colebrook offers an Anthropocene theory that is hinged on problematizing the idea of an impending climate apocalypse that humanity must act on. The notion of the apocalypse implies that Earth's planetary drama is staged for Anthropos exclusively, and culminates in the hero's dramatic death – the annihilation of humanity as a species. For Colebrook, humanity must instead accept that 'there will not be complete annihilation but a gradual witnessing of a slow end' (Colebrook 2014: 40). The task for Anthropocene ontology is thus 'not an apocalyptic thought of the "beyond the human" as a radical break or dissolution, but [orientation in] a slow, dim, barely discerned and yet violently effective destruction' (Colebrook 2014: 40). Like Stengers, Colebrook worries that an Anthropocene politics sketched out by the not-yet-destroyed modern Anthropos will endow the liberal subject with 'the right to continue in the same manner' (2014: 55) and thus miss its mark. Any political action 'in the name of the sustaining of human life, and of human life as it is already formed, already politicized and already organized' (Colebrook 2014: 114) does nothing to address the ontological fixtures, divides and barriers that form the root cause of the Anthropocene.

For Colebrook, the lesson to be drawn from the Anthropocene's ecological changes is the need for a posthuman ontological decentering to the planetary. The Earth's deep time, from which 'the human is an emergence and intrusion' (Colebrook 2014: 222) provides us with a non-subjective reference point for re-assembling ontology in the Anthropocene. More important than 'man's capacity to think beyond himself' (Colebrook 2014: 221) is the 'thought of a world without man that is released from the orbit of evolving time' (Colebrook 2014: 221). Deep time, for Colebrook, releases a posthuman creative force behind the world's becoming, a 'geological sublime' (Colebrook 2014: 225), alternative to the ordering principles devised by human reason. The time of the Earth is non-linear and unfolds through a dialogical interaction between past, present and multiple futures. Thinking in the mode of deep time 'requires a multiple and intensive mode of scientific calculation, concerned with positive and negative feedback loops and multiple timelines' (Colebrook 2014: 55) that can no longer be captured as unified, and uniform, natural environment. There is precisely no such thing as *the* Anthropocene that is caused, experienced and demands concern by everyone in the same way, or at all.[3]

Radicalizing Colebrook's fracturing of the Anthropocene, Karen Yusoff's *A Billion Black Anthropocenes or None* (2019) targets the colonial baggage that Western modernity – and Anthropocene theory – has to come to terms with before a new 'geologic subject' (Yusoff 2019: 19) can emerge. As a critical intervention into Anthropocene theory – albeit a sympathetic one, written by one of its leading thinkers – Yusoff's book starts from the presumption that broadening our gaze beyond Western modernity in the Anthropocene quest of writing a new ontology for an ecologically entangled humanity is urgently necessary, but requires the posthuman Anthropos to reckon with some uncomfortable truths. Yusoff shows how the Anthropocene, both as a geoscientific fact and as a mode of philosophizing, is entangled with the history of imperial subjugation, colonial extraction and racialization. Not only were the modern scientific and economic advancements that catapulted humanity into the Anthropocene only possible against the background of the systematic exploitation of non-Western humans and nonhumans who never got to share the privileges for which they paid the price. Native communities and their lands, for example, have long lived in a state of ecological emergency that settler states had created by polluting native lands, rendering them uninhabitable and thereby threatening their biological and cultural survival (Yusoff 2019: 55–8; see also: Povinelli 2021).

Anthropocene posthumanism, Yusoff suggests, shares the dark, colonial underside of liberal modernity. For the white citizens of Western democracies, the posthuman embracing of thing power, becoming-animal and becoming-vegetable (Deleuze and Guattari 1987: 272) might appear like an intriguing novelty and promisingly radical way of rethinking human existence and its place vis-à-vis the Earth. But for those on the other side of the demarcating line of modern-Western privileges, being linked to nonhuman life is neither new nor intriguing. Quoting Aimé Césaire's equation of 'Colonization = thingification' (Césaire 1972: 42), Yusoff draws out how blackness has long been the product of an ontopolitical apparatus that renders available nonhumans to exploit without guilt, and without violating the ethical codes that Western modernity has developed for those it counts as subjects (Yusoff 2019: 60–78). The nonhuman outside of liberal modernity is not innocently untainted by its epistemic, economic and political mechanism of production – it has long been serving the former.

This history of racialized dehumanization, Yusoff suggests, cannot simply be undone by developing ontological categories, politics and ethics for the Anthropocene that now aspire to extend beyond modern binaries. The exclusion of the dehumanized other is inbuilt into the idea of normative and ontological universality itself. Against this background, any conceptualization of existence in the Anthropocene must accommodate the radically different historical timelines through which peoples and subjects arrived here, and the dynamics of inequality they create in the present. 'The move towards a more expansive notion of humanity', Yusoff suggests, 'must be made with care. It cannot be based on the presupposition that emancipation is possible once the racial others and their voices are included finally to realize this universality but must be based on the recognition that these "Others" are already inscripted in the foundation formulation of the universal as a space of privileged subjectification' (2019: 58).

Yusoff's critical intervention is exemplary for a broader desire to critically examine, and overcome, the ontological and methodological whiteness of Anthropocene thinking that characterizes current scholarship (Satgar 2022; Baldwin and Erickson 2020; Chipato and Chandler 2022). A central source of inspiration is here the work of Sylvia Wynter, which analyses the subjugation of the Earth and that of non-Western humans as the interrelated constituents of liberal modernity. The Copernican Revolution, following Wynter, subsumed God, humanity and the world under the parameters of rational knowability and measurability by its universal standards. The same epistemic motion that dethroned the Christian church and replaced it with the Enlightenment's rational subject allowed the newly empowered subject to conquer and exploit the world it had rendered measurable (Wynter 2003: 278–80). But it also, importantly, not only allowed but justified the use of its universalized parameters to demarcate those that did not fit the mould of 'Enlightenment man' as outside others defined only negatively, by the absence of Western reason and civilization and therefore not to be granted the same rights and protections (Wynter 2003: 300–5; see also: Wynter 1979).

As Wynter puts it, the West would remain

> unable, from then on, to conceive of an Other to what it calls human – an Other, therefore, to its correlated postulates of power, truth, freedom. All other modes of being human would instead have to be seen not as the alternative modes of being human that they are 'out there,' but adaptively, as the lack of the Wests ontologically absolute self-description. (Wynter 1979: 282)

Wynter reveals the universalization of ontological whiteness and the exclusive suppression of alternative ontologies as the foundation that allowed the modern *Anthropos* to wield its planetarily destructive force. Viewed against this background, a critique of anthropocentrism that leaves this history of Western ontological supremacy unexamined, and thus allows it to continue in explorative formulations of living and governing for the Anthropocene, are destined to fail in their radical pursuit of distancing themselves from liberal modernity. For Wynter, leaving the present impasse of racist violence and planetary erosion therefore requires 'collectively undertaking the task of rewriting knowledge as we know it' (Wynter 2015: 17). For Anthropocene theory, this necessitates an ontological push beyond the idea of a pluriversal Anthropocene, which still takes the form of a theoretical truth claim and towards ontological forms and expressions that are resolutely external and otherwise to modernity's certainties and category systems (Satgar 2022).

Elizabeth Povinelli's work has made a decisive contribution to linking critical reflections on the colonial operativity of modern thought to ontological Anthropocene scholarship. The difficulty, Povinelli shows, is here that both our understanding of ontology and our tools for theoretical critique are imbued with the epistemic figures of liberal modernity and thus, at all times, run the risk of recuperating the former even within a theoretical project that is precisely intended to envision its otherwise (Povinelli 2021, 2016). In *Geontologies*, Povinelli argues that in the Anthropocene, the interplay between this recuperative pull of liberal capitalism and a resistance that displaces and escapes its social and epistemic structures plays out in the *geontopolitical* field between what the former defines as life and what it excludes as nonlife. Povinelli shows how Indigenous art, emergent from communities banned to Nonlife, is able to produce creative ontological expressions and political manoeuvres outside the confinements of modernity's ontopolitical apparatus (Povinelli 2016: 13–15).

Povinelli makes it clear that the Indigenous autonomy she theorizes is radically different from, and in fact disrupts, 'the [modern] romance of the autonomous soul' and comes close to a 'form of toxic sovereignty' (2017: 305). She cites the Indigenous Karrabing collective's film project *Windjarrameru, The Stealing C*nt\$. Windjarrameru* as an example that highlights how the otherwise to liberal capitalism she seeks to capture is not so much located on the completely detached outside of the former but rather emerges from its cracks and displacements. The film contains a scene where a group of young Indigenous men, falsely accused of stealing, are able to ward off the policemen chasing them by fleeing to an area marked as contaminated wasteland, disrupting and ambiguating the modern-liberal distinction between safe and unsafe ontological spaces (2017: 306–7).

Three theses on Anthropocene theory

Our structured overview of Anthropocene theory divides the existing scholarship into a catastrophic strand focused on how humanity can politically respond to the climate crisis and an ontological strand that seeks to utilize the Anthropocene as an opening in the way we make sense of the world to reconceptualize Anthropos, the Earth, and their relationship beyond their modern binary division. Having drawn out this divide, we propose three theses on Anthropocene theory that will ground this book's critical intervention.

(I) The ontological strand of the scholarship importantly advances Anthropocene theory by undoing the remnants of scientific positivism and modern-liberal human exceptionalism that catastrophic perspectives on the Anthropocene at times latently, at times blatantly, hold on to. The theorists of the Anthropocene catastrophe all criticize the exploitative excess that rendered possible liberal modernity and maintain that shifting away from the former requires us to fundamentally alter the way we think about and engage with nature. However, more or less explicitly, they all continue the trajectory of Western modernism by advocating for the pooling of rational human inventiveness to counteract and survive the Anthropocene catastrophe. The liberal subject has created the Anthropocene mess – but a different kind of human subject can get us out. The ontological strand of Anthropocene theory dismantles the modernist hope underpinning this line of argumentation. Thinkers of the ontological Anthropocene show how using the modern master's governmental and scientific tools to dismantle the master's house, built of steel and brick, might offer short-term 'techno fixes' for mitigating the Anthropocene condition, but ultimately leaves the anthropocentric ontology that grounds and sustains the exploitation of nonhumans unaddressed. Acting on the Anthropocene here requires, first and foremost, de-centring our understanding of being to the planetary and rethinking human communities as produced, shaped and limited by their many nonhuman entanglements. The creative complexity of the entangled Earth fractures the Anthropocene totality that the catastrophic strand of the scholarship challenges humanity to act on. It creates analytical space for a radically diverse Anthropocene present produced via multiple evolutionary pathways shaped by both local cultural contexts and global power structures.

(II) While the ontological scholarship advances the theoretical-conceptual tools of Anthropocene theory, it does however not effectively resolve the political questions raised by its catastrophic counterpart. We suggest that both strands of the scholarship must be understood as operating in different registers, the political and the ontological. The arguments that each strand develops in its respective register are not cancelled out by the points and criticisms developed by the other strand because they do not easily translate to the former. Both strands offer in themselves complex, logical and well-justified but incongruent accounts of the Anthropocene. Because they do not speak to each other, one strand cannot readily be identified as 'winning' the contest of theorizing the Anthropocene. The ontological strand of Anthropocene theory has effectively shown that the urgent call to collective action in the face of the climate catastrophe cannot belie, and does not do away with, the fact that such action, without a fundamental ontological reconfiguration of modern thought, must make use of political tools that are at best ill-equipped for their task, at worst worsen rather than improve the repercussions of human intervention into a poorly understood planetary ecology.

However, on the other hand, pointing out the inferiority of the ontological basis employed by the catastrophic perspective on the Anthropocene does not do away with the real social and ethical concerns that the former calls us to urgently address. Despite Latour's insistence that his Gaia theory is returning social thought to actual matters of concern, the danger is that the prioritization of ontology returns Anthropocene theory instead to the academic ivory tower because ecological political action is here rendered secondary to and dependent on ontological reconfiguration. For ontological Anthropocene theory, as shown earlier, the subjects of Western industrialized democracies have to become posthumans, Terrans or citizens of Gaia first to be able to think and then enact a politics worthy of the Anthropocene (Colebrook 2014; Stengers 2015; Latour 2021). Because the master's modernist tools simply will not do, we can only act once we have crafted new weapons from our Earthly entanglements. The catastrophic perspective's powerful rejoinder, which does not subvert but is also not devalued by this insistence on ontological reconfiguration, would be that any mitigating action that can protect lives and livelihoods and relieve suffering is better than none, and should be undertaken regardless of its modernist ontological baggage and recuperating effects.

(III) The third thesis that will guide the arguments of this book is that post-colonial and non-Western alternatives and challenges to modern ecology cannot readily be contained in either branch of Anthropocene theory but span across them, and call into question their division. All Anthropocene scholarship is critical of the workings and ecological effects of liberal capitalism and of the political frameworks that facilitate its workings. But radical calls to overcome liberal modernity towards a fundamentally different ontology that does not contain the seed corns of possessive liberalism are firmly located on the side of ontological Anthropocene theory. As exemplified by Yusoff's decolonial critique, it is here that Anthropocene theory investigates whether its own ontological propositions do not still carry the marker of ontological whiteness and thus reveal the long road ahead before the scars of colonial violence will be healed and the legacy of modernity can finally be put to rest. The relationship between ontological Anthropocene theory's battle cry for a novel understanding of being and its emergent self-awareness as a fundamentally Western-modern ontological approach will form the context and the topic of investigation for the arguments developed in the following chapters.

Chakrabarty's intervention quoted earlier reminds Anthropocene theory of the fact that industrial-technological progress is not an exclusively Western aim, and, at least for a brief moment in time, was closely interwoven with projects of decolonial liberation. The post-colonial challenge seems thus not readily overcome with an ontological turn away from rational advancement and societal progress. On the contrary, the insistence that Anthropocene theory's Western whiteness must be addressed and can be overcome on an ontological level might in fact situate the former more thoroughly within the path-dependent logic of modern thought. In her recent book *Between Gaia and Ground. For Axioms for late Liberalism*, Povinelli points out how operating according to an 'ontology first, politics second' logic is not only the particular marker, but also the particular shortcoming of Western ecology. The ontological turn, following Povinelli, has subsumed all critical engagement in the Anthropocene under the ontological axiom of 'entangled existence', to which historical and political contexts and specificities are secondary. Here, 'the different toxic accumulations of racial and colonial catastrophes are refigured as a coming catastrophe for humanity that can be solved only by returning to a set of first conditions – to ontology' (Povinelli 2021: 16).

For Povinelli, the primacy of the ontological axiom vis-à-vis the historical and the political places Anthropocene theory firmly in the tradition of modern liberalism that it so desperately seeks to escape. The explorations developed in the following align with Povinelli's insights in many ways. But instead of turning to the sites that allow for glimpses beyond the Anthropocene's hegemonic ontological modernity, as Povinelli does, we remain with and in the ontological Anthropocene. We explore the space spanned between its foundational presumptions and its political implications. Doing so, we draw out how the Anthropocene's continuous modernism manifests in its ontopolitical parameters. We further challenge the necessity of these parameters with the help of Indigenous knowledges and scholarship, where environmental political practice is not ontologically overdetermined in the modern fashion. In the following chapter, we bring Indigenous ecology into the Anthropocene equation of environmental crises, ontological reconfigurations and post-colonial politics. Indigenous thought and political activism aim to resist the modern-Western colonial State not only as a political institution but also as an ontopolitical apparatus. But at the same time, Indigenous ecology is only partially congruent with the planetary ontology of Anthropocene theory, and stands in a complex relationship to modernity.

Repoliticizing ecology

Indigenous knowledge in the Anthropocene

Now that the theoretical ground has been prepared, this chapter will install and bring into position the methodological tool of this book's critical intervention, the assemblage of Indigenous ecology as a critical mirror. This chapter creates an encounter between Anthropocene theory and Indigenous scholarship. In the critical mirror of Indigenous ecology, we will further interrogate the binary between the catastrophic strand and the ontological strand of Anthropocene thought, and the narrative of smooth theoretical progress from the former to the latter. We draw out how ontological Anthropocene theory parallels Indigenous knowledges and cosmologies in some of its foundational assumptions, including a relational understanding of Being, a conception of agency that is open to nonhuman shaping power and thus a responsive, local and adaptive governance.

At this point, we engage with Critical Indigenous Studies scholarship on the multiple political claims, local struggles and particular anti-colonial projects that the aforementioned ontological tenets are interwoven with on the side of Indigenous communities (Whyte 2017a; Todd 2015). Doing so, we bring into position a critical mirror of Indigenous ecology that problematizes the necessities, path-dependencies and limitations that an internally multiple but totalized entangled ontology sets up within ontological Anthropocene theory. The mirror renders visible stories of Anthropocene Indigenous ecology that cannot easily be accommodated under the umbrella of the ontological Anthropocene, both because they politically reject any such connection and because the approaches to agency, temporality and governance do not fit the parameters that the former has staked out for political action. The critical mirror of Indigenous ecology complicates the lessons to be learned and the political pathways of actualization that follow from the Anthropocene's ontological turn.

Enter the Indigenous: The Anthropocene's opening up to radical alterity

As drawn out in the previous chapter, the ontological perspective on the Anthropocene that dominates the current critical scholarship views climate change not as an apocalyptic threat but instead as an opportunity to rethink the ontological foundations of creativity and agency on Earth. Because this creative drive is motivated by the desire to make the world differently from what liberal moderns have come to accept as true and necessary, it is hardly surprising that some thinkers of the ontological Anthropocene have begun to engage with nonmodern peoples, and here particularly with the 'lived knowledge kept and created by Indigenous peoples across the Earth and over millennia' (Mitchell 2017: 15).

For Colebrook, non-Western thought and Indigenous cosmologies offer a mode of thinking and knowing that has avoided the Cartesian error of separating ideas and matter, and can thus support our ontological mapping of the human condition in the Anthropocene (Colebrook 2017a). If 'we suffer in the West from centered, disembodied, linear and instrumental notions of mind, then we would do well to pay attention to the eastern tradition of mindfulness' (Colebrook 2014: 137) and the 'embodied-relational modes' of awareness that render them distinct from the 'Western instrumental consciousness' (Colebrook 2014: 137) of 'managerial man' (Colebrook 2014: 184). Latour, in his Anthropocene ontology, endorses the epistemic tools that non-Western knowledges offer beyond our 'pathetic resources' (Latour 2017: 108) of linear ordering, planning and steering with similar enthusiasm. Indigenous peoples, following Latour, are versed in a different kind of 'diplomacy' (2021: 257) that mediates between humans and nonhumans within the networks that connect them. For this reason, he suggests that it is from these 'extramoderns' (2021: 257) 'who we put in danger that the industrialised can learn how to survive as if, to civilise themselves anew, they'd said to themselves "Let's be *rewilded* by these guys'" (Latour 2021: 258; emphasis in original).

In *The Ends of the World*, the Brazilian anthropologists Déborah Danowski and Eduardo Viveiros de Castro offer a more nuanced, less simplistic exploration of how the '[m]etaphysical problem' (2017: 6) of the Anthropocene interlinks with and can draw from non-Western, particularly Ameridian, ontologies that have always been de-centred away from the human subject (2018: 21–2). Following Danowski and Viveiros de Castro, Ameridians do not face the laborious task of crafting a posthuman subjectivity because they have never been modern in Latour's sense. Ameridian ontologies counter the Western-liberal teleology of progress with a mythology that instead posits the past as a rich, dynamic and productive resource for orientation. Nature, not humanity, is the creative force behind the becoming of the Earth and its multiple interwoven timelines. In Ameridian cosmologies, it 'is Nature that is born out of or "separates" itself from Culture, not the other way round, as in our anthropophilosophical vulgate' (Danowski and Viveiros de Castro 2018: 67). These cosmologies manage to resist universalizing and homogenizing human ideas, norms and pursuits because each contains an internal multiplicity of 'alignments among the various world peoples or "cultures" with several other nonhuman actants and peoples [. . .]. The multiverse, the ante-nomic or precosmic background state, remains non-unified, on the human as well as on the world side' (Danowski and Viveiros de Castro 2018: 90).

Danowski and Viveiros de Castro oppose the Western-liberal striving for linear growth and eternal life with the loop-like movement of Ameridian mythologies that are marked by consecutive Apocalypses and where death, rather than life, marks the existential human condition (2018: 76, 103). Similar to Latour and Colebrook but based on a much more profound engagement with non-Western thought, they conclude that Ameridians have much 'to teach us about the end of the world' (2018: 78). While Danowski and Viveiros de Castro acknowledge that the world's Indigenous peoples, existing in the present against the background of a long history of colonial violence, exploitation and oppression, might not have much appetite for coming to the rescue of a Western modernity that faces not only a climate crisis but with it also an identity crisis, they nevertheless conclude somewhat optimistically that the Indigenous masters 'of technoprimitivist bricolage and politico-metaphysical metamorphosis [. . .] are one of [humanity's] possible chances [. . .] of a *subsistence of the future*' (2018: 123; emphasis in original).

Donna Haraway points to opportunities for 'making multi-species kin' (2018: 70–82) in Indigenous communities that have experienced the injustices of losing human and nonhuman relatives. For other scholars, Indigenous communities remain a source of nonmodern planning and management practices that come to represent a different mode of subjective experience and a different form of entangled agency beyond human control (Salick and Ross 2009; Jojola 2008; Alaimo 2008). In sum, the cosmologies and realities of Indigenous peoples have become intrinsically linked to the project of reconfiguring ontopolitics for the Anthropocene. This is not just because they represent the voices of dispossessed subjects who have fought to survive and thrive in the face of genocide and exploitation, but also because their cosmologies contain elements that are particularly close to the entangled ontologies advocated by what we identified as ontological perspectives, from Latour's emphasis on relational Gaia to Colebrook's posthuman decentring and Stenger's Anthropocene characterizing – even if only some thinkers explicitly explore these links, as shown above. At this point, we would like to stay with the parallels that position the ontological Anthropocene in proximity to Indigenous ecology in its cosmological basis and its practised reality for a moment. We suggest that this parallelism is upheld by three distinct cornerstones of worldmaking: nonhuman agency, resilience and non-linearity.

In the first instance, Indigenous practices are commonly drawn upon as examples of ontological connectivity to an environment with autonomous shaping power. Indigenous worldviews are seen as affectively responding to, rather than seeking to tame, the nonhuman forces that affect them. Indigenous communities have built cultural practices around a relational engagement with their immediate environment that provides them with the means to sustain communal life through a combination of mutual support and adaption. Many Indigenous cosmologies highlight the agency of nonhumans and promote radically intertwined ways of thinking about nature, culture and humanity at the cross-section of the three (Agrawal 1995; Johnson and Murton 2007). As in ontological Anthropocene theory, reflecting on ecological situatedness here does not begin or end with acknowledging 'individual or cumulative effects of environmental change' (Harrington 2016: 481) that are clearly measurable and manageable. Indigenous cosmologies rather 'express protocols that often represent humans as respectful partners or younger siblings in relationships of reciprocal responsibilities within interconnected communities of relatives inclusive of humans, nonhuman beings, entities and collectives' (Whyte, Brewer and Johnson 2016: 2).

Since Indigenous communities do not have an ontologically reified 'nature', the landscape wherein human cultures live, work and play is not clearly delineated as an environmental outside 'other' to be feared or subdued (Van Horn 2017: 3–4). In discussing the Menominee communities' relationship to the forest, for instance, Jeff Grignon and Robin Wall Kimmerer point out that what is viewed as wilderness according to techno-scientific categorizations of the landscape, for example as applied by satellites, is actually the product of intensive Indigenous management (2017: 69). These landscapes, the authors claim, emerge and are maintained through reciprocal practices of care involving humans and nonhumans (Grignon and Kimmerer 2017). Though unintelligible to 'modern' scientists (see Peña 2017), these practices are guided by the ordering principle of respect for multiple beings rather than human supremacy and control (Peña 2017: 93).

On the other hand, Indigenous communities have long had to contend with actions of colonial powers that fundamentally disempower them or destroy cultural value, sometimes in the very name of sustainability for all, as it can be seen in the banning of fire in burning ceremonies in North America (Whyte 2018b). Because of this, Indigenous communities have developed strategies to maintain their cultural integrity under changing conditions shaped by the political and ontological hegemony of the settler State, which are akin to the adaptive resilience called for by ontological Anthropocene theory. As Peña notes, Indigenous communities are not 'ghosts of the primitive accumulation, of a forced separation from the land' (2017: 93). Instead, their practices evolve 'within cycles of epochal Indigenous resistance to capitalist colonial enclosures', as representations of communities that are 'vibrant coactants and shapers of the world' (Peña 2017: 93).

Because Indigenous communities have already experienced the enduring existential catastrophe of settler colonialism, their ways of living in and with nonhuman environments have adapted to spaces that are 'physically, emotionally, and spiritually toxic' (Simmons 2019: 175). Indigenous acts of resilience express a situated, dynamic politics that responds to, and productively utilizes, the particular, local, material entanglements in which the human actors find themselves. In her keynote address at a 2014 conference on Anthropocene Feminism by the Centre for 21st Century studies, Myra Hird describes an Inuit town's rejection of recycling waste as an example for such adaptive politics. By refusing to hide and remove trash and instead leaving plastic materials strewn out in the streets 'as they would a seal carcass, the Innuit community allows it to remain on the surface, refusing to make waste and wasted landscapes disappear' (Hird cited by Swanson, Bubandt and Tsing 2015: 155). Similarly, even formalized acts of ecological management, such as the establishment of Indigenous local planning regimes, allow for the continued exercise of Indigenous practices of land tenure based on collective rights against a backdrop of planning approaches coming from the West, which have – and continue to – usurp or undermine 'traditional' knowledge and cultural identity (Jojola 2008). These are but two instances of Indigenous practices as exercised in the end times; because 'for the native people of the Americas, the end of the world already happened' (Danowski and Viveiros de Castro 2018: 104), thinkers of the ontological Anthropocene seek to learn from Indigenous communities how to think and act after the (modern) world has ended, 'in a post-catastrophic time, or, if one wishes, in a permanently diminished human world' (Danowski and Viveiros de Castro 2018: 95).

The ontological Anthropocene employs deep time to conceptualize a non-linear and relationally dispersed shaping power, which extends indefinitely and beyond a certain end of history. This Anthropocene temporality mirrors the non-linear order of time constitutive of the way many Indigenous communities frame present actions and interactions as taking place in a productive dialogue with ancestral pasts to collaboratively establish futures. Indigenous understandings of time are intergenerational and fold back on themselves (Whyte 2018a). 'Spiralling time', as Whyte et al. describe Indigenous temporality, is characterized by a continued 'dialogical unfolding' of 'questions about how ancestral and future generations would interpret the situations we find ourselves in today' (Whyte, Brewer and Johnson 2016: 7). Indigenous communities 'have different orientations towards time, and theorizations of this alternative time [. . .] require scholars to rethink the scale of climate change within a longer historical trajectory' (Simmons 2019: 175). Like Indigenous resilience, spiralling time is intrinsically linked to the experience of colonial extinction. Describing the effects of colonialism, Davis and Todd point to the 'slinky-like' quality of disaster that compacts and expands time, destroying languages and legal orders by moving in 'a seismic sense' (2017: 771–2). In this sense, deep time makes it possible to view climate change as akin to the drawn-out, still ongoing end-of-the-world ushered in by colonial dispossession (Gross 2014; Danowski and Viveiros De Castro 2017: 75).

Indigenous thought and practice on planning and steering

So far, Indigenous ecology appears to have folded smoothly into the narrative framework of the ontological Anthropocene. But this is the case because we only told a particular set of stories from the realm of Indigenous ecology, and we told them in a way that aligns with Anthropocene ontology. Rupturing this smooth enfolding, the following passages highlight how Indigenous cosmologies and Indigenous politics exhibit a mode of ecological engagement that diverges from, and in some instances actively clashes with, the presumptions and postulates of ontological Anthropocene theory. Engagement with Indigenous thought and scholarship reveals distinctly different modes of translating ontological relationality and non-linearity into practical action. Beyond resilience, Indigenous ecologies hold on the role of intentional steering and futurity; they do not preclude planned action altogether but instead highlight the power dynamics inherent in the management of environmental relations (Watson 2013), as well as the fluid and evolving role of the 'human' in more-than-human relations.

Within Indigenous scholarship, Indigenous planning refers to 'practical activities whereby a collective [. . .] envisions different futures that are more or less desirable for itself and its members' (Whyte, Caldwell and Schefer 2017: 155). Planning here '"unsettles" "Western" [. . .] theory and in particular its globalising/totalising tendencies', providing 'an intellectual and political space for Indigenous peoples to define themselves, to spatialize indigeneity and, most importantly, mark out their future' (Porter et al. 2017: 640). It is, therefore, 'planning by/with (not for) Indigenous peoples' (Porter et al. 2017: 641). Indigenous communities have developed materially grounded planning systems to govern on the basis of 'protocols', that is, collectively established regimes sketching out various ways in which 'a group ought to proceed or behave in any given situation' (Whyte, Brewer and Johnson

2016: 2). For instance, in the territories of the Ngarrindjeri nation, located along the Murray river in the Coorong and Encounter Bay region in South Australia, Indigenous methodologies were deployed to 'resist, negotiate with, and transform NRM [Settler natural resource management]' and 'develop a sustainable economy and healthy community' (Hemming, Rigney and Berg 2011: 99).

The methodology employed as an Indigenous mode of planning here, known as Kungun Ngarrindjeri Yunnan, guides 'significant interactions with government and other non-Indigenous interests impacting on Ngarrindjeri *Ruwe/Ruwar* [country/body/spirit, encapsulating the inner-connection of people, their lands, waters and all living things including the spirits of Ngarrindjeri Ancestors]' (Hemming, Rigney and Berg 2011: 99). In this sense, as Ted Jojola suggests, Indigenous planning marks a way of actively re-appropriating shared land-tenure and collective rights approaches to community development that have been, until recently, 'subsumed by non-native practictioners' aimed mainly at the assimilation of Indigenous tribes into mainstream environments (2008: 41). Jojola also highlights that Indigenous planning represents an ideological movement to unite Indigenous approaches and distinguish them from liberal governance practices (2008: 42). The re-appropriation of traditional approaches to land management here not only represents a way to counter the 'slash-and-burn economics' (2008: 43) fuelled by private property rights, but is also an expression of collective agency, understood as the exercise of human stewardship for the fostering of a 'balanced and symmetrical interrelationship between humankind and the natural ecosystem that it occupies' (2008: 43).

Indigenous scholarship identifies Indigenous planning as an important form of self-governance that embodies resistance against continued erasure and colonial dispossession (Davis and Todd 2017: 774; see also Coulthard 2007). The environmental stewardship it sets up is resolutely non-Western but envisages a prominent position for the humans that practice it. 'Wildness is the dissolution of the boundaries of the self, accepting an invitation to follow a niche-abiding way of life in gentle relation with more-than-human beings' (2017: 90), Peña suggests, adding that such life is 'cognizant of the coupling of culture and nature as defined by the conditions of the self willing bioregional ecosystem' (2017: 90). Human stewardship happens in a context where nature has never been clearly distinguished from culture. Consequently, the desire for ontological safeguarding against the (modern) human will to control, subsume, appease, save or be saved from, which sparks the insistence on absolutely flat entanglements without any particular human shaping power or responsibility, is absent here. Indigenous guardians, un-selfconsciously, plan and manage expressions of care for kin and life (Davis and Todd 2017: 775). Since preserving or discarding, once and for all, the nature/culture dichotomy is of no interest here, 'humans have a role to play' in cultivating 'an ongoing relationship, one in which human cultures become attuned to the community of life and constitutive of the well-being of the places' wherein they exist (Van Horn 2017: 3).

The land-ethics encapsulated by Indigenous planning regimes counter liberal conceptualizations of territorial enclosures promoted and enforced through capitalism and settler colonialism. At the same time, they express an active human politics within an entangled world where human shaping power remains tantamount to posthuman collective action and 'relational solidarity' (Peña 2017: 96). Another example of this is the Anishinaabeg concept of *Akiing,* explained by Hausdoerffer as an invitation for humans to become 'cocreators in addition to preservers' (2017: 202) – 'akiing, then, is both land to which people belong *and land that requires people*' (2017: 202; emphasis added). This sustainable cocreation is radically different from both the capitalist exploitation of cheap nature and from solutions that seek to protect the environment by keeping it separate from human interference. For Peña, both are inadequate forms of ecological politics rooted in the modern-liberal inability to think nature and culture not just together, but as indistinguishable (2017: 97).

Divergence from ontological Anthropocene theory can also be found in Indigenous attitudes towards the future, and the notion of future success in particular. Against the background of a relational ontology, Indigenous scholars expressly clarify that Indigenous planning protocols are driven by the desire, and the manifest possibility, to achieve some form of anticipated future 'success' even under uncertain and unpredictable conditions. An example in the context of ecological planning is the reintroduction of the sturgeon to the Manistee river in Anishinaabeg territory (Whyte, Brewer and Johnson 2016: 4). While making it clear that Indigenous protocols are produced by collectives that are not exclusively human, this type of governance remains unapologetically insistent that targeted and directed human agency is possible: 'Indigenous ecologies physically manifest Indigenous governance systems through origin, religious and cultural narratives, ways of life, political structures, and economies' (Whyte, Caldwell and Schefer 2017: 159). The ecologies that emerge are 'systematic arrangements' where human agency is acknowledged to have 'shaped the lands and waters' (Whyte, Caldwell and Schefer 2017: 158) of ancestral territories. Through planning that cannot fix or predict but does anticipate and seek to shape a non-linear future, Indigenous knowledge places communities in the position to not just react passively to disastrous changing circumstances, but to actively promote 'practices that secure human benefits' (Whyte 2017b: 157) from relations between humans and nonhumans. Far from being merely the expression of ad hoc, resilient actions aimed to secure survival in the face of apocalyptic environmental changes (caused by human or nonhuman shaping power), human action is here situated within a framework that recognizes knowledge gathering, planning and policy making for the environment as the territory where Indigenous struggles over land ownership and sovereignty play out (Porter et al. 2017) and ultimately can bear fruit.

Relational ontology in the critical mirror of Indigenous ecology

What are we to make of the parallels and incongruences between Indigenous thought and scholarship and ontological Anthropocene theory drawn out earlier? In the following, we propose to read them through the politically charged debates of Critical Indigenous Studies (CIS) scholarship. It is against the background and through CIS's politicization of Indigenous ecology that we draw together ideas, stories and actions from Indigenous cosmologies and Indigenous environmental action towards this book's methodological device of a critical mirror of Indigenous ecology. CIS is held together by its locally specific, activist approach. As argued by Justice, it is 'an interventionist analytic of transformation committed to and dependent on local specificity within a broader network of relationships' (2016: 20). CIS provides not only ontological and epistemological alternatives to Western modernism but a way to 'contravene in, respond to, and redirect European philosophies [in order to] offer crucial new ways of conceptualising an after to empire that does not reside within the obliteration of Indigenous lives, resources and lands' (Byrd 2011: 229). Turning to the way Critical Indigenous thinkers respond to the Western Anthropocene debate, we can see a combination of ontological alignment and political complexity that does not neatly fit the frame of either approval or rejection and diametrical opposition. The parallels between Anthropocene ontology and Indigenous ecologies drawn out earlier have not gone unnoticed among CIS scholars. Several authors have cautioned against the danger that Indigenous ideas and practice would be enveloped by the Western canon of environmental scholarship in and against which they are developed. Liberal modernity, CIS thinkers point out, seeks to use Indigenous knowledges as an ontological resource for moving from the Anthropocene catastrophe towards a post-apocalyptic living in the end times – but for Indigenous communities, such a post-apocalyptic state, which would imply the end of colonial authority of their lands, resources and cultures, is nowhere in sight. As Elizabeth DeLoughrey suggests, 'the lack of engagement with postcolonial and Indigenous perspectives has shaped the Anthropocene discourse to claim the *novelty* of crisis rather than being attentive to the historical *continuity* of dispossession and disaster caused by the empire' (2019: 2; emphasis in original). In a similar vein, Métis scholar Zoe Todd asks,

> [W]hat 'modernist mess,' as Fortun eloquently describes it, characterizes this moment of 'common cosmopolitical concern' – Latour's term to describe the fact that the climate is a shared heritage, cross-roads, site, or milieu that we all inhabit, and one which deserves our deep attention as a commons and context for engaged involvement in the crises of climate change – that is the Anthropocene? And, finally, who is dominating the conversations about how to change the state of things? (Todd 2015: 244)

Indigenous critics highlight that the concept of the Anthropocene itself erases violent histories, meaningful diversity and intersectionality because of its universal claim (Day 2021; DeLoughrey 2019). For Eric Gary Anderson, the ghost of violence does indeed '[course] through and [inform] the Anthropocene' (Anderson 2021: 146). Indigenous critics view the theoretical perspective that Anthropocene ontology offers for making sense of the planet's posthuman condition as fundamentally unsuitable because it falls 'short of naming who is doing what to whom' (Anderson 2021: 146) in a radically – and path-dependently – unequal global present. Indigenous communities have developed ways to be resilient under conditions of ecological shaping power as necessary tools to survive continuous settler colonialism. Against this background, theoretically enfolding elements of their cosmology, uprooted from this colonial context, within Anthropocene ontology places them side by side with the ideational frameworks of settler states. This enfolding would further assist the former in making sense of the world in the face of the Anthropocene's environmental effects via becoming 'metaphorically Indigenous, shrinking-humanist subjectivities and recasting ourselves in reciprocal relations with more-than human beings' (Lemenager 2021: 102).

CIS scholars also point out that Indigenous concepts run the risk of being significantly distorted in the process of linking them to or encorporating them within a Western theoretical canon. Where Anthropocene ontology links to Indigenous ecological relationality, for instance, the former becomes imbued with the possessive liberalism of distinctly modern ownership models. In the entangled relationship with dirt, theorized by the Anthropocene ontologists Latour and Stacy Alaimo with reference to Indigenous cosmologies, the implications are that 'humans are responsible to land the way an owner might be responsible for a pet' (Watts 2013: 29). At the same time, Aboriginal scholar Virginia Marshall (2019) cautions against the presumption that Indigenous peoples per se reject property-based and human-centric forms of ecological guardianship, which she again attributes to ontological Anthropocene theory. The Anthropocene idea, as LeMenager suggests, offers a critique of capitalism and colonialism inspired by the imperative to 'learn "how to die"' (2021: 102). Enveloping Indigenous cosmologies and politics within the former renders Indigenous communities the embodiment of the posthuman condition that White and settler subjects must learn to embrace, once again erasing Indigenous agency. CIS scholars such as Vanessa Watts, Zoe Todd, Eve Tuck and Kyle Whyte have problematized the Anthropocene scholarship's metaphorical and selective engagement with Indigeneity in the name of imploding the imperialistic tendencies of Western knowledge from within (Watts 2013).

As Scott suggests, using Indigenous ideas within 'a Eurocentric framework as narrated through Western philosophy is not required or really even appropriate' (2016: 79) from the perspective of an Indigenous scholarship that seeks to achieve political recognition rather than epistemic representation. A Western turn to the 'Indigenous' as an essentialized body of knowledge not only continues to other Indigenous thought as 'epistemologically distinct' (Watts 2013: 26) but also opens, CIS scholars warn, 'a gateway for non-Indigenous thinkers to re-imagine their world' (Watts 2013: 26). The risk, here, is that Indigenous stories, principles and practices could come to be flattened 'to imply that – words, principles, morals to imagine the world and imagine ourselves in the world' equivalent to the abstract principles of Western ontology. Indigenous ideas and practices would thereby uphold the hegemony of the former in determining how we imagine and re-imagine the world – as one world, and through one lens, even if the former is fractured in the Anthropocene (Carter 2018). Watts (2013) critiques Haraway's use of the Indigenous concepts of the Coyote or the Trickster (Haraway 1991) to do the conceptual work of 'imploding' the boundaries of dominant Western concepts like heteropatriarchy. Following Watts, the consequence is that Western concepts are here re-assembled in an improved fashion that is able to accommodate the Indigenous alternatives that previously challenged them. For Watts, Haraway's engagement with Indigenous thought is symptomatic of a wider tendency within the contemporary Anthropocene scholarship to selective expropriate Indigenous concepts and images and turn them into abstract principles that advance Western knowledge production. At the same time, Chris Andersen has warned of the danger of limiting Indigeneity by framing it as a distinct, disciplinary form of knowledge sitting necessarily outside the (in part always also Western) academy (Andersen 2009: 81).

While CIS, its role, and its disciplinary boundaries, are very much a continued subject of debate, the density and multiplicity of Indigenous experiences lie at the heart of all of its expressions (Champagne 2007a, 2007b). Simone Rowe, Eileen Baldry and Wendy Earles (2015) thus suggest that, while Indigenous studies is a research paradigm underpinned by common fundamental principles pertaining to ontology, epistemology, axiology and methodology, these should not be understood as representing a multiple but ultimately shared Indigenous mode of being in the world. The methodological underpinnings of CIS thus challenge us to take Anthropocene heterogeneity seriously. The fractured multiplicity that CIS draws from Indigenous experiences, knowledges and politics cannot be accommodated in one entangled planetary condition – even if the former is radically diverse and fractured. CIS responses to the Western scholarship's turn to the Indigenous oscillate between the critique that the – politically charged – alterity of the former is not taken seriously, and the challenge of essentializing Indigenous peoples as the eternal 'Other' of Western modernity. In other words, some Indigenous scholars view the world they think and inhabit as distinct from the Anthropocene, and separated from the former by a gap that, under the conditions of settler colonialism, cannot be bridged epistemologically or politically. Others reject being positioned outside of Anthropocene entanglements. CIS highlights divergences and contestations so fundamental that they include the unity or plurality of the entangled planet itself. Taking CIS seriously means that this ontological ambiguity has to be retained.

In line with CIS' provocative challenge, this book brings together ideas, experiences and stories of Indigenous ecology that do not reveal a new – uniform or internally multiple – essence of being in the Anthropocene. Rather, they render visible complexity of different, situated, in themselves valid and purposeful, pathways of thinking and acting ecologically. The critical mirror of Indigenous ecology 'provincialises' the Anthropocene discourse, 'much as postcolonial studies "provincialized" the universalizing discourse of Europe' (DeLoughrey 2019: 2). It challenges 'absolute knowing' not through an essential Indigenous 'otherness' but because its politically situated complexity resists all overarching ordering and 'raise[s] the spectre of knowledge unintelligible to Western rationalism' (DeLoughrey 2019: 2). The ideas and acts of Indigenous ecology assembled in our critical mirror relate back to 'a cultural geologic that is not reducible to a universalized climate science of the Anthropocene' (DeLoughrey 2019: 4) – neither of a modern nor of a nonmodern kind. Here, 'culture, climate, experience, knowledge and the Anthropocene are all placed in disjunctive relation' (DeLoughrey 2019: 4). As a consequence, the certainties and uncertainties of the ontological Anthropocene are not so much undone as they are rendered particular, contextual, and open to alternatives.

Through its emphasis on relational connectivity and productivity, ontological Anthropocene theory seeks to distance itself from the modernist nature/culture and nature/scientific rationality binaries that modernity relies on. Rejecting the idea that nature is absolutely external and can thus be objectively measured and shaped by sustainable politics, the ontological scholarship insists that in the Anthropocene, 'you are inside it while hearing the loud crashing of outside/inside boundaries' (Latour 2017: 62). In undoing modernist binaries in favour of an essentially entangled Anthropocene, the ontological scholarship risks rendering the Anthropocene a realm of absolute immanence that swallows and thereby does away with all lines of division. While the Anthropocene is no homogenous whole, it is a relational totality that does not leave room for disconnected, genuinely resistant 'outsides'. Employing a related criticism that Melinda Cooper and Jeremy Walker have levelled against resilience-based governance approaches, it can be argued that the central achievement of Anthropocene ontology is to 'internalize and neutralize all external challenges . . . to metabolize all countervailing forces and inoculate itself against critique' (Walker and Cooper 2011: 157). Again, we find ourselves 'in the same boat'. This time, it is the Anthropocene as a theoretical perspective with the analytical pretence to accommodate not just all life on Earth but the productive capacity of the Earth itself in its totality.

Ontological Anthropocene theory performs an all-encompassing theoretical 'hugging' that replaces the scientific discovery of a catastrophic discontinuity with the ontological claim of an Anthropocene that has no outside because its multiple productive relations are always-already and indefinitely unfolding. 'If there is something like "Anthropos" unified by way of its capacity to generate planetary destruction, then it is this world that becomes the only horizon and only end. There is no "planet B" and no other world [. . .] and ends are no longer the sweeping away of deadened worlds for the sake of a future' (Colebrook 2019: 271). Because the continuous Anthropocene incorporates alterity (in the form of different speeds, feedback loops and multiple experiences and networks of agency), there is no outside to its ecological entanglements, which predates and will outlive human societies. The Anthropocene's ontological force of 'geopower has no outside, no "place" or "time" before or beyond it: it is the force, the forces, of the Earth itself: forces which we as technical humans have tried to organize, render consistent and predictable, but which we can never fully accomplish insofar as the Earth remains the literal ground and condition for every human, and nonhuman, action' (Grosz, Yusoff and Clark 2017: 135).

An entangled Anthropocene that introversively enfolds all differences and multiplicities it encounters immunizes itself effectively from critiques that highlight global differences, multiplicity and alterity. Anthropocene ontology thus renders innocuous alternative and resistant political claims – such as those of Indigenous groups – that contain diversity that cannot be accommodated in a unifying whole. This is especially problematic where these differences amount to a fundamental challenge to the meta-narrative of the continuous Anthropocene 'as a complex set of overlapping emerging processes in which all subject-objects are embedded' (Chandler 2013: 12). In this sense, the critical mirror of Indigenous ecology reveals how human-directed agency can generate different and emergent forms of management, planning and steering. It also, importantly, shows how a shared ecological-relational ontology can go hand in hand with multiple and partially clashing political claims.

Our critical mirror of Indigenous ecology is not assembled to achieve what Watts critically refers to as 'imploding' – that is confronting Western philosophy with its nonmodern outside in order to shatter the category systems of the former and draw them again in a better, more inclusive fashion. What we intend to make visible in the critical mirror is not what is missing from (Western) Anthropocene ontology but rather what has been there all along, a complexity of pathways that link ontological frameworks to political action. Rather than expropriating Indigenous thought and preparing its incorporation into a Western canon, the critical mirror is designed to spark reflection on the internal, irresolvable multiplicity of the (Western) Anthropocene that it renders visible. As DeLoughrey reminds us, 'in grounding the abstract discourse of the Anthropocene by tying it to specific histories and places we can learn much about the contextual nuances of narrativizing the relationship between human and more-than-human nature' (2019: 7). Resisting enfolding these contextual differences in a totalizing discourse of an Anthropocene that is ontologically absolute, we argue, will allow its thinkers to engage not just with 'localised' or 'provincialised' politics on their own terms but with the often overlapping, diachronic and dialectic relationship between part and whole (2019: 7).[1]

In an Anthropocene thought as plural 'all the way down', ontological relationality and political planning and affirmative transformation, catastrophism and continuity, can coexist in tension. They coexist without a theoretical or political meta-narrative holding them together and providing an analytical key with which the unsettling unintelligibility of the Anthropocene world can be unlocked. To some, this may require acknowledging the 'gap between Indigenous and modern ways of knowing' (Randerson and Yates 2017: 27) that underpins different registers (and potentially motivates different attitudes to steering and futurity as outlined earlier). But it also requires acknowledging that these differences are meaningful not because they represent absolute and clearly delineated lines but because they point to sites of situated, creative ontological and political emergence that can both maintain and transform these registers dependent on the particular needs and demands of the humans and nonhumans acting here. The complexity and diversity of political claims that unfolds, and of the principles that inform them, goes far beyond a simple Western/non-Western or modern/nonmodern binary and can thus not easily be reduced to the question of overcoming one in favour of the other.

The zooming out – to deep, planetary time, to an internally multiple anthropocenic world decentred away from Anthropos – which ontological Anthropocene theory demands, seems to provide, if not a secure ground, then at least a comforting certainty regarding the 'insecurity' of the ontological ground on which a fundamentally different politics must be assembled. The Anthropocene can neither be fully understood nor effectively governed. However, somewhat paradoxically, this acknowledgement here produces the theoretical tools necessary to somewhat accurately conceptualise these limits to human reason and action. We believe that critical ecological scholarship should be weary of internalizing this 'comforting' certainty. At best, ontological Anthropocene theory depoliticizes ecology by framing it as an ontological, aesthetic practice primarily aimed at freeing worldmaking from the constraints of modern subjectivity's will to govern. As Swyngedouw and Ernstson note, the risk implicit in such approaches, 'in spite of their internal differences, is the off-staging of the politics of dissensus that animated the historical-geographical dynamics of modernity' (2018: 10). At worst, the meta-theoretical enfolding that ontological Anthropocene theory performs risks delegitimizing the political struggles and claims, such as those to Indigenous self-determination, made by those who find themselves enfolded in the totalizing Anthropocene framework. To avoid both risks, we argue that a critical scholarship that embraces ontological relationality and nonhuman agency must bid farewell to anthropocenic certainties. This includes the idea that we must understand being in the Anthropocene before we can act on it, and the certainty that any sharp distinction from liberal-modern governance can give us a more confident insight to what the right kind of ecological politics for the Anthropocene is.

Tell the truth in the face of the extinction

Exceptionalism and depoliticization in Anthropocene activism

In the evening of 15 April in 2019, Extinction Rebellion (XR) erected the first traffic blocks in what would become an eight-day series of protest marches all across London, marking the group's largest and most visible public activism to date. Those who attended or passed by the road blockage on Oxford Circus, or followed the events in the news, will remember the striking image of a bright pink sailboat, floating in a sea of activists, carrying a single demand addressed to the UK's political leaders on its side: 'tell the truth' – the truth about climate change. The movement, founded only one year earlier by activist Roger Hallam and bioscientist Gail Bradbrook, now comprises of 485 activist groups in more than seventy countries (Extinction Rebellion 2022). As there is no official member list, it is difficult to establish the exact scale and reach of XR. However, it is undoubtedly the biggest single, centralized ecological movement to this date. As a sign and catalyst of XR's popularity, one of the April 2019 protests was attended by Greta Thunberg, the young Swedish climate activist who has spoken at the UN and met high-profile political figures from Barack Obama to Justin Trudeau.

The previous chapter has shown how Indigenous ecologies accommodate both a non-linear, relational ontology and the focus on context-specific, directed political action. Indigenous ecology disrupts the relationship between ontology and political practice that Anthropocene theory sets up. The critical mirror of Indigenous ecology has revealed that there is no single political lesson to be drawn from the realization of our planetary entangledness, because pathways for political action are not pre-determined by an Anthropocene ontology with absolute primacy over context-specific practical action. This chapter will explore the link between ontology and politics in the Anthropocene further, but this time from the other side, that of environmental political activism. This chapter will unpack XR as the most prominent example of contemporary Western environmental activism in its ontological and political underpinnings, dynamics and implications. We certainly do not suggest that XR activists are readers of Anthropocene scholarship driven by its principles and by the ambition to practically implement them. We merely suggest that XR activism, as a case of environmentalism in the Anthropocene present, can help us to interrogate the necessities that link ontological premises and practical politics within Anthropocene scholarship, not only but in part because both respond to the climate catastrophe with the attempt to do things fundamentally differently from the status quo of liberal modernity. The parameters, alliances and lines of division that the XR case reveals will then be blurred, problematized and ultimately subverted in the critical mirror of Indigenous ecology just like they have been for ontological Anthropocene theory.

The chapter speaks to existing criticisms that draw out how XR's white, middle-class activism superficially allies itself with Indigenous struggles without actually being able to accommodate the experience of non-white, non-Western subjects and communities in the face of climate change. However, we suggest that the critical mirror of Indigenous ecology reveals more than these grave but rather obvious limitations of XR's environmentalism: it renders visible the depoliticized nature of an environmental activism that detaches the nonhuman environment from the concerns and projects of a dynamically changing social community. The chapter will show that XR upholds a binary division between nature and society by sharply prioritizing action to protect the former over human cultural or economic causes. Expressions of Indigenous ecology, on the other hand, approach nonhuman nature as interwoven with human communities and their cultural and economic concerns, meaning that the protection of nature, at all times, needs to be balanced with the latter. Where XR activism works to establish an inwards-looking ecological normativity centred on a detached nature as object of affective practices, confessional truth-telling and subjective guilt, Indigenous ecologies employ long-standing ideas, values and cultural practices to reach outward- and forward-looking aims.

While Indigenous cosmologies inform and motivate environmental activism in practice, they do so not by removing a deified nature from human concerns but through a dynamic understanding of relationality where the status of and link to nonhumans changes dynamically together with Indigenous social communities and their political projects. Compared to Indigenous environmentalism, XR activism is both ontologically too liberal-modern and, in a way, politically not liberal-modern enough. Refusing to engage with the political means of the liberal state, XR ends off offering a depoliticized, primarily normative framework for engaging with the climate catastrophe whose practical implementation – because it would need to rely on third parties within the established institutional system – ultimately leaves the power structures that enact and sustain the violent exploitation of humans and nature intact. Indigenous environmentalism, on the contrary, combines radical ecological aims with the pragmatic readiness to use all available political pathways to realize the former.

We acknowledge the risk that some of the arguments developed as follows could be understood as fuelling the image of XR as a movement for middle-class vegans that right-wing and conservative establishment critics frequently indulge in to ridicule and delegitimize their protests (Sales and Feehan 2021; Liddle 2019). In those accounts, XR is presented as an 'eco rabble who want to kill off free speech' (Aitchison, Bucks and Henn 2020) and disrupt the lives of hard-working citizens from a 'vegetarian café in [a] leafy market town' (Thompson and Duell 2019). Emphatically, we would like to make it clear that this chapter is not intended to further such criticism, nor does it aim to cast doubt on the legitimacy and importance of XR's political aims and actions. Rather, we seek to understand better the political functioning and limitations of the Western environmental activism XR represents. The Indigenous mirror constructed and employed here is without depth – no 'better' or 'more authentic' ecological politics are hidden within or behind it. However, we hope that it can make apparent, and prompt reflection on, the dynamics and limitations of XR activism as an important example for Western Anthropocene environmentalism in practice, in order to render visible different pathways for ecological political action.

Extinction environmentalism and its discontents

Especially in its early years, in 2018 and 2019, achieving strategic arrests to block the UK's legal system and attract political as well as public attention was a vital part of Extinction Rebellion's strategy. Over 1,000 activists were arrested during the April 2019 protests; the movement's co-founder, Gail Bradbrook, was arrested in May 2021 for conspiracy to cause criminal damage after the group had smashed windows at the HSBC and Barclays buildings in London. However, one of the movement's founding aims is to create awareness for and spark action on climate change beyond the political left. For this reason, XR explicitly sought to distance itself from the traditionally tense relationship between left-wing activist groups, such as Antifa, and the police. Activists at different XR protest sites were captured marching to the chant 'police, we love you, but we are doing this for our children'.[1] The group's 2019 manifesto *This Is Not a Drill* frequently emphasizes how well protesters were treated by the police, and how many police officers had expressed support for the movement's aims. Ken Marsh, chairman of the London MET police, commented on the 2019 arrests by emphasizing that the XR protesters were 'very, very passive people, probably quite nice people, who don't want confrontation whatsoever with the police or anyone else' (quoted in BBC 2019), supporting XR's narrative of an explicit contrast to other activist movements.

Critics from the realms of academia and political activism alike have pointed out how the dual strategy of arrest for non-violent civil disobedience and a pro-police attitude is not only geared to activists who are white, middle-class and have little to fear from (short-term) imprisonment but also marginalizes violence committed by an institutionally racist police apparatus. In October 2019, legal scholar Nadine El-Enany commented on a tweet from the MET police showing flowers and a card, sent by XR, that thanked the Brixton police for their 'decency and professionalism' that this gesture captured 'everything that's wrong with #ExtinctionRebellion in one tweet. Brixton police station is where Sean Rigg died at the hands of police, none of whom has been held accountable'.[2] 'Meanwhile', UK Youth Parliament member Athian Akec notes in a think-piece for *The Guardian*, 'the tactic of being purposely arrested strikes an uncomfortable note for many people of colour, given the adverse experiences people in my community have had with the police' (2019). Seeking strategic arrest, as critics point out, is a viable political strategy only for those with no experience of police violence and with enough disposable income to miss a few days of work and, if necessary, to pay for legal defense. Reporting on a violent clash between XR protesters blocking rush hour travel and angry commuters, one of them reportedly shouting 'I have to go to work! I have to feed my kids!', even the centrist mainstream broadcaster CNN ponders whether Extinction Rebellion is 'too white, too middle class and lacking in empathy' (Lewis 2019).

The impression that XR is a climate revolution specifically designed for the educated middle class that make up most of its activists (Saunders, Doherty and Hayes 2020) is illustrated pointedly by passages like the following recommendation for 'feeding the rebellion' from *This Is Not a Drill*:

> **Cook vegan:** besides being good for the planet, it ensures maximum inclusivity and top health-and-safety standards. [. . .] Presentation and a mix of textures are important to meal planning. Add some salads, greens, something crunchy that looks good on the plate. (Haque 2019: 175)

Contesting the notion that what they describe as 'white veganism' indeed ensures maximum inclusivity, non-white and Indigenous scholars and activists unpack how the emphasis on vegan food contains notions of Western moral superiority that brackets questions of where and to whom a vegan diet is accessible, and how the industrial production and consumption of food is embedded in colonial and neo-colonial systems of production and extraction (Nieves 2019; Yazbeck 2018). In an open letter from 2019, the activist collective 'Wretched of the Earth' issued a friendly but urgent challenge to XR to reflect on its Western, comparatively wealthy positionality and 'centre those experiences and recognise those knowledges' of the Global South and Indigenous populations for whom the fight against extinction is not a matter of normative guidance towards the future but an issue of past and present survival without alternative.[3]

It is possible to both nuance and add to this critique by taking a look at how XR accounts for non-white and particularly Indigenous perspectives. In *This Is Not a Drill*, Hindou Oumarou Ibrahim speaks for the Indigenous communities surrounding the quickly drying Lake Chad, emphasizing precisely how the climate emergency is here not 'abstract . . . but reality. A reality that comes from elsewhere' (2019: 87). While it is the external forces of colonial extraction that have exposed Indigenous communities to the effects of climate change, Oumarou Ibrahim emphasizes that they do not intend to remain their silent witnesses. Instead, Indigenous peoples 'are ready to share their traditional knowledge, and to (re) teach humanity how to live in harmony with nature' (2019: 91). On their website and Facebook pages – which are important platforms to connect the loosely organized XR movement as well as share plans and record activities – XR carefully reiterates its commitment to and solidarity with all global environmental movements in their diversity and local specificity. In 2020, a group of Brazilian Indigenous XR activists organized a women's march in Brasilia,[4] and the movement's London branch collaborated with Indigenous activists to stage a protest on Trafalgar Square to mark the International Day of the World's Indigenous Peoples (Rea 2020). Vanda Shiva writes in the foreword to *This Is Not a Drill* that the 'extermination of biological diversity and of Indigenous cultures [. . .] are one indivisible process, and they began with the idea of the colonization of the Earth as the "civilizing mission" of a "superior race"' (2019: 23).

It is thus not the case that XR is not interested in the experience of Indigenous peoples in the face of ecological destruction, or not open to their political participation. However, XR's engagement with Indigenous ecological activism contains aspects of an orientalizing 'ecological Indian' narrative. They depict Indigenous peoples as communities whose primitive culture has retained a closer bond with nature than the industrialized, highly technologized West and from whom Western countries can now learn how to live 'simply' and in tune with nature (Tallbear 2000; Willow 2009). Following Gregory Smithers, the idea of an Indigenous authenticity that guides the ecological politics of native communities not only 'remains a part of the colonial and racial matrix of US colonialism' (2015: 92) – because it implies that Indigenous communities do not mind living 'simply' in reservations – but is also clearly still visible in 'contemporary environmental politics' (2005: 92). A few pages after Shiva's foreword in *This Is Not a Drill*, Sam Knight emphasizes that the non-Western 'majority world needs no lectures from us [Extinction Rebellion]' because they 'have been on the frontline of this struggle for centuries' (2019: 31). Indigenous communities do not need to learn from the XR, but XR *can learn from them*. Present within XR's expression of allyship with Indigenous struggles is the notion that the 'ecological Indian' knows better how to act sustainably, and how to create and sustain norms, economic frameworks and political rules that render the former foundational for community life. The authentic ecology of Indigenous peoples here becomes a resource for XR to draw on for their political action: 'we bow to their wisdom and their experience' (Knight 2019: 32).

What this narrative of Indigenous peoples as authentic ecological activists disregards is the fact that Indigenous sustainability is not merely an 'authentic' part of Indigenous cultures but in part also, as outlined in the previous chapter, the product of a struggle for survival under conditions of continuous colonization (Erickson 2020: 119–23). Beyond this, XR's engagement with Indigenous voices is selective, and flattens the breadth of Indigenous political voices to those that align with their aims and political methods. The Haida journalist and writer Geoff Russ develops a highly critical account of the XR movement, suggesting that they are 'speaking up for Indigenous rights when it fits their goals, and not in other instances like Indigenous people going missing' (2022). Russ references a video depicting a member of the Pacheedaht First Nation challenging a group of XR protesters with the words 'You want to be an ally, stand up when we need you. [. . .] People's lives are more important than a tree' (Russ 2022). Following Russ, what XR misses out is that Indigenous knowledge and ecological activism cannot be integrated into XR's ecological mission in any simple way because it is underpinned by an in itself already complex relationship between ecology and culture, environmental- and anti-colonial politics, sustainability and Indigenous sovereignty. Recalling the naming of the 2019 protest 'flagship', two activists explain that they had 'decided to name the boat after Honduran activist Berta Cáceres' who had been murdered in 2016 in order to 'memorialize her incredible sacrifice' (James and Ruby 2019: 180). The Indigenous leader, however, had not campaigned for environmental protection in general, but specifically against the destruction of ecosystems in Honduras that threatened the culture, livelihood and health of the Lenca people.[5] While her activism was certainly not unrelated to XR's cause, its complexity and its relationship to Indigenous and Western politics is bracketed in the posthumous enfolding of her activism in the XR cause. This chapter aims to recover some of this complexity at the intersection of Western environmentalism, Indigenous ecology and Indigenous environmental activism.

One threat to rule them all versus dynamic ecology

While the Extinction Rebellion does formulate political demands and action points, its first and foremost aim lies in advocacy. XR seeks to make the general public aware of the climate crisis, hoping that collective democratic pressure on political leaders will force them to act on the former (Hallam 2019: 156). Co-founder Roger Hallam's PhD research in social movement studies is clearly reflected in XR's dedicated attention to messaging, presentation and performative action. Everything XR does is intended to attract public attention, and via attention, to generate widespread support. The 'XR brand' that is being marketed is carefully curated as engaging but inoffensive, impactful but not divisive, from the choice of colour for the sailboat that spearheaded the 2019 protests – 'Pink is a calm colour, without being soft. Red is angry, pink is fun' (James and Ruby 2019: 179) – to the overall festival-like set-up of the protest marches. At the same time, XR diversifies the way they frame the effects of ecological destruction for different audiences, seeking to appeal to conservative voters with the emphasis that climate change is 'a threat to national security' and 'a threat to the economy'.[6]

At the heart of XR's bid for public attention lies the immediate and undeniable climate emergency, which transcends all political and social divisions. 'The story Extinction Rebellion has to tell is one of universal importance. Its audience is, ultimately, as big as it gets: namely everyone' (McNern 2019: 194). In the Extinction Rebellion narrative, the effects of climate change are context-specifically coupled with other threats and mechanisms of exploitation, such as the legacy of colonialism, and thus globally diverse. However, climate change nevertheless poses an unprecedented threat for all of humanity that trumps all other threats. 'The stakes are higher now than ever before. This time, we are literally fighting for our lives' (Burns and Reiman 2019: 165). The narrative underpinning XR environmentalism is that of the catastrophic Anthropocene that drives one strand of contemporary ecological social theory: climate change is an urgent, lethal threat of universal status insofar as its scale and destructive power is unprecedented, and inescapable, for all of humanity.

But XR environmentalism does more than universalize the singularity of the climate catastrophe – it also renders the former an umbrella threat under which all other social issues and activist causes can be flexibly accommodated. The challenge XR seeks to tackle, as Knights writes in *This Is Not a Drill*, is so 'extremely daunting' because 'the problem, unfortunately, is not just the climate. The problem is ecology. The problem is the environment. The problem is biodiversity. The problem is capitalism. The problem is colonialism. The problem is power. The problem is inequality. The problem is greed, and corruption, and money, and this tired, broken system' (2019: 32). One could argue that XR is here simply, and rightly, acknowledging the complexity and interwovenness of ecological challenges. But the issue that the critical mirror of Indigenous ecology will bring to light in the following lies in the fact that other social issues and political focal points are subsumed under an introversively expansive ecological meta-threat that here always has priority. As a consequence, XR environmentalism makes no provisions for tensions or clashes that might arise from acting on the different challenges that the ecological umbrella contains, which might require balancing competing demands, prioritizing certain issues over others, or even abandoning one aim in favour of another.

Within many Indigenous knowledge systems, there is no clear separation between nature and culture. Notions of sustainability and survival always concern the living environment of Indigenous communities at the same time as they require consideration for the physical, cultural and economic health and welfare of these communities and their members. Because humans and nonhumans are entangled in complex relationships, but can never be separated from one another, activism in this context must always be based on a negotiation that weighs up different needs (Whyte 2018a; Muller, Hemming and Rigney 2019: 406–9). The effect of this ontological entangledness of human – biological and cultural – and nonhuman life is twofold. First, the preservation of a nonhuman environment that is never completely separated from the cultural communities of Anthropos does not simply take precedence over fully human political concerns, such as those related to cultural survival, education or economic sustainability (LaDuke 1994b). What has priority for an Indigenous ecological activism that always aims to secure the survival of a particular Indigenous community in its human and nonhuman relations (Stevenson 1998: 7–9; Stevenson 2006) must be worked out through negotiating, balancing, and potentially resolving tension, between the different component parts of this relational sustainability. Second, as a consequence, the ecological sustainability that Indigenous activism seeks to achieve is flexible in its meaning, and defined locally and on a case-by-case basis.

In *On the Streets and in the State House* (2004), Diane-Michelle Prindeville explores the aims and motivations of New Mexico Indigenous women to engage in environmental activism. Prindeville notes that only a third of the activists she interviewed identify as "environmentalists" even though they espoused values that included respect for nature and preservation of the Earth's resources' (2004: 125). A lacking sense of belonging in the US' mainly white, mainly middle-class environmental movements has certainly contributed to this perception (Prindeville 2004: 126; Di Chiro 1992: 94). However, the Indigenous environmental activists do not just feel like they have no place in white, Western environmentalism. Rather, their ecology follows a fundamentally different logic. One activist explains this distinction by emphasizing that Indigenous ecology 'believes in the spiritual value of nature' and 'sees nature not only in a patch of forest, but also in the middle of downtown. An Indigenous environmentalist does not see anything "wild" about nature' (Linda, quoted in Prindeville 2004: 125).

A second activist, Marta, supports the notion that Indigenous environmental action must distort any strong difference between nature and culture: 'keeping the culture strong is an environmental mission' (Prindeville 2004: 126) because it is Indigenous culture that grounds ecological knowledge and sustainable ecological action. This sentiment can also be found in the writings of Anishinaabeg scholar Winona LaDuke, who explains that it is difficult to separate Indigenous action on environmental sustainability and on cultural sustainability because both are so intertwined. Discussing the "White Earth Land Recovery Project", LaDuke makes it clear that the 'struggle to preserve the trees of White Earth is not solely about forest preservation and biodiversity. It is also about cultural transformation, for the Anishinaabegg forest culture cannot exist without the forest' (2015: 169). For Indigenous environmental activists, the interwovenness of human and nonhuman concerns does not mean that both go together without tension, or that the ecological knowledge and spirituality that grounds their activism means that concerns for the nonhuman environment automatically come first. 'I believe in ecology, in the restoration of the human spirit, of the Earth', one activist explains, 'but people need to work to eat. We have to have jobs, responsible industries' (Dalia, quoted in Prindeville 2004: 127).

Indigenous ecology, as an ontology and ethics, is here the condition for environmental activism, but importantly not its primary driving force. Around 98 per cent of the Indigenous activists Prindeville spoke to suggested that 'maintaining the integrity of their culture, language, and lifeways' (Prindeville 2004: 86) was their motivation for political action. While this includes concerns for environmental protection against destruction, ecological sustainability is not prioritized over more immediate, more human concerns such as community health and safety (Prindeville 2004: 88). The acute awareness of having to weigh up and negotiate between different concerns related to a holistic sustainability is rooted in the experience of colonialism. Whereas XR bases its political claim on the unprecedented urgency of the climate catastrophe, for Indigenous communities surviving in the face of the continuously unfolding apocalypse of colonialism has long required balancing actions on threats to physical survival and safety, cultural integrity, economic welfare and ecological sustainability (LaDuke 1994a).

In the early 1990s, the Campo Band of Mission Indians received widespread public attention for their plan to construct a solid waste landfill on their territory. The construction was widely and vitriolically rejected by local farmers, who feared that the landfill would pollute their land. Ralph Goff, at the time the chairman of the Campo tribe, defended the landfill by emphasizing the economic benefits, for the tribe, of a project that 'environmentally [. . .] can be done' (Goff quoted in Smithers 2015: 91). The case went to court, where the ecological safety of the project was confirmed, and the landfill was built in 1993. In 1998, the Oglala Sioux Tribal Council of the Pine Ridge reservation voted in favour of a plan to grow industrial hemp on their land in order to create employment and income for the community (Ecoffey 2019). As in the case of the Campo landfill, environmental protection was a concern here – the tribal leaders mindfully chose to focus on a plant that could be farmed sustainably – but so was addressing poverty and unemployment, which legitimized the controlled modification of tribal land. The Oglala Sioux's plan was rejected by the federal government, revealing, like the resistance to the landfill, the pervasiveness and political impact of the 'ecological Indian' stereotype, which prompted authorities to act when 'the Oglala Sioux were acting in ways that ran counter to stereotypes about how ecological Indians should behave' (Smithers 2015: 96). Masked by this stereotype is the fact that tribal sovereignty, building economic, educational and social opportunities and ecological responsibility are interconnected in Indigenous ecology in a way that transcends any simple prioritization of environmental protection and further calls into question the binary between environmental sustainability and economic productivity that characterizes XR's Anthropocene environmentalism.

This does however not mean that Indigenous environmental activism has no points of contact or alignment with Western ecological activism like XR's. Gwich'in leader and Indigenous environmental activist Sarah James, for example, emphasizes the importance of acting on the threat of climate change, stressing that Indigenous communities, like the West, 'must learn to share more, to reuse, recycle, and use less energy' (quoted in Mankiller 2004: 204). However, the complex and nuanced Indigenous concept of ecology draws attention to the fact that environmental sustainability needs to be sensitive to the needs of both the humans and nonhumans involved; the protection of the Earth, if it is to be successful in the long run, cannot take place in a way that brackets human needs, and not at the expense of the human communities populating it. As Prindeville notes, for Indigenous environmental activists, the environment is 'defined broadly to include "where we live, work, and play"' (2004: 126). Renewable energy, viewed in this light, offers 'native solutions' not just because it is environmentally sustainable but also because it 'supports local economies by providing income, jobs, and tax revenue' (LaDuke 2006: 6).

The flexible and locally specific ecology that underpins Indigenous environmental activism allows for a strategically differentiated public presentation. LaDuke's Honor the Earth activist group, which aims to influence environmental policy, strategically shapes the framing and styling of its demands and actions depending on the particular audience they target. As Nicholas Cragoe observes, the movement has available both a 'cultural' and a 'procedural' narrative to ground its claims. Public events to raise funds and awareness place an 'emphasis on performative aspects of Anishinaabe cultural tradition' (Cragoe 2017: 51). 'Immediately before the traditional drumming and singing begins', Cragoe recounts one such event,

> Winona delivers a short speech to the audience of mostly-white Unitarians sitting behind plates of amaranth crackers and mashed whitefish. She provides a traditional Anishinaabe introduction in Ojibwemowin, followed by a blessing over the meal [. . .] no one understands the words Winona has used or specifically what has been said, but their appreciation, admiration, and fascination are evident on their faces. (Cragoe 2017: 50–1)

On the contrary, when presenting their aims to the mainstream media or to governmental bodies and non-Indigenous organizations, Honour the Earth does not dramatize the link between nature and Indigenous culture but instead focuses on legal and economic concerns to substantiate their environmental claims and demands (Cragoe 2017: 54–5). As political outreach 'gets farther from the corridor' of Honour the Earth's community 'the stories surrounding Honor the Earth become . . . decidedly more legal or procedural in focus' (Cragoe 2017: 56).

At a first glance, Honour the Earth's ecological narratives appear similar to the XR's strategically differentiated self-presentation, with a focus on national security and the economy in public messaging to attract voters with more traditional political concerns and staging festival-like protests to create community among its predominantly young, left-wing, middle-class members. While the two are certainly not unrelated, we suggest that the effectiveness of XR's differential messaging is limited by the fact that what changes is the framing, but not the actual message. Communicated to both audiences is the idea that action against climate change is urgently necessary but without any regard for how such action sits alongside other human concerns that could be identified as equally weighty, such as pensions, wages or living costs. The nonhuman environment frames as, for instance, 'economic concerns' remains primary and does not have to be mediated with (other) economic concerns.

On the contrary, Indigenous environmental activists, such as those of Honour the Earth, do not just present their story differently for different audiences – they have, and tell, *different stories*. Their environment is not fixed, distinct from human-cultural communities and superior to the former as a focal point for environmental political activism. A politics that aims to ensure ecological sustainability must here always have multiple focal points to capture the multiple relational links at work in an Indigenous sustainability that is always at the same time social, cultural and environmental. The critical mirror of Indigenous ecology confronts XR's monothematic focus on the climate catastrophe with a dynamic and multi-faceted understanding of ecological sustainability, which can balance and negotiate between the different concerns it encompasses as locally appropriate.

The ecological interconnectedness that characterizes many Indigenous knowledge systems creates the responsibility to interact with ecosystems in a sustainable manner that recognizes this reciprocity, but moreover also to challenge a Western environmentalism that is ignorant of the former (McGregor 2020; LaDuke 1994a). Simpson critically observes how Western engagements with Indigenous ecology pick up environmental relationality but bracket the fundamentally spiritual and fundamentally political character of the former (1999: 55–6). For Simpson, 'separating environmental knowledge from other kinds of knowledge . . . violates the fundamental belief system and understanding inherent in Indigenous Knowledge systems' (1999: 64). The political task that arises for Indigenous environmentalism as a direct consequence of Indigenous knowledge is to challenge 'the culturally limited worldview of many urban environmentalists' (1994: 139) and implement a logic of environmental proception that is not liberal-proprietary but relational in an expansive sense (1994: 129).

Where the ecological normativity of XR creates a spiritually loaded environment by removing the former from human practices and relations, Indigenous ecological relationality undermines any sharp distinction between human and nonhuman concerns. Mohawk leader Katsi Cook, for example, employs the value of relationality to focus her environmental activism on the situation of women (Cook 2018). As LaDuke comments on Cook's political work, the

> first environment, from Katsi's perspective, is the starting place for it all [. . .] The first environment is about a baby, a woman, and family. Katsi's approach [. . .] is that everything the mother feels, eats, and sees affects the baby. That is a part of the Mohawk belief system. That is why, whether it is GM contamination or the mental health of the mother, all must be cared for if the baby is to be healthy. (2015: 41)

This dynamic Indigenous understanding of the environment can accommodate changes in the nature and status of the nonhuman nature that activist action seeks to protect. Anna Willow (2009) explores the case of the Grassy Narrows First Nation's decade-long blockade intended to slow the pace of clear-cut logging in their traditional territory. Following Willow, over the course of the blockade, the pollution of the native lands and changing lifestyles meant that native communities now hardly consume food from the lands they protect. However, they maintain the blockade, and the narrative that links their culture to the products of the land they seek to protect, as a political project intended to stake and defend Indigenous claims. While the value of ecological relationality inspired the blockade, the conception of the environment to be protected, changed in the course of the environmental activism and shifted from a natural to a cultural-political focus.

Introversive norm-building versus culturally grounded political action

The drastically different conceptions of the nonhuman environment that drive XR environmentalism and Indigenous environmental activism are the product of different ecologies: where XR activism ultimately does not challenge the modern-liberal nature/culture binary, Indigenous ecological thought does not categorically distinguish between human and nonhuman sustainability. But beyond this, we suggest that the normative-cultural functionality of both types of activism is also fundamentally distinct. Indigenous environmental activism seeks to implement the political demands of a cultural community that pre-exists activist actions. In its critical mirror, the functioning of XR activism is revealed as primarily norm-building. Both within XR's public communication and in their protest marches, concrete political action points take a backseat compared to the central demand for the public to accept the reality and urgency of the climate emergency. *This Is Not a Drill*'s 'dispatches from the frontlines of climate change' (Knights 2019: 33), collected from all over the world, build the case that anthropogenic climate change is not only real but that its effects on human communities have already started to unfold. In the face of the climate catastrophe's immediate reality, the first imperative, painted on the side of the 2019 protest 'flagship', and running mantra-like through all XR content, is to 'tell the truth' (Griffiths 2019: 145) – to acknowledge this reality. 'The job of scientists is to tell the truth' (Ripple and Houtman 2019: 53), two researchers affiliated with XR declare, while the Extinction Rebellion manifesto urges 'governments to tell the truth by declaring a climate and ecological emergency' (Knights 2019: 31). On the movement's website, a campaign video shows an XR activist beginning a public talk with the emphasis that what comes first is 'to tell the truth . . . and asking people to act as if the truth was real' (2022).

The scenario conjured up by XR mirrors the plotline of the 2021 Netflix satire *Don't Look Up!*, in which two increasingly desperate astrophysicists try to convince the US government and the public to take seriously an impending asteroid impact. The scientists have proof that the asteroid, if not destroyed or diverted in its course, will wipe out all life on Earth. But politicians and citizens, distracted by prospects of financial gains or their smartphones respectively, choose to ridicule fact-based concerns as hysterical fearmongering. In the face of such widespread climate change denial, acknowledging the truth of the climate catastrophe becomes a normative demand that XR's activism responds to. Hinged on the belief in the reality of climate change, XR sets up a framework of ecological normativity for Anthropocene societies.

Of central importance is here the value of love, used as a counterpoint to liberal individualism and as a basis to call for the building of communal relations. Acknowledging the collective fragility and vulnerability of human life, and its dependency on the nonhuman environment, here opens up a relational ethics that XR members both espouse in their activist practice and aim to implement in wider society. 'We can and now must redesign human societies based on love, justice and planetary boundaries', Yamin writes, 'so that no person or society is left to face devastating consequences and we can learn to restore nature together' (2019: 49). *This Is Not a Drill* repeatedly invokes 'the love that we desperately need' (Knights 2019: 33), 'our capacity to love and our sense of justice' (Yamin 2019: 49), love as 'a way through despair' (Bendell 2019: 125), the obligation to welcome people the movement 'with love, food and music' (Legal Team 2019: 209) or the 'highest authority to love our neighbours as ourselves [. . .] to love the stranger and the one that is the enemy' (Williams 2019: 283).

Inclusivity is further central to the normative framework that XR expresses. In its publications, public presentation and networks, the movement aims to actively incorporate queer activists and non-Western voices from different parts of the world (Hague 2019; Extinction Rebellion 2022). The opening section of this chapter has shown how this inclusivity can be viewed as problematic insofar as it replaces attempts to genuinely engage with different perspectives on ecological activism, especially where they stand in tension with XR's supposedly universal cause of environmental protection. But we suggest that XR's aim of inclusivity should not be understood as a calculated attempt to utilize diverse voices to increase their political legitimacy while purposefully excluding their concerns and interests. On the contrary, XR's emphasis on inclusivity and diversity constitutes the declaration of a normative programme that is posited as an alternative to the value system of the liberal *homo economicus,* and thus as a suitable basis for Anthropocene societies.

In addition to the post-individualist relational ethics of love communicated here, a certain joyfulness is also characteristic of XR's self-presentation. The appearance of the protests, with activists wearing costumes, bright colours and body paint, accompanied by drums or a make-shift DJ set, is celebratory. Hallam emphasizes the strategic importance of making the protests appear 'fun' (2019: 155). 'We're going to show the media that we are not sitting around waiting to die any longer. We're gonna have a party' (2019: 155). Bradbrook similarly highlights how XR's colourful protests are not only attention-grabbing but also intended to de-escalate conflict through joy: 'it's hard for drivers to go ballistic if you're having a disco' (2019: 289). While strategic considerations are certainly important for XR's self-presentation as a revolutionary movement that allows you to dance (Hallam 2019: 155), they also underline the message of joy beyond the liberal-modern hope of progress that XR seeks to communicate. While there is no way out of the climate apocalypse, there is a way to live in it with 'the possibility of joy' (Williams 2019: 281).

While the ideas and actions of XR's ecological activism set-up a normative framework for post-liberal Anthropocene societies that are yet to come, we argue that this ethics draws from a Christian normativity that still shapes the value systems of Western democracies. Central to both Christianity and XR's apocalyptic normativity is the demand for truth-telling. The confession that XR calls for involves the admission of guilt on the part of both political and economic leaders and the general public. Climate change is here the original sin that renders all citizens of industrialized democracies collectively and determinately guilty. We might not have individually willed the destruction of nature, but we have all been tempted by the fruits of global capitalism, and enjoyed them at the expense of the planet. We are all sinners, for we are all wilfully contributing to the pollution of the Earth, and now the Earth has to die for our sins. As in the Christian original, this confession, while necessary, cannot allow those confessing to escape their sinfulness – there is no return to the Garden of Eden, or the Holocene. However, confession and repentance for the ecological sins committed nevertheless promises salvation – the possibility of a life after death, here the climate apocalypse. The pathway towards the former is not active-political but reflective-ethical and unfolds from the confession of climate guilt. Recalling the lesson of Michel Foucault's *History of Sexuality* (1978), Christianity's truth-telling creates the flawed subject to be guided and governed by pastoral power and thereby works hand in hand with modernity's political and economic apparatuses. Against this background, the residual Christian normativity underpinning XR's sketch of an Anthropocene ethics renders it unfit for purpose because it ties its moral guidelines to an epistemic apparatus that has, for a long time, operated in service of the modern liberalism that it seeks to counter.

At this juncture, the critical mirror of Indigenous ecology does not only reveal the epistemic baggage of XR's normativity but also allows us to contrast its inwards-looking, community-building and subjectivizing environmental activism with the culturally grounded, outwards-oriented political actions of Indigenous environmentalists. Indigenous environmental activism is, by its very nature, interwoven with the traditional knowledges, values, beliefs and practices of a particular cultural community. As Anishinaabeg scholar and activist Deborah McGregor notes, this means that Indigenous ecology has one face turned towards the past and one towards a future that needs to be secured through practical action: 'pathways to environmental sustainability are based in part on ancient philosophies. They reflect the persistence of Indigenous peoples' influence and their role in creating an expanded dialogue of sustainability informed by their understanding of Mother Earth and humanity's obligations to her. The ideas are both ancient and innovative' (2020: 138). Where XR's environmentalism aims at norm-building, Indigenous environmental activism draws on and expresses Indigenous beliefs and cultural practices that long precede particular activist contexts.

The aim of strengthening community through shared, joyful experiences that marks XR activism is certainly present in Indigenous collective action. Describing an Anishinaabeg procession in Peterborough, Canada, Leanne Simpson recalls how 'that day we turned inward to celebrate our presence and mark our resurgence' (2011: 24) through 'songs, dances and performances' (2011: 21–2). LaDuke similarly notes how Indigenous environmental activism purposefully incorporates singing and dancing to strengthen the affective dimensions of political action. 'In our communities', she writes, 'Native environmentalists sing centuries-old songs to renew life, to give thanks for the strawberries, to call home fish, and to thank Mother Earth for her blessings' (LaDuke 2015: 20). For LaDuke, the Seminole tradition of the Green Corn Dance exemplifies the affective power of Indigenous culture. The century-old yearly event was cancelled in the 1990s when Seminole tribes were forced off the land that constituted its traditional site. When it was reignited in 1998, the 'new homecoming of the Green Corn Dance [. . .] lifted the spirits of many Seminoles and the Indigenous community everywhere' (2015: 69).

However, the affective quality of the collective practices embedded in environmental activism is not necessarily joyful. Lakota Standing Rock protester Chas Jewett describes the Sundance Ceremony that experienced resurgence during the movement in 2016 with violent images: men and women either 'tie themselves to a tree with hooks of eagle talons embedded in their flesh or tie themselves in a similar way to buffalo skulls which they drag around a tree. They stay like this for four days and nights, fasting and singing' (Jewett and Garavan 2019: 44). Jewett explains the significance of the ceremony both with a view to the importance of sacrifice for the Lakota ecology and as a practice that fosters healing from the colonial experiences of humans and nonhumans. 'The key word here to listen to is trauma. The healing is needed not to help participants feel good but to recover – personally, culturally, and ecologically – from trauma' (Jewett and Garavan 2019: 44–5).

Different from XR's use of 'joyful' protest methods, Indigenous dances, songs and cultural practices, both of the joyful and of the violent kind, do not constitute methods of community mobilization chosen for their affectively binding quality. On the contrary, they are genuine expressions of Indigenous ideas, values and beliefs that, if they function to mobilise activism, do so because of the cultural significance they carry. Returning to Simpson's recollection of the Anishinaabeg procession in Peterborough, she emphasizes how the joyful affect of the dances she witnessed was a genuine expression of the Indigenous ecological relationality that was celebrated as cultural value and lived practice. 'Our culture is beautiful and loving, and it nurtures our hearts and minds in a way that enables us to not just cope but to live. We always *feel* good after being out in the bush, or after ceremony' (Simpson 2011: 26–7). Here, music and dance are not inserted into the activist context to build a political-cultural community, but are immanent products of cultural bonds. Expressing them as part of environmental activism renews the bonds between Indigenous humans, but thereby also their cultural connectedness to nonhumans. Protecting and expressing Indigenous culture thereby becomes and important cornerstone of an Indigenous environmentalism with deep and intricate cultural roots. A vivid illustration of this link is the following retelling of an Indigenous prophecy by Cherokee leader Wilma Mankiller:

> The man had warned the Cherokees that the Mother of the Nation was unhappy. She was unhappy that we had given up planting corn. [. . .] According to the oral tradition, it was during this time that a great Cherokee prophet called Charley claimed to have received a message from the Great Spirit, the creator of life and breath. Charley emerged from the mountains accompanied by two wolves. Charley told an assembly of Cherokees that the Great Spirit was displeased that we had given up our old ways in favour of the white man's mills, clothing, and culture. He told them that the Great Spirit was angry and wished the Cherokees to take up the old dances and feasts [...]. Charley warned that if they ignored the message he delivered, they would face death. [. . .] [S]ome of us realize that the death Charley talked about may not have been physical death, but the death of the spirit. (Mankiller 1993: 929–31)

Indigenous ecological values and beliefs directly inform environmental activism, but in a way that is dynamically dependent on the conditions and needs of a particular community at a particular point in time. While XR's environmental normativity thus detaches the environment to be protected from the guilty subjects unworthy of the former, Indigenous spirituality establishes a practical, reciprocal and malleable link between humans and nature that drives political projects to transform the societies that human–nonhuman relations set up. The cultural-normative community that activists belong to precedes and grounds their activism and directs outwards-oriented political action that aims at the preservation of this community in its human and nonhuman relations. 'The Earth is a very important female entity to me, as an Indian woman and as a Pueblo woman raised with very strong traditional beliefs' (Valerie quoted in Prindeville 2004: 88), states one of the Indigenous New Mexico politicians interviewed by Prindeville. 'And so it becomes an obligation for me personally, to do whatever I can [. . .] to protect it' (Prindeville 2004: 89). Another activist explains how her political work is rooted in her upbringing within an Indigenous community where she learned to be 'a part of the environment; not a separate entity' (Prindeville 2004: 132). McGregor draws out how the spiritual importance of water for Anishinaabeg tribes inspired Indigenous women led by the elder Josephine Mandamin to instigate the environmental campaign Mother Earth Water Walk in the early 2000s to seek legal protection for the Great Lakes in Canada's Ontario province (2012). In these examples, the cultural connectedness to a particular ecosystem does not just function as abstract justification for a particular act of Indigenous environmentalism, but motivates individual activists spiritually and emotionally. '[T]here is a profound spiritual dimension to our natural environment, and without it, the war would not be worth fighting' (Small 1994: 12).

While Extinction Rebellion puts forward concrete demands addressed to political decision-makers – acknowledge the reality of climate change, act on it and listen to your citizens – its mode of operation is not actually geared to the implementation of these political demands. Rather, it aims at the creation of an ecological normativity hinged on those demands among its members and its audience. Where Indigenous activism can draw on a solid normative foundation that informs its political actions, the politics of the XR aim to build such a shared ecological normativity first. Cheyenne scholar Gail Small draws attention to this 'spiritual gap' between Indigenous and Western ecological activism when discussing why Western activists might feel compelled to join Indigenous movements. 'Some white people look to us for help in their struggle with loss of identity, spirituality, and a sense of security' (quoted in Mankiller 2004: 35).

Interpreting the inwards-orientedness of XR favourably, one might argue that such norm-building is a necessary first step to generate the social conditions under which meaningful political and economic change is possible because it would be carried by a social normativity that supports the political prioritization of ecology. Understood in this sense, norm-building is part of a necessary catching-up process that Western environmentalism has to go through in order to achieve the collective ecological awareness that already grounds Indigenous communities. But viewed less favourably, its inwards-orientedness renders XR, despite its radical appearance, a fatally depoliticized, politically toothless lifestyle movement whose primary function consists in providing its members and supporters with an ecological identity. In the movement's manifesto, the normative focus on the climate emergency ties in smoothly with concerns from sexual inclusivity to post-colonial awareness and veganism, offering a focal point and umbrella for a loosely progressive social identity that exhausts itself in the continuous performance of normative inclusion. It lacks the politically transformative impetus of Indigenous environmental activism that is based on a socially expansive and dynamic understanding of ecological relationality.

'This is not about politics' versus pragmatic institutionalism

Zooming in on XR politics, the movement formulates three distinct political aims for its activism: first, the need for the government to acknowledge the climate emergency, second to act towards achieving net zero by 2025 and third to create a Citizens Assembly On Climate and Ecological Justice that guides governmental decision-making on environmental matters (Extinction Rebellion 2022). Out of the three aims, only the third reflects and requires a demand for the movement to be part of, and shape, democratic procedures. The Extinction Rebellion's relationship to established politics, both of the extra-institutional and of the institutional kind, is ambivalent. *This Is Not a Drill* hardly spares a thought for the Green movements of the 1970s and 1980s which, long before XR's birth, used protest marches accompanied by music and dance as well as acts of non-violent civil disobedience to draw public and political attention to ecological issues from the risks of nuclear energy to air pollution. While their participants should be commended for their efforts, so the XR narrative, they ultimately failed in raising mainstream awareness for environmental destruction and thus did not create public pressure sufficient to force political leaders to act.

XR's mass civil disobedience is designed to both strain executive and legal systems and generate significant public attention to exercise political pressure via two pathways. The underlying aim is to shape the dynamics and power relations of the political mainstream but without entering the institutions of democratic politics and risking political co-option by its dynamics and pressures. The inability of institutional democracy to address climate change adequately is foundational for XR's political strategy. 'Normal politics', Yamin writes, 'has brought the whole planet to the brink of ecological disaster' (2019: 43). For this reason, ecological activism 'cannot rely on the inadequate legal tools of the past thirty years that have allowed this crisis to happen' (2019: 43). Demanding a move beyond party politics, personal politics, oppositional politics, identity politics and Westminster politics, XR suggests that the 'challenges we face and the decisions that need to be made are simply too big for our broken parliamentary democracy' (Extinction Rebellion 2022).

Two points appear particularly central to XR's demand for a radical reimagining, and restructuring, of democracy in the Anthropocene. The first point is moving beyond the divisions of ideologically driven partypolitics and identity politics towards unity and collaboration with a view to developing shared, effective environmental politics. Unpacking the public branding of XR, two activists explain that they 'avoid aggressive colours. No obvious left-wing reds or conservative blues, no alienation or division' (Glyn and Farrell 2019: 183). XR position themselves explicitly against, and beyond, existing political party lines. Because the climate catastrophe trumps all other social challenges as a matter to be politically addressed, the XR narrative goes, ideological divisions pale, and must be set aside, in the face of the former. The ontologically unifying force of the extinction threat here leads to the demand of a united political front to mitigate the former.

The second notable point is the radicalness of XR's demand for political change. Echoing Mark Fisher's *Capitalist Realism* (2019), the movement starts from the presumption that addressing climate change requires, first and foremost, addressing the 'utter failure to imagine any meaningful alternative' to liberal democracy and global capitalism (Shiva 2019: 33). *This Is Not a Drill* repeatedly emphasizes that an adequate response to the climate crisis requires moving beyond the exploitative, expansion- and revenue-driven logic of liberal capitalism, both in ideational and in economic terms (Shiva 2019: 29; Yamin 2019: 49; Rafaeli and Woods 2019: 77–9; Raworth 2019: 237). The intention to radically transform democratic politics comes to light in the movement's third aim of instituting a citizens' assembly focused on environmental political matters at the heart of democratic politics. The assembly would be composed of randomly selected laypeople (composed of both citizens and non-citizens) that are advised by scientific experts and then produce recommendations for the government on a consensus-basis. Mirroring the composition of the UK's national population in terms of gender, age, ethnicity, education level and geography, and following a deliberative logic, the citizens assembly is designed to produce better, more just decisions on environmental protection. It does so, XR proposes, not only by disrupting the aggregative, elite-centred logic of representation and by ensuring that democratic politics includes diverse voices but also by limiting the weight of economic interests: the 'wealthiest 1% only have 1% representation on the assembly' (Extinction Rebellion 2022).

Like the first two political demands, XR's proposition of a citizen's assembly however must be viewed as serving the overarching goal of achieving better actions on climate change from existing political elites. The movement's overriding aim is quick and effective environmental political action – to achieve this, it is easier to put pressure on existing political institutions and actors than to lobby for a laborious political reform first. XR's stance on the necessity to render their citizens assembly's recommendations binding illustrates this clearly; changing the political system through Parliamentary vote 'not only potentially delays action [on the climate emergency], it also is no guarantee that commitments won't simply be rescinded in the future' (Extinction Rebellion 2022). Consequently, XR focuses on building and sustaining public support for radical environmental politics through which the 'government will be obliged to take the [citizen assembly's] recommendations on board' (Extinction Rebellion 2022). Despite its radical claims that the climate catastrophe must be tackled at its modern-liberal social roots, XR does not put forward plans to rework the liberal foundations of democratic politics. Instead, pragmatic considerations lead XR to focus on making use of existing political channels from the outside to achieve quick and impactful political action on environmental protection.

A strategic pragmatism that prioritizes the aims achieved over the means used for achieving them also features prominently in Indigenous environmental activism. However, while XR compromises on radical political transformation in favour of achieving concrete political action on climate change, Indigenous environmental activism reluctantly employs the institutional-political tools of the settler state to achieve environmental political aims, but never compromises on the aim of radically transforming it. Where XR can compromise on their political aims because these are ultimately secondary to the movement, transforming democratic politics in a manner that renders ecological relationality foundational for all considerations, processes and decisions is central to Indigenous environmental activism.

While XR's rejects the pathways of 'traditional' politics and adopts a strategy of exercising political pressure from the outside, a significant number of Indigenous environmental activists use democratic institutions to achieve their goals. Prindeville's research on New Mexico's Indigenous women environmental activists reveals a dual structure of formal and informal political action. Grassroots activists and elected politicians each make use of the specific sets of political means available to them in order to advance the intertwined aims of tribal interests and environmental protection. The grassroots activities adopted by the New Mexico activists here closely mirror XR's public-facing actions: protests and boycotts with a developed media strategy, public hearings where intentions and aims are discussed and seeking funding and endorsement from politicians and celebrities (Prindeville 2004: 150). However, here these grassroots strategies complement the actions of elected Indigenous office holders who review official documents, monitor compliance with environmental regulations and lobby local, state- and national political bodies for new legislation (Prindeville 2004: 151). Prindeville finds that the majority of actions undertaken by Indigenous environmental groups were what she refers to as 'mutually employed' (Prindeville 2004: 154) insofar as they incorporate and interlink both grassroots and institutional-political strategies. This interlinking ensures that elected officials retain an active connection to their grassroots base (Prindeville 2004: 155).

This does not mean that scepticism towards institutional politics, or even outright rejection, is not common among Indigenous environmental activists. Scholars who research Indigenous environmentalism from contexts as different as 1970s Canada and contemporary Bolivia note that grassroots activists who have purposefully chosen an extra-institutional arena for political action often mistrust elected officials and feel that Indigenous environmental interests cannot be adequately represented in political bodies geared to the values and interests of the Western colonizers (Piper 2019; Hess, Flores and Geiser 2017). This ambivalence is also notable in the accounts of Indigenous environmental activists that hold political offices. Indigenous politicians do not enthusiastically support 'the system' they have become part of, but rather pragmatically recognize the political opportunities that their position opens up (Hess, Flores and Geiser 2017). 'You kind of have to play a role and I hate to say that but it's true. If you want to get something done in the political arena, you have to play within those rules [. . .]. I've been coopted by the system' (Jacinda quoted in Prindeville 2004: 133), acknowledges one New Mexico politician. But at the same time, she emphasizes that she 'can be more effective from within the system. You still have to keep pushing, but from a political perspective, I can be more effective' (Prindeville 2004: 133).

Honor the Earth's founder LaDuke campaigned as Vice-presidential candidate for the Green Party alongside Ralph Nader in both the 1996 and the 2000 US elections. 'I am by my nature not someone who is inclined to participate in electoral politics', LaDuke states in her 1996 nomination speech, 'that is because the native community [. . .] was not given the right to vote until 1924' (LaDuke 1996). LaDuke links her scepticism towards US democratic politics to the fact that Indigenous communities have only been granted access to the former late and reluctantly, and that its procedures and decisions still do not reflect, and do little to address, the concerns of Indigenous communities (LaDuke 1996). However, exactly this shortcoming leads LaDuke to put aside her scepticism and campaign for political office to ensure sustainable living conditions for native peoples in the United States. The political demands LaDuke formulates are radical and far-reaching. Transcending a narrowly understood realm of Indigenous environmentalism, they concern ecological relations between humans and nonhumans in the United States in its multiple dimensions. Indigenous struggles for education, employment and infrastructure under precarious conditions, following LaDuke, reflect 'the situation of most other people in this country in some way or another' (LaDuke 1996). Addressing them requires a fundamental shift towards more sustainable economic production and agriculture and a more equal distribution of wealth and value in society. 'We don't want a larger piece of the pie', LaDuke makes clear, 'we want a different pie' (LaDuke 1996).

While the aim of changing the way societies approach the nonhuman environment leads XR to shy away from institutional politics, Indigenous environmental activism acknowledges that its powerful tools can be valuable for achieving such far-reaching ecological transformation. For Eric Swyngedouw (2010; 2011), the lack of any attempt to do the same on the part of contemporary Western climate activism, exemplified by XR's, is a marker of its ultimately post-political character. Following Swyngedouw, not only does the 'pure negativity' (2010: 219) driving the apocalyptic focus on the climate catastrophe offer no suitable ground for political action, but maybe even more importantly, the new ecological politics do not transcend, but rather play out within the parameters of technocratic-managerial liberal politics. Climate change, for Swyngedouw, demands 'that we have to change radically, but within the contours of the existing state of the situation' (2010: 219). For Swyngedouw, contemporary Western environmental activism is populist insofar as it avoids fundamental political conflict in favour of normative consensus-building and addresses existing political elites rather than aiming to subvert their status. Ecological populism, like any form of populism, is 'based on a politics of "the people know best"' (Swyngedouw 2010: 223). The 'participatory governance that operates beyond the state' leaves its liberal-capitalist order untouched and thereby 'non-disputed' (Swyngedouw 2010: 222). The populist cause 'is not about replacing the elites, but calling on the elites to undertake action' and it 'does not invite a transformation of the existing socio-ecological order' (Swyngedouw 2010: 223).

Not all of Swyngedouw's criticisms can easily be applied to XR's political activism. For instance, XR clearly do not seek to stabilize the climate as 'a condition for capitalist life as we know it to continue' (Swyngedouw 2010: 222). However, the critical mirror of Indigenous ecology renders visible that Swyngedouw's charge of a post-political environmental populism holds force here. XR does not seek to represent a particular social group – workers, women or an Indigenous community – but rather aims to speak on behalf of humanity as a whole, 'on behalf of life' (Extinction Rebellion 2019: 18), as stated in *This Is Not a Drill*. They do not enter the arena of political contestation in order to improve the position of a population they represent. Instead of aiming to transform society for the better, which requires a specific, socially situated vision of what a better society would look like, and for whom it would be better, XR's demands can readily be fulfilled through the mere 'management' of environmental decline by the existing political elite. XR's political aims are focused on achieving a shift in communication ('tell the truth') and action vis-à-vis environmental protection on the part of an existing government. Even their citizens assembly does not fundamentally transform the workings of democratic politics. It is designed to offer recommendations and scrutiny, not to participate in legislative decision-making itself, and its jurisdiction is limited to a narrowly defined environmental realm.

This stands in sharp contrast to Indigenous environmental politics, which is always immediately rooted in the political interests of a particular tribal community and intended to achieve environmental protection only insofar as the former sustains or advances the culture and livelihood of the community in question. While XR's political pragmatism leads them to formulate 'achievable' political demands that can easily be accommodated within the existing logic of liberal politics, the same political pragmatism motivates Indigenous political activists to enter the institutional realm of the modern State, but with the aim of achieving radical transformation through their participation. Not all Indigenous activists seek large-scale political and economic change on a national level, as LaDuke does. However, the intertwinement of environmental sustainability with Indigenous cultural and political rights, but also with the social distribution of wealth, welfare and opportunities beyond Indigenous communities means that Indigenous activism always aims at both environmental conservation and radical social transformation. Indigenous environmental activism pragmatically opts for incorporating the institutional systems of the colonial masters in their political tool box – but they always do so with the ultimate aim of dismantling the master's house. The critical mirror of Indigenous ecology on the contrary reveals a fundamental disconnect between problem diagnosis and action on the part of the contemporary Western environmentalism exemplified by XR. While the structures and institutions of modern liberalism are recognized as the root cause of climate change, the movement ultimately does, or even proposes, little to address these. Like ontological Anthropocene theory, it gives priority to the rethinking, and here especially the normative reordering, of the Anthropocene condition.

Rights of nature and Indigenous threshold politics

In April 2022, Spain became the first European country to recognize an ecosystem as the holder of legal rights. By overwhelming majority, the Spanish Congress of Deputies voted in favour of awarding the Mar Menor saltwater lagoon the status of a legal person.[1] Over the past decades, a growing number of landmark decisions on the nonhuman rights of nature from across the globe had prepared the ground for the Spanish case. In 2008, Ecuador was the first country to inscribe the rights of nature in its constitution, which was soon followed by Columbia and Bolivia. Australia, New Zealand, India and the United States, among others, passed legislation that recognized the legal personality of particular nonhumans such as rivers, lakes or local ecosystems and in some cases installed political bodies specifically dedicated to their protection. The Global Alliance for the rights of nature, one of the many lobby groups that seek to advance the enshrinement of nonhuman rights in international law, defines the rights of nature in their 'Proposal Universal Declaration of the Rights of Mother Earth' a set of fundamental rights that apply to all living entities 'without distinction of any kind, such as may be made between organic and inorganic beings, species, origin' to secure not the welfare of human subjects and communities but instead the 'wellbeing of Mother Earth, now and in the future' (GARN 2010).

Like climate change activism, the rise of the rights of nature as theoretical buzzword and actualized legal practice must be understood as a consequence of the anthropocenic shift in public discourse. Their proponents present it as a pathway for ecological politics in the Anthropocene that radically departs from the anthropocentric law that safeguards human exceptionalism and the exploitation of nature through extractivist politics (Viteri 2002; Gudynas 2011;

Cullinan 2011). 'The world can no longer deny that the planet is on the verge of an Anthropocene catastrophe' (Viane 2022: 202), and as urgent debates on humanity's political reaction unfold, the central governmental means of 'law cannot stay behind' (Viane 2022: 202). In some cases, the call for posthuman Anthropocene legislation is directly embedded in the theoretical discourse of the Anthropocene. Chakrabarty, whose assessment of human life in the Anthropocene is centred on the political tools suitable to govern the former, suggests that an Anthropocene expansion of the legal realm to encompass nature is indispensable. In the Anthropocene, 'our concern for justice cannot any longer be about humans alone' (Chakrabarty 2021: 178).

The recognition of nature's intrinsic rights is both political and ontological insofar as it produces concrete legal prescriptions to be politically upheld, but these are hinged on and further impose a certain understanding of being. However, at the intersection of their political and ontological dimensions, critical legal scholarship has recently started to question whether the rights of nature are fit for their Anthropocene purposes, or whether they remain tied to the principles of extractivist liberalism by design. Both endorsements and critiques of the rights of nature zoom in on their link to Indigenous ecologies to substantiate their claim. For those defending posthuman rights as useful tools for Anthropocene politics, the fact that these rights often draw on Indigenous cosmologies and are sometimes the product of Indigenous political activism underlines their genuinely progressive quality. But for those problematizing their recuperative liberalism, the fact that the rights of nature expropriate Indigenous ideas from their ontological and cultural context and shoehorn them into a theoretical framework where the ontology of the Western colonizers remains hegemonic further disqualifies them.

Located at the intersection of Anthropocene ontology and environmental politics in the Anthropocene, this chapter will unpack the rights of nature as another case where the critical mirror of Indigenous ecology renders visible political trajectories alternative to those that ontological Anthropocene theory presents as necessary for a posthuman condition. Juxtaposing ontological Anthropocene theory with our critical mirror on the one hand allows us to highlight what the former *can* bring to contemporary environmental politics: the critical tools to draw out the pervasiveness of liberal epistemic frameworks and to interrogate their intertwinement with national and global power structures in which the modern-Western state still dominates. But it also, as in the previous chapters, brings into view the shortcomings that follow from the deterministic link ontological Anthropocene theory sets up between its ontological and its political claims and which causes it to miss political complexities – including both contestations and opportunities – escaping or running across any sharp modern/nonmodern distinction. Grounding critical readings of the rights of nature in ontological Anthropocene theory draws out how the former adapt and recuperate rather than successfully subverting the ontology of modern liberalism. But at the same time, in the critical mirror of Indigenous ecology, the idea of a unitary rights of nature project collapses into a multiplicity of diverse political contexts and contestations where success or failure are not pre-determined by the 'right' or 'wrong' ontological ground but result from the very particular power relations present in each scenario.

As we will show in the following, Indigenous cosmologies are neither incompatible with rights – and property – based understandings of nature nor per se opposed to anthropocentric environmental guardianship. Where Indigenous communities reject the rights of nature, this rejection is not the consequence of a diametric opposition between Indigenous ecologies and the ontological underpinnings of the rights of nature. In the cases examined, rejection and endorsement rather depend on locally specific political projects and strategies where ecological protection is always intertwined with the fight for Indigenous sovereignty. The plural and politically situated understanding of the rights of nature that emerges from this chapter resists a sharp distinction between 'Western-liberal, humanist and thus politically regressive' and 'non-Western, posthuman and therefore politically revolutionary' because, we argue, the more Anthropocene thinking relies on binaries and constitutive outsides to define a posthuman planetary condition the deeper it remains entangled in the order of modern-liberal thought that it seeks to overcome.

The case for nature's rights

The idea that nature has inalienable rights just like the human subjects of social contract theory predates the Anthropocene discourse. The first substantial proposal for rethinking nature as a rights holder within Western legal scholarship was made by Christopher D. Stone in his 1972 article, '*Should Trees Have Standing?* Toward Legal Rights for Natural Objects'. Stone's ideas were developed further by a number of legal thinkers and practitioners, recently most prominently by the South African environmental lawyer Cormac Cullinan. Cullinan calls for an ecocentric 'wild law' 'based on the idea that humans are only one part of a wider community of beings' where 'the welfare of each member of that community is dependent on the welfare of the Earth as a whole' (Cullinan 2011: 12). However, it is only in the course of humanity's slow awakening to the reality of climate change that the rights of nature have found both widespread academic interest and support within mainstream politics, which prepared the ground for their practical implementation.

Existing cases where legal rights have been granted to nature follow one of two legal routes. A set of rights for nature can on the one hand be set out in a founding legal document, such as the Ecuadorian constitution. Here, Chapter 7 lays out that nature, 'or Pacha Mama, where life is reproduced and occurs, has the right to integral respect for its existence and for the maintenance and regeneration of its life cycles, structure, functions and evolutionary processes' (Ecuad. Const. 2008: ch. 7, art. 71) and that nature 'has a right to be restored' (Ecuad. Const. 2008: ch. 7, art. 71). The advantage of the general rights model is that the threshold for defending the rights of nature is low; everyone, not only Ecuadorian citizens, can, per Ecuador's constitution, act an advocate for nature's rights and take action to have them defended in court (Ecuad. Const. 2008: ch. 7, art. 71). The flip side is that this general approach diffuses responsibilities and ambiguates the implementation of the rights of nature – everyone *can*, but nobody is *directly required* to protect nature's rights (Whittenmore 2011). The first landmark decision where Ecuador's rights of nature were upheld took place in 2011, when two American citizens brought forward the rights of the Vilcabamba River that was damaged by road construction work. The claimants achieved a judgement that obliged the provincial government of Loja to halt the construction work and to restore the river to its pre-construction state (GARN 2011). More recently, in 2021, Ecuador's Constitutional Court upheld the rights of the Los Cedros Ecosystem to the effect that mining rights granted to the state company Enami had to be revoked.[2]

The second route of legislating natural rights, which is favoured in the rights of nature scholarship, on the other hand employs a guardianship model where a specific guardian, either an existing political authority or a newly created governing body, is appointed to uphold the rights of the specified nonhuman rightsholder (Kauffman and Martin 2017; Tănăsescu 2020). The guardianship model underpins two High Court judgements in India, where first the Ganges and Yamuna rivers, and later all natural objects in the State of Uttarakhand, were recognized as legal subjects. In the Uttarakhand case, the judges state that the rights of the ecosystem 'shall be equivalent to the rights of human beings and the injury/harm caused to these bodies shall be treated as harm/injury caused to the human beings' (Lalit Miglani v State of Uttarakhand 2017: 63). As O'Donnell observes, both court judgements invoke the *parens partriae* doctrine where the state intervenes on behalf of a legal minor in need of protection who cannot protect themselves (2018: 138–40). In both cases, existing local authorities are entrusted with the obligation to protect the nonhuman right-holders, resolving the issue of ambiguous responsibilities that characterizes the general rights approach (O'Donnell 2018: 141–2). The guardianship model also underpins the Te Urewera Act (2014) and the Te Awa Tupua Act (2017) in New Zealand, which grant legal rights to the two ecosystems they are named after. Both acts recognize the significance of the right-holding ecosystems to the Indigenous communities that inhabit them and acknowledge that the long-standing intertwinement between nature and Indigenous cultures that marks these spaces means that granting rights to nature must here also mean granting power of environmental governance to Indigenous communities. The Te Awa Tupu act installs a legal guardian comprised of one representative nominated by the Whanganui iwi and one by the New Zealand state. The guardian is created for no other purpose than protecting the integrity of, and working to restore where necessary, the ecosystem of Te Awa Tupu (Pain and Pepper 2021: 328–30).

Advocates for a widespread implementation of natural personhood emphasize its radical potential not only to combat the continuous environmental destruction that marks the Anthropocene, but also to transform social power relations within the former. Emphasizing the norm-building quality of law, rights of nature scholars suggest that a posthuman legal order can function as a catalyser for changing the knowledge structures and value systems of Western societies. As Seth Epstein argues in his recent paper 'Rights of nature, human species identity, and political thought in the Anthropocene', rights 'have served to construct a particular human identity resting on notions of capability and freedom, but used differently they may instead highlight humans' vulnerability and interdependence' (2022: 17).

Granting legal rights to nonhuman actors, in this view, initiates a transition away from an anthropocentric juridical system designed to protect the rights and foster the interests of human subjects at the expense of the Earth and towards an ecocentric position that recognizes human obligations to care for and sustain nature (Kotzé and Villavicencio Calzadilla 2017; Kauffman and Martin 2014, 2017).

Stone, in his early formulation of nature's claim to rights, already emphasizes that rendering nature a holder of legal rights necessarily implies a profound shift in thought. Comparing the extension of rights to nonhumans with granting legal equality to women and black Americans, Stone suggests that each such extension of the sphere of legal persons had to challenge and move the boundaries of what modern societies considered 'unthinkable' (Stone 1973: 456) first. Explicitly positing his call for rights of nature against the 'human chauvinism' of his 'economist friends' (1973: 475), Stone demonstrates remarkable sensitivity to what could, in hindsight, be described as Anthropocene questions. Recognizing that nature 'is a continuous theatre in which things and species (eventually man) are destined to enter and exit' (1972: 480–1), Stone, beyond merely advocating for the legal subjecthood of nonhumans, ponders avenues towards their political representation. Stone is here acutely aware that the shift towards a posthuman reconfiguration of liberal politics will require 'subordinating some human claims to those of the environment *per se*' (Stone 1973: 490). Within the contemporary scholarship on nonhuman rights, thinkers who propose to incorporate rights for nature within a juridical and epistemological system of liberal rights that remains otherwise unchanged, form a minority (see for example Wood 2014). The majority of scholars working on rights of nature echo Stone's idea that awarding legal standing to nature is milestone and stepping stone for a more general shift away from the human exceptionalism that grounds modern-Western societies (Epstein 2022; Tănăsescu 2020; Pain and Pepper 2021).

Vital to the post-liberal, progressive nature of the rights of nature is the fact that many of their legal formulations explicitly draw on, and thereby also legally enshrine, Indigenous cosmologies. Ecuador's constitution codifies nature's rights as part of a larger commitment to wellbeing for humans and nonhumans, which is described with the Kichwa concept *sumak kawsay,* or buen vivir in Spanish. For Alberto Acosta, the Marxist economist who presided over the constitutional assembly that drafted the 2008 constitution for the progressive government of Rafael Correa, *sumak kawsay* offers an alternative to the modern-liberal imperatives of growth and progress that have driven colonial and environmental exploitation and still underpin global markets and international development agendas (Acosta 2012). As the Uruguayan rights of nature scholar Eduardo Gudynas puts it, *sumak kawsay* 'can only occur in a community, which is social but also encompasses nature' and 'goes beyond the Western dualism where nature opposes society, and the individual opposes the community' (2011: 441). In both Ecuador and Bolivia, the constitutional recognition of rights for nature followed long-standing, organized political campaigning by networks of Indigenous communities. Indigenous activists advocated for *sumak kawsay* as a political orienting principle that would interrupt colonial (neo-)liberalism (Kauffman and Martin 2014; Gudynas 2011).

In New Zealand, Indigenous communities did not endorse the rights-based approach to environmental safeguarding reflected in the Te Urewera and Te Awa Tupua acts. However, the legal documents reflect the Tūhoe Iwi tribe's claim to their homeland against the Australian state.[3] While the acts do not restore Tūhoe sovereignty over the Te Urewara and Te Awa Tupua ecosystems as such, they replace settler sovereignty with a shared governance model that recognizes the Tūhoe people as their legitimate guardians. The acts thereby not only acknowledge the legitimacy of the Tūhoe land claims but also the cultural significance of the protected areas – their protection is not only necessary in recognition of nature's nonhuman rights, but also because the former is intertwined with the cultural survival of the human subjects of the Tūhoe people (Kauffmann 2020). The explicit intention of validating Indigenous ontologies as equal to Western-liberal rights is reflected in the writing of the acts themselves. As Craig M. Kauffman notes, the Te Urewera Act on the one hand recognizes the forest as a legal person with 'all the rights, powers, duties, and liabilities of a legal person', but also 'recognizes the Tūhoe view of Te Urewera as a living, spiritual being with its own *mana* (spiritual authority) and *mauri* (life force)' (2020: 2–3). Against this background, the Te Urewara Act does not impose a Western proprietary logic of rights, but instead installs the Indigenous *Te Kawa* as guiding principle for Te Urewara's guardianship. For the Tūhoe,

Te Kawa is about the management of people for the benefit of the land – it is not about land management [. . .] Te Urewera predates us and that we are her creation living with and amongst all of her kin. As her children, we are born with responsibility; we are not born with power and rights. The most difficult of virtues, yet most important to accomplish, is our sense of belonging, to know our place and contribution to creation. (Te Urewera Board cited in Zelle et al. 2021: 310)

The Te Urewara Act inserts Indigenous cosmology into the framework of liberal rights and thereby alters its functional logic – neither the liberal state nor the Tūhoe are given ownership of Te Urewara but are instead appointed as shared guardians of a living ecosystem that defies liberal appropriation. Different from the Indian Uttarakhand case, the guardianship does not follow the paternalistic logic of *parens partriae,* but instead foregrounds the responsibility of both the Tūhoe and the New Zealand state to sustain an environment that is neither inferior to nor separate from its human guardians. Against this background, Kauffman views the Te Urewara Act as a remarkable victory for Indigenous ecology. The act 'empowered the Tūhoe to retake their traditional place as *kaitiaki,* or guardians of Te Urewera. This created space for the Tūhoe to begin the long process of recovering ancestral knowledge, customs, and practices to reconnect the people to the land' (Kauffman 2020: 2).

Liberal property, Indigenous expropriation

As told so far, and through the eyes of their advocates, the story of the rights of nature is one of remarkable success. It appears to warrant at least careful optimism that awarding legal standing to nonhumans offers a meaningful avenue for acting on anthropocenic environmental changes because it does not only generate a set of directly useable political tools but also promises to reconfigure the modern-liberal logic of rights, obligations and the functioning of legal protection. In the countries and cases where rights of nature have been legally enshrined, however, it is far less clear whether this implementation can be understood as successful in terms of aiding environmental protection and advancing posthuman awareness. In Ecuador and Bolivia, the constitutional codification of nature's rights goes hand in hand with the continuation of rapid and large-scale deforestation (Laing 2015; Kotzé and Villavicencio Calzadilla 2017). Neither in South America nor in New Zealand and Australia has the participation of Indigenous communities in drafting and guarding the rights of nature changed their socially, culturally and politically marginalized status or provided a steppingstone for political sovereignty. To a number of critical scholars, the rights of nature's failure to live up to their radical promise is anything but surprising. Rather, they argue that the rights of nature were destined to fail because they reinscribe, with only superficial alterations, precisely the modern-liberal ontology that the Anthropocene has powerfully rendered untenable (Rawson and Mansfield 2018; Viane 2022; Burdon 2020).

Critics of the rights of nature suggest that individual rights, of both the human and the posthuman kind, are fundamentally unsuitable for protecting the environment because of the proprietary logic they follow and reproduce (Burdon 2020: 316). In John Locke's foundational account of the inalienable liberal rights to life, liberty and property, it is the latter that conditions the former two: because we have property in ourselves, both our bodies and our minds, any external – individual or collective-political – interference in the former is illegitimate. The right to property grants the property-holder a freedom from external interference. But the property in ourselves is, in Locke, also what generates commodity ownership – through labour, we mix our bodies with whatever we produce from environmental resources, thereby making it irrevocably and unquestionably our human property (Wood 1984: 53–4). The dual function of Locke's property in oneself – grounding liberal rights and grounding commodity ownership – inscribes the human prerogative of property acquisition and property ownership at the heart of liberal rights. Locke's rights are those of an 'agrarian capitalist' (Wood 1984: 81) because 'self-possessed individuals constitute and sanctify property in objects and themselves precisely by treating the environment as a buffet' (Ephraim 2022: 675). Designated by God to populate the Earth, humans are not only entitled but morally commanded to take hold of, use and even destroy whatever they need for the advancement of mankind, because he 'who appropriates land to himself by his labour, does not lessen but increase the common stock of mankind' (Locke 2005: §37).

Locke's liberal rights are not only built on the human prerogative to exploit and capitalize on nature, but also exhibit a latent anthropocentrism. Rights unfold in a negative logic – they set up a freedom from external interference that the right-holder can legally demand and protect with the help of executive authorities that can be alerted in the case of transgression and issue punishment. Nonhuman right-holders, however, are not able to demand the policing of their personal property in the way that human right-holders do (Epstein 2022: 16–17). For this reason, legal protection via property in oneself means that the ownership of nature's legal standing is, indirectly or directly, as in the Indian cases, transferred to a legal guardian to enforce it in practice. But because Locke's theory leaves the boundary between rights and property ambiguous, transferring liberal rights to a political authority always also opens the door for the commodification of the nonhuman right-holder. Finally, Locke's conceptualization of liberal rights lays the ground for their now widely problematized 'affinities with colonial rationalities' (Esmeir 2006: 1545) because rights are here given to some, while others are dehumanized as belonging to the sphere of nature waiting to be appropriated. 'Those who fail to fully utilize food or food-producing land – failures he associates with women, native people, and laborers – are disqualified from ownership. In short, Locke holds that ingestion both entails and justifies appropriation' (Ephraim 2022: 675).

Designed in the image of Locke's liberal rights, the rights of nature firstly do not disrupt the logic of liberal commodification but can peacefully coexist with the former if the political authority instructed with guarding them chooses to pursue an extractivist politics of human advancement. In Ecuador and Bolivia, granting constitutional rights to nature has achieved little in halting large-scale environmental destruction through deforestation, mining and fishing. Instead of offering a genuine alternative to the neoliberal development agenda, critics suggest that the focus on the intertwinement of human and nonhuman wellbeing – that must be upheld by the state – has extended the power of the latter to implement its agenda of economic growth under the guise of fostering such holistic wellbeing (Kotzé and Villavicencio Calzadilla 2017; Pain and Pepper 2021). In one of the first instances where new legislation referenced the Ecuadorian buen vivir constitution, nature's rights were evoked to evict small-scale artisanal miners in a remote region of the country where the Ecuadorian state has since expanded corporate mining, to a significant extent on Indigenous land (Tănăsescu 2020: 118–19). Rather than advancing Indigenous political claims, the Indigenous principle of *sumak kawsay* is here perverted to facilitate their continuous violation.

Because the rights of nature are practically implemented by granting property rights to particular humans, the protection of nature secondly impacts human power relations depending on how, and to whom, ownership is granted. In

Ecuador, the introduction of *custodias* arrangements for fisheries, which gives Indigenous communities the rights to act as property-holding guardians for coastal ecosystems, preceded the recognition of nature's constitutional rights within an Indigenous logic but was further strengthened through legislation that followed the buen vivir constitution (Beitl 2016: 328–9). In her overarching analysis of coastal management in Ecuador, Christine Beitl notes the overall positive impact of buen vivir-style Indigenous guardianship arrangements on both environmental protection and Indigenous empowerment. However, she also points out that implementing environmental guardianship under the umbrella of property-ownership comes with certain challenges for Indigenous communities. In order to apply for guardianship, they must form an association recognized by the state, meaning that in order to implement both the rights of nature and their own cultural practices, Indigenous communities must reconfigure themselves within the political-legal logic of the liberal state, with the latter holding decisional power over who can and who cannot act as a guardian (Beitl 2016: 331–2). Even in New Zealand, where Indigenous activists successfully resisted a guardianship model based on ownership, the guardianship arrangement nevertheless requires that ecosystems are in practice managed as property, meaning that the hegemony of Indigenous principles is here theoretical rather than politically actualized (2020: 449–50). As Tănăsescu notes, the 'self-ownership of Te Urewera . . . comes very close to corporate personhood, which further makes it available for integration within already existing legal infrastructures' (2021: 85).

While the rights of nature literature is distinct from the discourse of Anthropocene theory, the interplay that unfolds between the advocates of legal personhood for nonhumans and its critics parallels the dynamic between the catastrophic Anthropocene and its ontological critics. In both cases, the original proposition – of governing (in the face of) the climate catastrophe and of protecting nature by awarding it individual rights – is driven by the desire for urgent political action on the Anthropocene condition. In both cases, the founding mistake that leads critics to object to what is being proposed is that of using and improving rather than discarding the ontological and political tools of liberal modernity in the Anthropocene. Ontological Anthropocene theory is hence perfectly suited to situate and further explore what, from the perspective of an entangled Earth, is wrong with the rights of nature. Understood in this sense, the issue with rights for nature lies deeper than the proprietary logic of Locke's individual rights – with their continuation of ontological anthropocentrism. While the rights of nature, on the surface, overcome the anthropocentrism of modern-liberal law by granting rights to nonhumans, the inclusion of nonhumans expands the reach of the liberal legal sphere as it is rather than substantially altering its functioning.

Stone's early call for the legal standing of nature illustrates clearly how the rights of nature accommodate the explicit rejection of anthropocentrism within a theoretical framework that nevertheless remains anthropocentric. As shown above, Stone drafts his rights of nature against the 'human chauvinism' (Stone 1972: 475) that drives modern-liberal thought and its legal application. But the rights of nature he proposes follow the pattern of liberal human rights: like Locke's rights of life, liberty and property, they are 'inalienable' (Stone 1972: 455) and held by the rights holder, 'the environment *per se*' (Stone 1972: 481), qua their existence as rights holder, without any justification necessary beyond the tautology of liberal subjecthood. For Stone, modern-liberal ontology is not only a perfectly suitable way to guard the protection of nonhumans, but indeed a superior way. He references Earl Finbar Murphy's *Has Nature Any Right to Life?* to comment dismissively on the idea that non-Western relational ontologies, which regard humans and nonhumans as existentially entangled and ontologically of the same status, could be more effective in grounding environmental protection than modern liberalism. For Stone,

> the spiritual beliefs of the Chinese and Indians 'in the unity between man and nature had no greater effect than the contrary beliefs in Europe in producing a balance between man and his environment'; [. . .] in China, *tao* notwithstanding, 'ruthless deforestation has been continuous.' I am under the impression, too, that notwithstanding the vaunted 'harmony' between the American Plains Indians and Nature, once they had equipped themselves with rifles their pursuit of the buffalo expanded to fill the technological potential. (Stone 1972: 949)

Modelling the rights of nature after liberal human rights has immediate implications for how the environmental protection they set up functions: rendering natural entities legal subjects disrupts the ecological relationships that link them to humans and other nonhumans. By coupling legal protection to an individual private sphere, the legal personhood renders nature passive and extra-political. The rights of nature thereby reproduce the sharp binary between a static, passive nature and dynamic human relations that is germane to modern thought (Tănăsescu 2020: 436–8). They are incapable of adequately capturing the demands of living, growing and changing ecosystems for which static sustenance might be detrimental, and which are so intertwined with human relations that withdrawal to a protected sphere of pure nature untainted by human interference is illusionary. To safeguard fundamentally entangled Anthropocene environments, our political-legal tools must be re-thought on the basis of a relational, contextual and fractured understanding of being in the Anthropocene. Viewed from the critical perspective of the ontological Anthropocene, Indigenous ecologies offer exactly such relational and context-sensitive ways of understanding the legal and ethical relationship between humans and nonhumans.

However, the rights of nature preclude, or even worse, pervert, any insight to be gained from Indigenous ecologies by isolating their ethical-legal principles from their cultural and political context and forcing them into a framework of modern-liberal rights with which they cannot readily coexist. As Ariel Rawson and Becky Mansfield put it, 'by treating rights for nature as a natural truth, RoN [rights of nature] is not only contradictory but naturalizes the colonial history of legal personhood. To clarify, RoN enacts a contradictory logic, where in the name of overcoming western human-nature dualism, and its concomitant anthropocentrism, it turns to western notions of rights, personhood, and holism as the solution' (2018: 100).

For the case of Ecuador, this raises the question to what extent *sumak kawsay* has not only been strategically uprooted and emptied of its original meaning when incorporated into Ecuadorian political management and planning as *buen vivir* (as for instance argued in Cuestas-Caza 2018) but was rather always insufficient as a vehicle for Indigenous ecology because it is designed in the image of a modern-liberal ethical principle. While the concept was introduced to the rights of nature discourse by the Indigenous academic Carlos Viteri Gualinga in 2004, scholars query whether *sumak kawsay* is actually rooted in Indigenous cosmology in a meaningful way (Domíngues, Caria and León 2017; Sánchez Parga 2011; Whitten and Scott Whitten 2015; Quick and Spartz 2018). While *sumak kawsay/buen vivir* is presented as a native alternative to and 'conceptual rupture' (SENPLADES 2009: 7) with the Western concept of development, it nevertheless folds neatly into a framework of progressive human advancement that is however fundamentally alien to the Indigenous cosmologies it is attributed to.

This highlights that the concept, even at its conceptual core, should not be understood as an originally Indigenous idea but rather as the product of Indigenous and Western cultural blending in Ecuador. The mixed heritage of the concept not only means that it is 'necessarily reductive and cannot account for the semantic richness' (Vanhulst and Beling 2014: 56) of Ecuador's Indigenous ecologies. As a one-dimensional ethical principle that offers guidance on how to engage with nonhuman life but is emptied of the sociopolitical implications that are an intrinsic part of Indigenous ecologies, *sumak kawsay* is ready-made for functioning as the environmental 'add on' to liberal socio-economic programmes. For this reason, Ecuador's National Plan for Good Living 2009–13, developed by the National Secretariat of Planning and Development to implement the principle in political practice, can easily integrate the former in an agenda of human, societal development and advancement.

> Buen vivir seeks to achieve the satisfaction of necessities, the attainment of the quality of life . . . the healthy flourishing of all, in peace and harmony with nature . . . . in a manner that they permit a simultaneous achievement of that which society, territories, diverse collective identities and each one – seen as both an individual and UNIVERSAL HUMAN BEING value as the objective of a desirable life. (SENPLADES 2009: 6)

Because the cultural-epistemic blending that has produced the concept does not take place on an equal playing field, but rather on one where the Indigenous side has significantly less epistemic and political shaping power, '*buen vivir* as development is the State. And it is the State that signifies in technocratic, economistic, and humanistic terms what is development and *buen vivir*' (Walsh 2010: 20). For José Sánchez Parga, who dismisses *sumak kawsay* as a political ideology forced onto rather than representative of Ecuador's Indigenous peoples in this sense, the concept misrepresents Indigenous ecology as frozen in an idealized pre-colonial past by rendering it a normative framework that relates to untouched nonhuman nature only (Sánchez Parga 2011).

Designed to operate within a political framework centred on human development, *sumak kawsay/buen vivir* constitutes an instrumentally expropriated version of Indigenous relational sustainability. It immunizes the Ecuadorian state against the charge of exploitative neoliberalism while at the same time allowing it to continue its development agenda. Against this background, it is hardly surprising that Ecuador's Indigenous activists have responded critically to *sumak kawsay/buen vivir* (Altmann 2014; Quick and Spartz 2018). In 2010, only two years after the new constitution was ratified, CONAIE, the umbrella organization of Ecuador's Indigenous communities and political movements that had represented the former during the process of writing the new constitution, severed all ties with the government. CONAIE justified the end of the dialogue with the government's use of *sumak kawsay*. CONAIE's public statement expressed their dissatisfaction with how the principle was politically implemented in no uncertain terms, describing the government as 'a false socialist traitor, populist, genocidal, fascist to the principles of the sumak kawsay' which abuses the former to cover 'up the colonialism of the XXI century' (CONAIE 2010 quoted in Altmann 2014: 90).

While the ontological and political displacement of Indigenous ideas through their integration in a liberal rights of nature framework is more obvious in the case of Ecuador, a similar observation can be made for New Zealand's Te Urewera and Te Awa Tupua acts. Here, the Tūhoe were successful in lobbying for a stewardship model nominally not based on the Western notion of property ownership but which instead followed the non-proprietary authority of *tikanga* – in fact the acts even avoid reference to the Western notions of 'guardianship' or 'stewardship' altogether (Tănăsescu 2020: 445). Tănăsescu (2020) emphasizes the revolutionary potential of the Te Urewera and Te Awa Tupua acts because they recognize the legal standing of the ecosystems they protect in a way that is taken out of the framework of liberal law and set up a politically open governmental model *sui generis,* which grants Indigenous actors significant shaping power (see also Epstein 2022). However, because of this political openness, it is at the same time far from clear whether and to what extent the conceptual dominance of Māori terms in the two acts translates into a political dominance in managing Te Urewera and Te Awa Tupua for the Tūhoe (Jones 2016: 52–6; Tănăsescu 2020: 447–8).

Commenting on similar co-managed guardianship models that exist to preserve ecosystems with legal standing in Australia, the Indigenous scholar Virginia Marshall suggests that any such arrangement must fall short from an Indigenous point of view because it does 'not fracture the skeletal frame of Australia's legal system' (2019: 241). For Marshall, questions of environmental protection and cultural and political sovereignty for Indigenous peoples are intrinsically intertwined. This means that compromise arrangements like the shared management of water resources in Australia – or like the New Zealand acts – can only be understood as successful if they advance both causes at the same time. 'The key failure of the rights of nature advocacy', for Marshall, 'is that it acknowledges "Indigenous wisdom" and moves on to characterizing a collective human behaviour that rejects their "Earth community" philosophy, which of itself imparts trauma and fails to recognize the impact on usurping the nation status of First Peoples' (Marshall 2019: 236).

The critical lens of the ontological Anthropocene reveals the liberal underpinnings of the rights of nature as an inbuilt ontological flaw. It destines them to failure as a political tool for tackling the human and nonhuman exploitation that has given rise to the Anthropocene. Liberal rights operate through the demarcation of right-holders from those they exclude, which can be flexibly assigned. Following Rawson and Mansfield, 'extending personhood to nature as an alternative to the commodification of life and human–nature dualism (i.e. RoN) attaches properties of whiteness to nature and naturalizes being human as a property of whiteness' (2018: 105). The rights of nature do not disrupt the liberal, colonial ontology of nature as the property of a white, Western Anthropos and thus not only fall short in protecting nature from exploitation through the liberal state instructed with its safeguarding, but also reinscribe the subordination of non-Western peoples through the 'largely unacknowledged imbrication with the supposed "West" [they] reject' (Rawson and Mansfield 2018: 100).

Political primacy, property and obligation in Indigenous environmental governance

If we assess the case of the rights of nature through the lens of ontological Anthropocene theory in the earlier manner, we can end here. The evidence is clear and the verdict inevitable. As a pathway for environmental politics in the Anthropocene, the rights of nature were doomed to fail from the get-go because they do not achieve distance from the recuperative pull of modern liberalism. All political potentiality they can unfold will thus, in one way or another, reproduce the epistemic formations that found the political and economic status quo of hegemonic liberalism. With the help of our critical mirror of Indigenous ecology, we will in the following reopen the case and re-examine the evidence. Importantly, this re-examination does not intend to invalidate the insight that the rights of nature carry liberal-colonial baggage established earlier through the critical perspective of Anthropocene ontology. However, the critical mirror of Indigenous ecology does call into question how decisive these ontological flaws are for their political failure, and whether mapping the rights of nature as diametrically opposed to and per se incompatible with Indigenous thought and practices does justice to the latter. Against the Anthropocene critique of the rights of nature, we suggest that they are not doomed by their theoretical make-up, but rather fail in practice. In other words, their failure to unfold a genuinely creative political potentiality is not the necessary result of their 'taintedness' with the mark of modern liberalism, but rather the specific effect of their particular political configurations, in which the forces of the liberal state and market hold disproportionate power. Understood in this sense, the lack of Indigenous bargaining power within the arrangements that implement the rights of nature in practice is here not a direct, necessary result of the lacking, simplistic or perverted application of Indigenous cosmologies, but simply that – a lack of political power within the structures and processes of settler-colonial states.

The first case to be revisited here is that of Ecuador's *sumak kawsay.* Returning to the sharp criticism that Ecuador's political programme for good living received, it is notable that its Indigenous critiques do not target the legitimacy of *sumak kawsay* as an Indigenous concept, or how it is being used to frame policy, but rather the political implementation of good life policies. Ecuador's multiple Indigenous communities (with fourteen being officially recognized peoples) have a long-standing history of collective, organized political mobilization. After the failure of the 1973 land reform, which was supported by Indigenous leaders, Altman notes that Ecuador's Indigenous organizations loosened their alliance with left-wing state politics and instead adopted a collective 'identity politics' as the new strategy for advancing Indigenous interests on the level of national politics (2014: 87–8). Altman's observation opens up a different perspective on the constructedness of *sumak kawsay* as Indigenous ecological principle. Andreu Viola Recasens advances this reading of *sumak kawsay* as a strategically invented tradition, identifying it as an attempt to employ the master's 'juridical' (2014: 63) tools to dismantle the master's house on the part of Ecuador's Indigenous communities. Viewed as an expression of strategic essentialism, the value of the concept is not determined by its Indigenous foundational essence but instead by its functionality as an ontopolitical tool for collective Indigenous politics.

An Anthropocene ontology critique of Ecuador's rights of nature, which is centred on their all too Western, insufficiently Indigenous conceptual roots remains limited by the *in itself inherently modern* primacy of ontology over politics. It struggles to adequately capture the stakes and battle lines in the political struggles of Indigenous peoples for whom ontology does not necessarily hold the same grand, foundational meaning – and for whom the strategic invention of a universal ontological principle in the style of Western modernity is thus not original sin but rather a viable political strategy that must be judged by its effectiveness. Several Ecuadorian scholars note the intentional vagueness of the concept, which connects expressions and ideas that exist in different Indigenous cultures rather than specifying a fixed set of rules and principles (Gudynas 2011; Cuestas-Caza 2018). In Viteri's foundational text, the good life is necessarily open-ended and flexible so that it can be adapted to local contexts and changing future circumstances (Viteri 2002). Specific and clearly defined is Viteri's *sumak kawsay* only in its opposition to the Western, neoliberal concept of development (Viteri 2002: 1; Altmann 2014: 86), albeit that this opposition failed to become impactful in the concept's political implementation, as shown earlier.

The concept of the good life was readily employed by non-Indigenous political activists as an ontopolitical tool against modern-Western liberalism. In the same year as Viteri's paper was published, Acosta (who would later, in 2013, run unsuccessfully as a Presidential candidate for the Indigenous-allied Patchakutik party against Rafael Correa) adopted *sumak kawsay* as an Ecuadorian alternative to Western development (Acosta 2002). But the concept also quickly became a tool of Indigenous politics: in 2003, only one year later, the local Indigenous organization 'Autonomous Territory of the Aboriginal Nation of the Kichwa People of Sarayaku' made use of the concept to ground their opposition to petroleum production in their territory (Sarayaku 2003). The Sarayaku document adopts the good life as an ontological principle representative of Indigenous lifeways without specification or qualifier, but inserts it in the context of their specific cosmological beliefs and traditions and their political demands for land rights. Here, the Kichwa argue that *sumak kawsay* can only be realized in a pluri-national state where Indigenous communities have full autonomy over their territories (Sarayaku 2003: 1–4).

In 2015, the Kichwa people presented 'Kawsak Sacha' – the living forest – as a proposal for nonhuman rights to the 2015 Climate Conference in Paris. The proposal is phrased in universalizing language and anchored in the concept of the good life: Kawsak Sacha 'grows out of the millennial knowledge of the Indigenous Peoples who inhabit the Amazonian rainforest' (Kawsak Sacha 2015: 1) and who have a particular authority to speak on matters of sustainability because of the 'continuous relation that . . . Indigenous People have with the beings of the forest [. . .] which, in turn permits a harmony of life among many kinds of beings' (Kawsak Sacha 2015: 1). The good life is here put forward not as confined to Indigenous communities but as a framework for 'global ethical orientation' that can become 'a planetary reality' (Kawsak Sacha 2015: 1). First and foremost, 'Kawsak Sacha' appears as an ideal-typical example for Indigenous thought that is cosmologically uprooted, Westernised and instrumentalised to 'save' liberal modernity. But noteworthy is also how the Kawsak Sacha document identifies the good life as an 'economic project' (Kawsak Sacha 2015: 2) directed against the 'large-scale neo-colonialist extractive projects' (Kawsak Sacha 2015: 2) undertaken on Indigenous lands by 'the very governments that put forth solemn discourses criticizing imperialism, capitalism, and colonialism . . . in the supposed name of democracy' (Kawsak Sacha 2015: 2).

While the Kichwa led the way in adopting *sumak kawsay* as an ontopolitical tool against liberal-modern development, other Indigenous organizations and institutions, including Ecuador's Intercultural University Amawtay Wasi, followed suit (Altmann 2014: 88–9). In their proposal to the 2007 constitutional assembly and consecutive documents, the Indigenous umbrella organization CONAIE also embraced the concept. The CONAIE argues that the good life demands 'the construction of a post-capitalist and post-colonial society' (CONAIE 2007: 1), in which a non-extractive and sustainable economy serves the wellbeing of both humans and nonhumans (CONAIE 2007: 7, 2010) and demands a pluri-national reorganization of the Ecuadorian state (CONAIE 2010). The diametrical opposition between Ecuadorian good life and liberal-modern development is here not ontological fact but rather political aim for Indigenous communities that have come to learn that liberal politics is anti-Indigenous (Viola Recasens 2014: 66–7). In the same sense, Whitten and Scott Whitten (2015) contrast the Kichwa's positioning of their ancestral wisdom as people of the forest in clear demarcation from modern societies in 'Kawsak

Sacha' with the daily lives of Indigenous peoples in Ecuador, who often move dynamically between being *sacha runa,* people of the forest and their identity as subjects of the Ecuadorian state, *alli runa.*

The artificiality, ontological simplicity and Westernized set-up of *sumak kawsay* are obvious; but there are good reasons to assume that Indigenous communities and organizations have adopted the concept not only regardless, but *precisely because of* these characteristics. Palatable to national and international policy-makers but inherently linked to Indigenous cultures, *sumak kawsay* appears as a suitable tool to open up space for Indigenous claims, most importantly the theft of territories and resources, within different political arenas. The explicit nonmodernity of the good life is here less *a priori* ontological fact than the secondary, deliberately produced effect of an Indigenous struggle against Ecuador's extractivist politics, which Indigenous communities hoped to further by providing it with ontological foundations intelligible to the modern-liberal opponent. Prioritizing access and bargaining power over ontological genuineness, some of Ecuador's Indigenous communities and organizations adopted the concept of the good life to arm their politics until it became clear that the Ecuadorian state only intended to greenwash its neoliberal development agenda with the 2008 rights of nature constitution, meaning that no actual political momentum could be gained from appealing to the good life. The failure of *sumak kawsay* as a vehicle for ecological politics is thus political, secondary to and conditioned by the inability to exercise sufficient shaping power on Ecuador's government on the part of Ecuador's Indigenous communities. Even this failure is not clear-cut, general and necessary: while CONAIE severs all ties with the *sumak kawsay/ buen vivir* politics of the Ecuadorian government in 2011, the Kichwa employ the concept to support Indigenous land claims at the 2015 Climate Conference.

Indigenous ecology cannot readily be mapped onto the various modern/ nonmodern distinctions set up by ontological Anthropocene theory. Both in their strategic endorsement of the rights of nature and in their opposition to the former, Indigenous communities are not the revolutionary Others of Western modernity, offering counter-ontologies and counter-politics for the Anthropocene. In the case of the Te Urewara and Te Awa Tupua acts, the Tūhoe's opposition to codifying land and water rights through legal personality is not so much based on a categorical rejection of legalism as it is on the recognition that Indigenous conceptions of land rights are difficult to accommodate within liberal rights frameworks because they link rights and obligations in a way that is locally specific to the nonhuman nature and the human Indigenous community that mutually sustain each other. As Australian Indigenous scholar Marcia Lynne Langton writes against the background of Australian Aboriginal cosmology, the 'concept of personhood of river systems is foreign within Aboriginal ideology, where there is no separation between land, water and Aboriginal cultural/legal obligations that derive from the fundamental Aboriginal belonging to the land and waters' (1997: 90). The implication is that Indigenous communities oppose the liberal personhood of nature because their own, culturally embedded frameworks of law, rights and guardianship are better suited to ensuring genuine ecological sustainability – not because conceptions of rights, law and ownership are per se alien to Aboriginal culture (Marshall 2019: 240–1). The legal recognition of nature is not antithetical to Indigenous cosmologies – only Western legal personality is, rendering it unfit for the protection of ecosystems that are intertwined with Indigenous cultural survival and the politics of Indigenous sovereignty.

Referencing the Australian *Gumana v Northern Territory* case, in which the Yolngu Peoples of north-east Arnhem Land sought to ban third parties from fishing in their traditional waters of Blue Mud Bay by citing their Indigenous land rights under the Aboriginal Land Rights (Northern Territory) Act 1976, Marshall writes that Aboriginal law for humans and nonhumans

> does not separate the land from the water, nor can Aboriginal laws allow unrestricted economic exploitation of the land or waters without compromising customs, practices, values and the obligation of caring for Aboriginal Country. Aboriginal peoples' relationship is embedded within the environment. Tied to the spiritual creation of the lands and waters, and understood as a relationship to an animate object of Aboriginal customary property rights bound by birthright, in a familial connection that includes the concept of ownership. (Marshall 2019: 239)

The intrinsically intertwined relationship between ecological protection and Indigenous cultural survival means that Indigenous ecologies sit uneasily not only with the ecocentrism of the rights of nature, but also with the flat ontology of Anthropocene theory. For Indigenous communities, it is not nature per se that holds rights and demands protection, but specific natural entities and ecosystems that stand in established spiritual, cultural and economic relations with particular human communities. The value of nature does not stem from a flat ontology in which all beings are fundamentally equal, or which ontologically prioritizes Earthly entanglements over particular subjects, but from its asymmetrical human-cultural entangledness.

The ontological Anthropocene recognizes this entangledness, but only reflects on its implications for human agency and responsibility. For Indigenous communities, ecological relationality means that nature has responsibilities towards humans too. Spiritual practices aim at the management of mutual ecological obligations – their neglect leads nonhumans to neglect human communities on their part. Elders from Guatemala's Q'eqchi' people discuss changes to the water resources in their territory as the result of such mutual neglect. 'Young people do not know the sacred sites of the river so they do not ask for permission and they violate the life of the river' (quoted in Viane 2022: 200), states elder Qana Elvira. For Qawa Flavio, this is 'why the water gets angry; that's why the community stream has dried up' (Viane 2022: 200). The Q'eqchi's spiritual relationship to water is not that between ontological equals but rather places the Q'eqchi' in the specific position of having to manage water, sustain its productive relationship with human communities and prevent its anger.

While the critical lens of Anthropocene ontology allows us to recognize how Indigenous perspectives undermine universalist nonhuman rights, they bracket how Indigenous ecologies also problematize the blanket rejection of anthropocentrism in the name of a universally flat ontology that drives the former. Indigenous ecologies assign the human subject particular, ontologically weighty responsibility alternative to that of liberalism's unencumbered individual, and centred on the multiple ecological connections of Anthropos, and the specific obligations these create. Marshall again expresses this pointedly:

> From an Indigenous perspective, this approach, that is, that all forms of life have intrinsic value, described above is highly problematic because it proposes that humans are one of many living species and organisms where none are superior to the other, existing as individual organisms with duties such as not to harm or interfere. First Nations relate to and contemplate value in terms of relationships in the environment where Aboriginal identity is integral and articulates both communal and individual rights and interests. (Marshall 2019: 244)

For Marshall, rights of nature declarations that place the relational Earth in a hierarchically superior position vis-à-vis the beings that populate it, including humans, are 'oppositional to the inherent role of Aboriginal peoples to manage and protect their country' (Marshall 2019: 245). But in the same vein, a flat Anthropocene where human subjects and their actions can hold no privileged position cannot accommodate the idea that the 'Indigenous peoples of Australia have a primary, unique, and inherent obligation to exercise the ownership, protection and wise management of the environment' (Marshall 2019: 246). Within an Indigenous logic, environmental protection is asymmetrically linked to the political and cultural rights of Indigenous humans, which hold primacy.

The ontological Anthropocene inflates and overstates the 'otherness' of Indigenous ecologies, bracketing all parallels and points of contact to modern liberalism. For this reason, it cannot grasp the complexity that unfolds where the rights of nature, as political practice, intersect with Indigenous cosmologies and Indigenous politics. Remaining bound to the modern/nonmodern binary that grounds the ontological Anthropocene, the former maps this framework onto the relationship between the rights of nature and their Indigenous 'other'. It fails to recognize how the 'nonmodernity' of Indigenous ecologies vis-à-vis the rights of nature is not original and foundational but unfolds in the politically loaded context of continuous settler colonialism and Indigenous contestation and political action. Beneath a deliberate and politically instrumentalized diametrical opposition to the liberal state, Indigenous ecologies parallel and interact with what Anthropocene ontology dismisses as the fallacies of an inherently modern rights of nature logic in many ways. Anthropocentrism, ownership and management are not foreign to Indigenous environmental protection but an intrinsic part of the cosmological frameworks and practices that locate and guard the environment for some Indigenous communities. While the logic of ecological interaction these ideas unfold here is distinct from, and in some ways opposed to, that of the liberal rights of nature, this opposition is the product of locally specific relations where ontology, cultural practice and political strategy blend dynamically.

The relationship between the Saami people and reindeer populations in Finland further illuminates how Indigenous environmental sustainability is grounded in a dynamically adaptive cultural relationship between humans and nonhumans and secondary to their preservation. Saami traditions of reindeer husbandry follow a rights-based logic of ecological protection that is not based on *a priori* rights of an abstract nature, but on the particular meaning that reindeer husbandry has for the Saami. The specific value of the ecological relation between Saami humans and reindeer grounds a political claim for Indigenous sovereignty. The Saami present their cultural and territorial rights as the ground for an effective environmental protection that is enacted through cultural relations specifically built around herding reindeer (Oksanen 2020: 1148–9). In this logic, protecting reindeer husbandry as an Indigenous cultural practice through granting rights and sovereignty to the *human* end of this cultural relation

> would also mean that the Saami's reindeer would gain some protection. Not necessarily the individual reindeer – the practice of reindeer herding typically involves the castration, branding and slaughter of individual animals. [. . .] But the Saami's right to their own cultural identity would provide some measure of protection for the *kind* of which those individuals are members. (James 2020: 6)

The Saami do not reject a rights-based approach to environmental protection but oppose expropriation by the liberal state through 'a unique expression . . . combining traits of modern nationalism with traditional Indigenous practices' (Oksanen 2020: 1155) that is neither antithetical to rights-based environmental and cultural protection nor to an asymmetrical understanding of human and nonhuman value and agency.

Beyond failing to reject the veiled anthropocentrism of ownership-based environmental protection, the Saami reindeer farmers more generally defy the idea of the good, 'nonmodern' ecological native. Where the Australian Aboriginal cosmology, as shown earlier, situates ecological protection in a logic of rights, management and ownership that is alternative to that of the modern-liberal settler state, the Saami logic of intertwined natural and cultural protection also includes ideas of property and competition, which are alternative, but in the understanding of being they unfold not completely oppositional to those germane to modern liberalism. For the Saami, reindeer are not only integral to their cultural protection, but also essential to their economic livelihood and community survival. Robert Paine introduces the concept of 'pastoral capital' (2004: 24) to capture how cultural and economic sustainability blend in the Saami practice of reindeer husbandry. While the 'immediate resource that becomes capital are the reindeer, [. . .] the maintenance of social relations between pastoralists are another regenerating resource' (2004: 24). Paine notes that Saami communities are characterized both by a pervasive egalitarianism and by a 'competitive ethos' (2004: 28) that comes to the fore in the way different reindeer herders compete for the most fertile pastures. Against this background, it would be misguided to argue that for the Saami, ecological protection emerges from meaning systems to which the ideas of ownership, rights, property and even competition are thoroughly external and alien. However, within Saami culture, the forementioned unfold a social logic distinct from that of modern liberalism because they are linked to and mediated by other social values, chiefly an idea of equivalence, which means that small herders are paired with those owning large herds so that the former have better chances to be successful in competing for the best pastures and the latter have additional support in looking after their large herds, as well as by a flexible idea of usufruct (Paine 2004: 27–9).

The extent to which Saami competition, capital and ownership are translatable into the liberal counterparts of the state is unclear. In Norway, such translation did not happen naturally but was enforced by the Reindeer Act of 1978, which fixed and standardized the property arrangements of Saami reindeer herders. However, this process of cultural-legal translation and blending was in part embraced and only in part critiqued by Norway's Saami communities (Paine 2004: 30–8). Sami reindeer herders themselves emphasize the importance of sustaining traditional knowledge, but at the same time also the necessity to flexibly adapt the former to changing environmental and sociopolitical conditions, which includes the use of modern knowledge and technology. In a comprehensive study based on interviews with several Saami reindeer farmers, Axelsson-Linkowski et al. found that the 'persistence of knowledge [. . .] was often related to the maintenance of traditional practices and the creation of so-called "hybrid knowledge" where traditional knowledge is able to adapt to a changing context' (2020: 488). Several of the herders emphasized that their focus must now be on principles of herding and teaching the children to think for themselves' (2020: 487). Whether Saami communities here support or reject the rights of nature depends on how their specific implementation relates to the political aims of cultural integrity and territorial sovereignty. Again, granting nature rights cannot be judged as advantageous or detrimental in a general fashion, but such judgement depends on the specific political configuration of their implementation, and the avenues it opens up for Indigenous agency.

Perhaps the most famous example blending nonhumans rights and Indigenous political and territorial claims is the Standing Rock water protection movement against the Dakota Access Pipeline. Built in 2016, the pipeline transports crude oil from the Bakken oil fields in North Dakota, through South Dakota and Iowa to Illinois, crossing the Standing Rock reservation. In July 2016, the Standing Rock Sioux Nation filed a lawsuit against the US Army Corps of Engineers, stating that the pipeline 'threaten[ed] the Tribe's environmental and economic well-being' (Clearinghouse 2016: 1–2). The Standing Rock water resources form the focal point of the tribe's political claim. In the cosmologies of the Wisconsin Sakaogon, water is recognized as an actor with powers in its own rights, which therefore demands recognition, relational care and protection like a human subject (Dhillon and Estes 2016). For the Indigenous scholar Glenn C. Reynolds, the agent-status of water is reflected in the names that the Sakaogon gave to their water resources. They 'called the small, wetland-enveloped creek flowing into Rice Lake from which they still gather herbs and medicinal plants Mushgigagomongsebe, meaning "Little River of Medicines"' (Reynolds 2003: 149).

The Standing Rock Water protectors on the one hand mobilize the right-holding status of water within their native cosmology to ground their opposition to the pipeline, which infringes on the rights of the reservation's waters to remain unpolluted. As Anna M. Brígido-Corachán writes, the 'Standing Rock activists are [. . .] activating "a relational experience" that Indigenizes the way we understand, communicate with, and act toward the land and its human and other-than-human inhabitants. Bodies of water deserve the same legal recognition that corporations or trust funds in the United States already have: human legal status' (2017: 75). The Indigenous activists found their political-legal claim on a native idea of 'commons' that spans both humans and nonhumans, and places the former in a position of specific responsibility (Jewett and Garavan 2018: 53). But on the other hand, the assertion of water rights in the Standing Rock case cannot be separated from the tribe's aim to protect and exercise their territorial sovereignty over the reservation lands.

In the course of the protests, native activists from all over North America came together in the Standing Rock camps, turning the water protection protests into a collective native movement. The native activists put forward a de-colonial, anti-capitalist, anti-patriarchal political agenda that far transcended the issue of local water rights and protection. The many female leaders of the movement linked the pipeline, and the oil boom in North Dakota that produced it, to what native activist Jewett describes as a Western, colonial and capitalist 'rape culture' (Jewett and Garavan 2018: 45), which is built on the violation of both humans and nonhumans, and to which the united native tribes seek to sketch out an Indigenous alternative (Jewett and Garavan 2018; Brígido-Corachán 2017: 78–9). The Standing Rock movement failed to close down the pipeline – a 2017 executive order by the newly elected president Trump had the protesters removed from the site and the building of the pipeline, which is in operation now, expedited (Ellis 2019: 173). As an act of Indigenous ecological activism, Standing Rock was unsuccessful. However, and maybe surprisingly, many Indigenous commentators nevertheless identify the protest as a success because it reinvigorated a collective native politics. For Jewett, the significance of Standing Rock lies in the fact that after '500 years the Indigenous voice has come back. Re-claiming our power. Re-claiming our voice as the people who walked that land' (Jewett and Garavan 2018: 55). Estes references the Standing Rock documentary *Awake* to underline the, among the activists present, pervasive sense that the movement was a milestone for Indigenous political action.

> The calm, steady voice of Floris White Bull, a member of the Standing Rock Sioux Tribe and the film's lead, cuts through the familiar cacophonic soundtrack for our era of mass dissent, the screaming and chanting of protesters and the repetitive, low concussive explosions of police flashbangs, rubber bullets, and teargas canisters. 'I am not dreaming. I am awake,' White Bull declares over the clamor. 'To be alive at this point in time is to see the rising of the Oceti Sakowin.' Out of chaos the Oceti Sakowin, the Seven Council Fires of the Dakota, Lakota, and Nakota nations, is reborn. (Estes 2018: 384)

Both Indigenous activists and the academic literature that engages with Indigenous politics highlight what Frank Hopper refers to as the 'ripple effect' (2018) of Standing Rock. 'Part of what makes [Standing Rock] historic' (Johnson 2017: 163), according to one of the movement's media coordinators, Said Desiree Kane, are the waves of support it generated on social media. At Standing Rock, Indigenous activists for the first time systematically used social media to share their narratives of the movement with a global audience rather than relying on established mass media (Deem 2019: 124; Kidd 2020: 241; Ellis 2019: 172–3). As Elizabeth Ellis observes, one of the crucial distinctions between how Standing Rock was portrayed in mainstream media and the self-presentation of the movement that motivated the turn to social media was the fact that mainstream news broadcasting was overly focused on the aspect of environmental protection and 'missed a crucial component of the issue, Native sovereignty' (2019: 180). The water protection activism was monitored and actively supported by millions of online followers. A Facebook call for a 'check-in' in solidarity with protesters under police surveillance, for instance, received over 1.5 million responses (Johnson 2017: 164). But the ripples of Standing Rock also reached other Indigenous activists in North America and beyond, which actively reference the water protection movement as inspiration and legitimating ground (van Gelder 2016; Hopper 2018; Kidd 2020: 234, 11). Indigenous filmmaker Shannon Kring, who also documented the Standing Rock activism, recalls how the protests influenced women activists in Scandinavia and Honduras. 'It gave them this boost of confidence, like "They can do it. We could do it too"' (Kring quoted in Draxler 2021).

The Standing Rock movement was unable to prevent the pipeline. However, the movement's planned, directed political action achieved a non-linear kind of success in a different register; it advanced Indigenous politics by invigorating the cultural-political relations of the Sioux locally, and by providing Indigenous activism with novel strategies, consolidated grounds and a wider audience globally. This political consolidation and advancement was ultimately not without effect on the case of the North Dakota access pipeline itself: in the years following the Standing Rock movement, and in direct response to Indigenous resistance, several of the European banks that financed the pipeline sold their shares and cut ties with the pipeline owner, Energy Transfer (Kidd 2020: 244). In 2020, a federal court first ordered a review of the pipeline's environmental impact by the US Army Corps of Engineers and then a temporary shut-down. While this decision was overturned in the same year, in 2021 the US Court of Appeals for the DC Circuit sided with the Standing Rock water protectors to suggest that the pipeline should never have been built without a thorough environmental review (Friedman 2020), which was affirmed by the US Supreme Court in February 2022 (Fritze 2022).

Returning to Ecuador against this background, the same primacy of politics underpins the fractured and changing Indigenous position here. The ontological framework of *sumak kawsay* is strategically endorsed not as truthful vehicle of Indigenous cosmologies but as a political tool to foster Indigenous interests and realise Indigenous political demands. CONAIE and the Kichwa understand perfectly that the umbrella of the rights of nature would grant Indigenous communities unprecedented access to powerful political fora, such as Acosta's constitutional convention, or the 2015 Climate Conference. The Kichwa proposal brought forth illustrates clearly that the assertion of the rights of nature is here, as in the example of Standing Rock, situated within the wider context of the political aims of the Indigenous activists presenting them, chiefly that of full territorial sovereignty. Kawsak Sacha makes it clear that 'the Rights of Nature are . . . closely related to our Human Rights as Indigenous People, guardians of the Living Forest' (Kawsak Sacha 2015: 3). For this reason, the proposal aims for 'attaining national and international recognition for [. . .] the Living Forest' (Kawsak Sacha 2015: 1), but its ultimate goal is 'to preserve the territory of Indigenous Peoples, and especially the material and spiritual relations that we establish in the Living Forest' (Kawsak Sacha 2015: 1). CONAIE makes this even clearer in their 2011 conceptualization of *sumak kawsay* when they suggest that the principle can only be realized in a pluri-national Ecuador where different Indigenous peoples have full autonomy over their territories and can enact the protection of their human-nonhuman networks according to local traditions, practices and needs (CONAIE 2010).

The Anthropocene critique importantly reveals that CONAIE's rights of nature proposal cannot be understood as an endorsement based on the genuine Indigenous ideas and values that the rights of nature encompassed, but was made in a context where, to use Gayatri Spivak's famous expression, the subaltern cannot speak – where discursive power relations did not provide space for a genuine expression of Indigenous cosmologies (Viane 2022: 199). This impossibility is certainly not unrelated to the political conditions that caused the rights of nature to fail as Indigenous projects. However, importantly, this chapter has shown that their relationship cannot be understood as a straightforward ontological determination of political outcomes. The Indigenous position towards the rights of nature changes with their assessment of its relationship to Indigenous political causes – once it had become clear that the constitutional codification of *sumak kawsay* did not translate into fostering Indigenous interests against the, still, neoliberal agenda of the Ecuadorian settler state, CONAIE ended all communication with the Ecuadorian government, but more generally re-focused their political activism away from the rights of nature approach that had turned out to be a political dead end. While Standing Rock, despite being a failure in terms of implementing rights of nature, can be deemed successful as an act of Indigenous politics, Ecuador's rights of nature, despite forming a precedent for their constitutional codification, ended up being a disappointment for the Indigenous political hopes attached to the former.

If we take these two cases as the ends of a continuum of Indigenous politics via nonhuman rights, New Zealand's Te Urewera and Te Awa Tupua acts are located in the ambiguous middle ground between them. On the one hand, Indigenous communities were successful in taking both ecosystems out of the exclusive territorial sovereignty of the New Zealand settler state and place them into a new, unprecedented legal arrangement that resists the modern-liberal framework of legal personhood. But on the other hand, this arrangement does not grant the Tūhoe full sovereignty over their territory, and instead sets up a guardianship arrangement that is shared between Indigenous representatives and the state. Emphasizing one or the other dimension, New Zealand's rights of nature acts could be viewed as unprecedented success for Indigenous politics or as a pyric victory that ultimately leaves the settler-colonial territorial organization of *terra nullius* unchallenged. Interesting at this juncture, and potentially suggesting a slight imbalance towards the former, is the intrinsic flexibility and inbuilt open-endedness of the legal arrangement, which, at least in theory, creates legal and political space for a reconfiguration of the guardianship of Te Urewera and Te Awa Tupua in an Indigenous image (Epstein 2022: 13, 16). However, whether such a radical reconfiguration will be possible will depend on the power relations that underpin and play out in the shared guardianship arrangement in practice.

Acting, resisting, surviving

Indigenous agency beyond the 'end times'

The previous chapters have shown how Anthropocene environmentalism, both in theory and in political practice, has recently performed an Indigenous turn driven by the desire to escape the ontology of modern liberalism via substantial alterity. So far, we have shown how the Anthropocene engagement with Indigenous ecologies successfully mobilizes ontological and political parallels especially between the former and the ontological strand of Anthropocene theory, but brackets, flattens and conceals political plurality and contestation that does not readily fit the Anthropocene's ontopolitical framework. We mobilized the methodological tool of the critical mirror of Indigenous ecology to render visible the creative potentiality of a diverse, fractured and activist assemblage of Indigenous ecologies. The critical mirror has problematized the depoliticizing functioning of the Anthropocene ontology that envelops, rather than sustaining, the political multiplicity of the former. It has further called into question the political necessities hinged on its political postulates.

Ontological Anthropocene theory prioritizes rethinking the human condition in the Anthropocene over tackling its practical effects. Politics first needs to become non-anthropocentric, posthuman, ontologically entangled and resilient rather than managerial before we can think of governing the Anthropocene condition without falling back into the operational mode of anthropocentric, expropriative governance that has caused it. The critical mirror of Indigenous ecology has revealed how the radical project of ontological Anthropocene theory however inscribes a deterministic link between its nonmodern ontology and the kind of nonmodern politics it deems appropriate for the former within its theoretical propositions. Indigenous ecologies challenge the necessity and rigidness of their ontological-political links by revealing how nonmodern ontologies can be coupled with political projects that link to, parallel or draw from Western modernity in complex ways. The Indigenous ecological scholarship and activism discussed in the previous chapters is not grounded in or defined by its ontological alterity to modern-liberal ideas, values or politics, but rather driven by Indigenous political claims and projects on which their ontological undergirding was dependent. Beyond the prescriptions of Anthropocene ontology, the critical mirror of Indigenous ecology has once again blown wide open the question of *what kind of political action* is possible, appropriate and legitimate in the Anthropocene.

Against this background, the final chapter of this book will hone in on the particular political potentiality that Indigenous ecology indicates as possible in an ecologically relational Anthropocene. In what follows, we will suggest that the type of Indigenous agency represented in Western scholarship as underpinning Indigenous environmental activism is understood primarily as a form of resistance against coloniality. This frames agency as a by-product of victimhood, a response to the end of the world of which Indigenous communities are passive casualties. The critical mirror of Indigenous ecology highlights how Indigenous activism, different from the Western scholarship invoking it in a spirit of allyship and as a source of inspiration, but importantly also beyond what the ontopolitical space of the Western Anthropocene renders possible regardless of whether or not it is theorized with reference to Indigenous alterity, does not propose a reactive politics centred on a post-political catastrophe. Instead, it drives a politicization of the environment through the folding of ecological, political and cultural projects. Here, the theoretical tools of Critical Indigenous Studies allow us to draw attention to the creative power of Indigenous activism beyond mere resistance to a hegemonic narrative.

Indigenous agency as resistance-based activism

Indigenous activist movements are usually understood as expressions of resistance against settler states and capitalist production and consumption encroaching on the lands and ways of life of Indigenous communities. Their central aim, within this framing, is to achieve protection for lands, ecosystems or cultural relations that have already been severely damaged by the violence of modern politics and economics. To be clear, resistance to enduring coloniality is certainly a crucial aspect of Indigenous activist movements. Indigenous sovereignty can be understood as a central, political-legal expression of Indigenous resistant activism that aims to seek, establish and reaffirm the self-determination of Indigenous people within and through the existing framework of International Law. As an umbrella for Indigenous activism, Indigenous sovereignty combines specific, practical political and environmental goals with more fundamental efforts 'to decolonise the conceptual and methodological outlook adopted to examine and investigate Indigenous histories' (Shrinkhal 2021: 74). Nevertheless, Indigenous scholars and activists alike have, at the same time, been weary of the dangers inherent in operating within an inherently exploitative and violent political-legal system.

For this reason, they have drawn attention to forms and practices of activism that transcend the formal and legalistic frames of modern law and the democratic state. This shift in focus places the ways in which Indigenous communities have continued to survive in the face of environmental degradation, settler-state exploitation and erasure centre stage (Hokowhitu 2009). The necessity for resistance is here grounded in the ontological principle of relationality that features prominently in many Indigenous cosmologies and practices. Because the complex relationships between humans, lands and their nonhuman inhabitants are threatened by capitalism, settler-colonial governance and climate change, resisting them becomes an essential means of survival. Long likens the close links between ecosystems and the Indigenous body politic to 'autoimmune relations' (2018) where threats to the former must trigger a defensive response in the latter. With the example of Oceanic communities in mind, Long suggests that the 'theology of interconnectedness' (Halapua quoted in Long 2018) underpinning Indigenous cosmologies indicates how fluid structures (human and nonhuman) pervade all aspects of life and community (Long 2018: 62). For this reason, ontological relationality grounds not only the political demands of Oceanic Indigenous communities but also their responses to the encroaching threats caused by the Global North's economic exploitation and pollution of the seas (Long 2018: 62). It is precisely because of this ontological relational condition that threats to 'land'[1] are then also seen as threats to Indigenous ways of life and life itself. Resistance to the structures that cause or worsen these conditions is then conceived as a way to shed light on the vulnerable position of Indigenous communities vis-à-vis the erosive structures of settler futurities.

Although understanding the vulnerability of Indigenous communities is an important part of acknowledging the structural nature of colonialism, Critical Indigenous scholars warn against overstressing the passive quality of Indigenous resistance through the (over-)emphasis on resistance. Focusing on the vulnerability that their ontological relationality places Indigenous communities in and that drives the need to resist, they argue, takes attention away from productive Indigenous agency. The example of the narratives that surround the management of invasive species in North America is here particularly telling. Indigenous communities in North America have certainly had to consistently defend their lands from invasive animal and plant species, particularly because the latter can pose challenges to traditional food sources and alter the pattern of hunting and farming. However, in the way this Indigenous struggle against invasive species is presented in mainstream discourses in the media, politics and academia, critical Indigenous scholars note how much of the emphasis lies on the vulnerability of Indigenous communities to environmental change (Reo et al. 2017: 203) rather than on the multiple ways in which these successfully work with and around invasive species. Indeed, as Watt-Cloutier explains in the context of Inuit communities, Indigenous peoples 'are not victims of globalization' but 'have a powerful history of strength, of wisdom, that can be offered back by integrating that kind of wisdom into the new institutions. But what's happened is that these institutions have taken over the role of parents, the role of the provider and have even helped to make it worse in many cases' (Watt-Cloutier quoted in: Reo et al. 2017: 215).

Indigenous experiences then tend to be mediated through understandings of activism that are intelligible and readily accessible to Western and non-Indigenous activists and scholars alike. Horton, for instance, highlights in the context of a surge of art-based Indigenous activism across the American continent in the early 1990s how, regardless of 'however much Native American artists' contemporaneous insights anticipated unfolding debates about the ecological toll of "crisis globalisation", they were read within the then-dominant framework of identity politics' (2017: 49). However, underlying the issue that Western discourses tend to put Indigenous cosmologies and politics in boxes they do not fit neatly, or at all, Indigenous scholars have problematized the default framing of Indigenous activism as resistance.

To be clear, we certainly do not suggest that all, or even much of, the ontological Anthropocene theory that engages with Indigenous cosmologies and scholarship is guilty of this 'resistance reductionism', as the earlier debate on Indigenous agency is somewhat separate from the Anthropocene turn to Indigenous ecologies. However, we do argue that the Indigenous responses to the Western framing of Indigenous agency are of crucial importance to Anthropocene theory because they contain ontopolitical configurations that transcend the space of possibility opened up by Anthropocene ontology. Following the aforementioned Indigenous critiques, the emphasis on vulnerability that underpins narratives of Indigenous activism as (mainly) resistant is problematic for a number of reasons. Most notably, it promotes understanding agency along a resistance/capitulation binary that does not allow engagement with the ways in which communities successfully govern their interactions within the dominant structures that affect their lifeways. Here, Indigenous agency can express itself beyond the binary indicated earlier. Going back to the example of invasive species, Reo et al. suggest that

> whatever Indigenous peoples are doing today to approach invasive species flows out of their own histories with environmental change and how these histories shape their assumptions today about the meaning or significance of their current interaction with novel species. These histories and assumptions – that do not flow out of nonIndigenous frameworks such as 'the anthropocene' – shape what Indigenous people view as appropriate approaches. (Reo et al. 2017: 213)

Importantly, these histories have been formed in the context of colonial governance and the hegemony of Western knowledge, and thus do not exclude elements of Western science. Taking action is therefore not necessarily predicated on choosing between accommodation/co-option and resistance/protest. Indigenous groups, as Veber argues, are rather unduly limited and constrained in their agency and its perception by this binary thinking, which reproduces a dominant/dominated logic where agency is only ascribed to them in the form of what he calls 'induced agency' (1998: 387).

In addition, scholars have also pointed to where such emphasis on resistance from vulnerability may conceal inherent misunderstandings regarding the agency of Indigenous communities. Eudaily, for instance, suggests that within this framework Indigenous activist groups are often presented as passive protesters accepting 'the rules of the game laid out by liberal democratic principles' (2004: 19) rather than being seen as actors who contest these and claim supervisor validity for their own laws and principles. For Eudaliy, this (mis-)reading of Indigenous activism is justified with the fact that Indigenous activists often employ the tactics and the language of the liberal world order (e.g. the language of the UN framework for Indigenous rights), which is understood to indicate a 'practice of taking those identities and liberties produced by the dominant form of power as tools for said power's subversion' (Eudaily 2004: 49) in a meaningful, substantial way.

Eudaily contrasts such a view of Indigenous resistance as merely responsive to and reactive within the hegemonic rules of settler-colonial politics and economics that are accepted as such with a tactical Indigenous resistance that takes 'the form of everyday/unobtrusive acts of defiance' (2004: 49). As Chapter 4 highlighted for the example of the Standing Rock water protection movement, Indigenous environmental activism, especially in its online self-presentation, not rarely appeals to the universalizing logic of Western environmentalism as it enables what would normally be family and place-based resistance to link up across the multiple borders of the settler-colonial geography (Barker 2015). However, the existence of such strategic links does not mean that Indigenous activism accepts the Western rules of the game, nor that it compromises on its radical aims of overcoming settler colonialism, accepting that it can only achieve transformation within the parameters of the former.

Although the productive power of everyday Indigenous resistance is acknowledged to some degree here, Eudaily's observations are, in themselves, emblematic of the problem, as an understanding of Indigenous agency that is primarily subdued continues to persist and takes clear precedence over its political potentiality. To be sure, scholars point out that the emphasis on back-seat 'civility' and small-scale political transgressions and reversals evident earlier can also be identified as predominant in accounts of Indigenous environmental activism more generally, with emphasis placed on particularly non-threatening and non-violent expressions of activism (Waitere and Allen 2011: 46).[2] Vine Deloria Jr (1995) suggests that such accounts are rooted in a misunderstanding of Indigenous agency, as Indigenous communities are here framed as powerless against (or potentially even complicit in) the structures that oppress them and threaten their survival. Like other critical Indigenous scholars, he argues that the emphasis on vulnerability as the bedrock of Indigenous resistance rests on hegemonic narratives that centre whiteness and non-Indigenous frameworks as the unmarked space that defines the default of political agency so that all alternatives are placed in the position of having to be defined against the former.

Leanne Simpson argues that Anthropocene scholarship that draws on Indigenous activism is guilty of framing the former as defined against hegemonic narratives of climate change in exactly this manner (Simpson 2016) and therefore always remains linked to them. Indigenous responses to environmental crises, and in this case specifically agential expressions identified with activist movements, are 'seen' under states of emergency decided by settler societies where 'green' political action becomes necessary (Clark, De Costa, and Maddison 2016: 8). The institutions and knowledge relations of settler colonialism sets the standards for what is a crisis and decide on the parameters of the solutions that must be considered to overcome the former – even if these lie with its nonmodern 'Others'. For Zoe Todd, the White discursive space of the Anthropocene continues to selectively appropriate and at the same time obscure Indigenous experiences because the decision to turn to alternative forms of political action, and their very framing as such, is still that of the colonial state (Todd 2015), within which Indigenous activism cannot easily be accommodated or replicated (Simpson 2016: 27).[3]

This overly narrow understanding of Indigenous politics as resistance in the context of Anthropocene environmental discourses, we argue, follows from a reductive view of the kind of politics a relational ontology renders possible. Nonmodern Indigenous agency is understood to be grounded by the ontological folding of nature into culture. Relationality is translated into 'land-as-culture' in order to generate a pre-contact, distinctively nonmodern and posthuman Indigenous community that not only serves as a point of contrast to ground critique of Western Anthropocene politics but is also posited as a way forward for the West's grappling with the Anthropocene condition. Yet, for many Indigenous communities, places (or 'land'), as Willow suggests, are not merely blank representations of a nonhuman nature linked to human culture in a state of pre-contact purity (2011: 263). They are deeply political and shaped by complex and often contradictory processes where Indigenous communities' experiences with both colonial extinction and adaptive cultural-political affirmation play off each other at the blurry intersection of and interaction between modernity and Indigeneity.

As such, struggles for land are forms of 'strategic' (Simpson 2016: 31) engagements where groups express their agency not simply to protect their environment, either as a part of their culture or as spiritually valuable in itself in an act of resistance directly inspired by the human–nonhuman relationality of Indigenous cosmologies and performed in the nonmodern, resilient, manner that the former necessitate. Rather, the expression and preservation of Indigenous cosmologies and traditional practices are only one aspect in a political struggle ultimately focused on political advancements and sovereignty where the role of Indigenous ontologies moves fluently between grounding and strategic mobilization (Sangster 2012: 35–7). If Indigenous politics is thus not constrained by the ontological relationality that grounds it and its alterity to liberal modernity, then a resistance that fits with the Anthropocene understanding of a posthuman, nonmodern politics is only one of the myriad ways in which political agency can play out.

Indigenous critiques from the side of CIS highlight that reading Indigenous activism through the lens of the Anthropocene's ecological crisis confines the former within the framework of an anti-modern resistance because this is the desired pathway of political action that follows from the posthuman Anthropocene ontology, as well as from the necessity to overcome the laws, economics and politics of liberal modernism that is expressed in Western Anthropocene politics, as shown in Chapters 3 and 4. As a consequence, the Anthropocene framing of Indigenous activism feeds into a reductive understanding of the former that foregrounds vulnerability and political reactivity and where Indigenous politics can only ever be 'Other to' the modern-Western hegemon it challenges, which Indigenous scholars have problematized in the earlier way. However, as for the aforementioned chapters, we seek to explore what the critical mirror of these Indigenous challenges reflects back on Anthropocene theory. Opening up the academic understanding of Indigenous activism to forms and practices that do not fit the framing of resistant otherness, we argue, highlights the openness and multiplicity of politics that can take place against the background of a relational ontology.

Reclaiming political space beyond the modern/nonmodern

Underpinning accounts of Indigenous activism is a notion associated in particular with the North-American context: resurgence. There is much disagreement over the details of what Indigenous resurgence actually is and entails, and what it is ultimately aimed at vis-à-vis the settler-colonial state. However, scholars largely agree on the ethos of resurgence, which is understood to lie in the 'radical transformation of the contemporary social world' (Elliott 2018: 64) through processes of 'grounded normativity' that represent 'profoundly different ways of thinking, organizing, and being' (Simpson 2016: 22). While resurgence is often equated with or conflated to resistance, Simpson highlights that resurgence is importantly distinct from the former (Simpson 2016: 25). Resurgence as a notion is tied to a specific geographical context, but the actions it refers to are not openly about 'the environment' or 'land'. Resurgence promotes an understanding of individual activism that is also inherently and simultaneously collective, nonhuman, complex and systemic. Resurgence frames activist individuals as 'hubs of networks. When an individual is hurt, then the system is out of balance' (Simpson 2016: 26).

Acts of resurgence are representative of deeply political agency, transcending any simple categorization of the purposes of activism. Though resurgence is framed primarily as ensemble of everyday, mundane acts of contestation and transformation such as those outlined earlier, critical Indigenous scholars also point out the importance of understanding these as part of wider processes of mass mobilization (Simpson 2016: 24) against settler-state structures more widely (Coulthard 2014). Resurgence, Corntassel suggests, 'means having the courage and imagination to envision life beyond the state' (Corntassel 2012: 89). Although this 'turning away' from the state system (Elliott 2018) is often not represented in the wider public discourse, it remains essential for the structural sustainability of Indigenous communities. As an example, Corntassel points to the Cherokees' honouring of the Kituwah mound which, in spite of continued encroachment by settler governments, has been sustained over time through individual Cherokees' efforts to travel to the site and bring the ashes of the sacred fire back to their homes and villages (Corntassel 2012: 90). Cortnassel's example focuses on drawing out the value of individual and collective informal acts of contestation stretching out over time and pertaining as much to the sphere of active resistance as to that of everyday life.

Indigenous resurgence is thus more than just resistance because it captures micro and macro practices that highlight and productively work towards an ethical, political or economic otherwise to the extractive forces of progress-driven settler societies (see for instance Recollet 2016; Gushiken 2019). This Indigenous 'otherwise' does not envision different futures in the liberal model of linear progress towards continuous modernization, a model which generally implies that past wrongs such as white racism 'can be modernized away' (Baldwin cited by Tuck and Gaztambide-Fernandez 2013: 80). As Tuck and Gaztambide-Fernandez point out, settler colonialism is not only invested in how the past is understood and produced, but also in practices of 'calculation, imagination and performance' though which the settler colonial past and present can be amended (but never removed, erased or uprooted) in order to secure a future where Indigenous peoples are merely incorporated and assimilated, but still governed by the structures of the settler state (Tuck and Gaztambide-Fernandez 2013: 80). Theories of action embedded in Indigenous resurgence instead employ 'forms of knowledge that persist outside of the colonial territory, and says, *no, you can't have them*' (Tuck and Gaztambide-Fernandez 2013: 85 emphasis in original).

Indigenous scholars draw attention to how Indigenous agency operates beyond (and against) formalized structures, including Anthropocene ontology's binary distinction between a liberal modernity marked by rational subjectivity, large-scale planning and active political shaping and its nonmodern other. In particular, they show how informal, everyday expressions of political creativity represent meaningful ways in which Indigenous communities exercise their sovereignty, defend their land and contribute to the sustenance and thriving of their communities. Art activism, for instance, features prominently in Indigenous approaches to political agency. Art, both written and spoken, is here understood to enable productive interventions from Indigenous artists and activists. Writing, story-telling, folklore and fairy-tales can, for instance, 'honor and discuss the ways in which Indigenous stories adapt to moments of political and social crisis' (Kuwada and Yamashiro 2016: 19), but beyond a merely commemorative and reactive practice also draw out pathways to 'live on in ways that sustain Indigenous culture, health, identity, and sovereignty and engender activism' (Kuwada and Yamashiro 2016: 19). Artworks can act as 'visual contestation of global capitalism' (Horton 2017: 49), asserting what Jolene Rickard identifies as 'visual sovereignty' (2011).

Using the example of Two Row Wampum (two strands of white and purple shell beads weaved together), Rickard suggests that centuries-old visual art communicates practices of diplomacy (including peacebuilding and reconciliation) exercised by First Nations, binding human and nonhuman elements alike (2011). Despite not being seemingly openly political or environmental in nature, art here constitutes a reservoir of Indigenous political potentiality from which active – both individual and collective – expressions of agency can draw. Similarly, also beyond the realm of formal activism, parenting is seen as a way for Indigenous communities and individuals to productively shape communal life and advance Indigenous futurities. The praxis of fatherhood, for instance, is understood as couched within a complex contemporary reality that ties together intimate Indigenous spaces with wider settler-colonial contexts. Corntassel and Scow (2017) examine fatherhood away from the private/public domain dichotomy typical of Western-liberal frameworks. Though their focus remains on the 'everydayness' of the praxis, the scholars are adamant that the mundane actions through which fatherhood is marked and performed are significant examples of acts of Indigenous regeneration. Remembering and recalling communal stories and ceremonies in a way that is flexibly woven into ideas and practices that mark the changing lived realities in which their children grow up enables Indigenous parents to make space for Indigenous ideas and practices towards what they suggest can constitute an 'assault' on attempts at erasure (Corntassel and Scow 2017: 60–4).

Likewise, work also expresses a productive Indigenous agency. Labour is not just a way in which individuals and their kin sustain themselves, but a process through which communities can express, articulate and secure politically significant demands. Frequently, Indigenous communities' work practices are set in stark contrast to the structures of neoliberal global capitalism 'centred on the exploitation of human and natural resources for private gain' (Baker 2011: 13). Since, as shown in the previous chapters, the Indigenous relationship with capitalism and the state system that supports it is not straightforward, Indigenous economic practices cannot readily be identified as clearly delineated from the former even if Indigenous politics target extractive capitalism as the root cause of continuous colonial violence (Baker 2011: 14). The focus on labour brings into view how the paradox of producing both with and against capitalist practices plays out at the granular level. Where capitalism has commodified land in Western societies (and beyond), severing labourers from the source of their livelihoods, Indigenous communities ground production and labour in land. In doing so, the economic model that Indigenous communities practice both links to and employs elements of capitalist production, monetization and consumption. At the same time it sets up a logic distinct from free market global capitalism because it integrates 'the natural economy, the sustenance economy and the market economy' (Baker 2011: 14) to specifically advance not only the livelihood of Indigenous communities but also the special grounding that constrains productions and profits and thereby actively works against capital accumulation in the hands of few.

An example for the operativity of such an alternative Indigenous economy is to be found in the development plans which Hawaii's Moloka'i's community developed for the island of Moloka'i. The island has long been subject to attempts at developing real estate for the tourism industry. Property development on the island has primarily been driven by the interests of transnational corporations. Yet, maybe surprisingly, the Moloka'i's attitude to commercial activity on the island has not been one of complete rejection. The development plan offered by the Moloka'i Enterprise Community presents a vision where tourism is central to the economic activity of the island but in a way that is distinct from the plans of property developers; 'the ruling principle on the island being 'Moloka'i: Not for Sale. Just Visit' (McGregor cited in Baker 2011). The Moloka'i proposal neither aims to resist capitalism nor to adopt its rules for their community's benefit but rather expresses a creative, transformative agency that seeks to install a (tourism) economy with distinct, Indigenous rules.

In addition, the focus on labour draws attention to processes that Karl Marx identified as 'alienation', but which critical Indigenous scholars such as Brendan Hokowhitu describe as forms of subjectivization through which particularly Indigenous bodies came to be framed. In the context of Aotearoa/New Zealand that Hokowhitu writes from, 'the Māori male body symbolised and came to embody the physical realm and, thus, was employed for its physical labour, observed for its performativity, and humanised through physical pursuits such as physical labouring' (2020: 183). The labour of Indigenous women, on the other hand, was often considered 'ancilliary', secondary to that of the men who contributed to nation-building in settler-colonial societies (Williams 2012: 8).

Williams and Hokowhitu show how the mechanisms of Western capitalism not only alienated Indigenous communities from the traditional fruits of their labour and productive practices, but thereby also extended a Western economic paternalism to Indigenous communities with a traditionally far more fluid labour distribution. Against this background, labour-based Indigenous activism represents a way of re-narrating the experiences of Indigenous individuals and communities that had been shaped by possessive liberalism in both their values and subjectivities and their productive processes towards a different future. Beyond merely recounting, remembering and highlighting how stories of intimate violence, stolen wages and forced labour are woven into the economic prosperity of settler states (Harkin 2020: 198), labour-based activism works to render inoperative the subjectivizing mechanism of Western capitalism and replace it with an Indigenous economy that works differently and produces different economic subjects.

What to do 'after Having Done'? Agency and futurity

In the earlier cases, ecological relationality operates as a (dis)ordering principle that sets up intimate relations, creative practices and economic structures that transgress their modern-liberal counterparts in a meaningful, substantive way. Again, the pull of the ontological Anthropocene's explanatory framework is strong – and tempting. Indigenous agency seems to fold smoothly into the theoretical order of ontological Anthropocene theory where a nonmodern, posthuman foundation not only renders possible but necessitate a political action fundamentally other to that of the Anthropocene's liberal status quo. Understood in this sense, Indigenous relationality, which goes beyond human/nonhuman and culture/nature divides, makes it possible to appreciate the plurality and creativity of ecological relations while guiding theoretical and political projects of critique and resistance against capitalism, settler futurity and the hubris of liberal modernity. Indigenous political projects works to unsettle settler futurity because colonial time at best cannot capture the complexity of 'Indigenous sovereign people, actions, knowledge and performances' (McKinnon 2021: 401) and at worst work to favour the logic of a global capitalist system whose 'sole purpose is the unity of people under a single system of time, bringing cohesion and formality to industry, the marketplace, religion, and politics' (Matamua 2021: 108). Emphasizing relationality as the descriptor of an ontological condition that ontological Anthropocene theory shares with Indigenous thought and political activism is helpful in foregrounding how both position themselves in critical, resistant opposition to modern liberalism. However, importantly, the practical implementation of a nonmodern ontological 'otherwise' that produces a politics radically different from that of the former is only one side of the story of Indigenous ecological politics.

Indigenous agency highlights how directed human agency in the Anthropocene is not only possible but also, even more crucially, that it does not have to be framed within a binary of modern/nonmodern in order to offer alternative futurities. Political projects directed towards Indigenous futurity reject and subvert labels and framings that retain or reinforce the modern/ nonmodern binary in which settler colonialism had, after all, positioned Indigenous communities (firmly on the side of the nonmodern). 'Indigenous futurity does not require the erasure of now-settlers in the ways that settler futurity requires of Indigenous peoples' (Tuck and Gaztambide-Fernandez 2013: 80) in the manner in which land ownership or governance structures are negotiated and implemented. This insight is telling because it highlights a fundamental rejection of the boundary-making processes that underpin Western ontologies – including that of the Anthropocene. While ontological Anthropocene theory effectively problematizes and dismantles the positivist catastrophism of those Anthropocene thinkers who insist that a distinctly different and distinctly threatening Anthropocene present necessitates unprecedented action, it does not, however, rid itself from modernity's epistemic mechanism of achieving a progress through distinction.

Ontological Anthropocene theory employs clear boundaries and cause-effect necessities to identify and correct the ills of liberalism, capitalism and modern Western settler governance. In outlining what remains fundamentally modern – and is thus ontologically tainted beyond any hope for reconfiguration – and what sits outside of the recuperative pull of modernity – and thus offers a viable way forward for thinking and governing the Anthropocene *differently* – Anthropocene scholarship has turned to Indigenous projects of resurgence and their fights against settler governmentality. However, because the theoretical curiosity of Anthropocene theory is limited to the markers of fundamental alterity within Indigenous politics, what is lost here is how these perspectives may further reduce our understanding of the complex ways in which relationality plays out in a practical, politically pragmatic and fluid manner. Indigenous agency is more than just an 'otherwise' understood as just the outside of settler futurity. Because the conditional of a grounding ontological distinction for theoretical and political progress does not underpin Indigenous thought and politics in the same manner as it does modern thought, Indigenous agency is not tied to the necessity of having to either win against or surrender to both settler colonialism and the Anthropocene and its effects.

As poignantly suggested by Melanie Benson Taylor (2021), the Anthropocene narrative ultimately reveals a need for continuous 'crowdsourced revision' as it trials different theoretical avenues for leaving behind the toxic wastelands of Western modernity. Drawing on Indigenous agency as one such promising avenue towards the 'otherwise' of modernity is tantamount, as Taylor Benson puts it, paraphrasing Chaat Smith, to treating it as 'ideological Vicodin', the utopian object of a desire for Anthropocene redemption through becoming-ecological and becoming-decolonial. Paradoxically, then, it is precisely this radical desire of ontological Anthropocene theory to progress beyond the past faults of modernity through becoming other that condemns it to offering 'nothing new' and unintentionally rebooting 'essentialisms and dangerous mystifications' (Benson Taylor 2021: 10). For Indigenous scholars, the implication for Anthropocene theory is clear. Taylor Benson's intervention represents a pervasive call to 'diligently clarify, as a matter of ethic course' (Benson Taylor 2021: 10) the culture of dispossession which, from the perspective of CIS, animates the Western Anthropocene and its theoretical myths of the ecological, nonmodern native alike. For many CIS scholars, this equates to a call to let the theoretical framework of the Anthropocene wither and die.

But the target of this book's critical mirror of Indigenous ecology is the functioning of the Western Anthropocene itself. Here, the aforementioned conceptualizations of Indigenous agency drawn from political projects and CIS scholarship show how the deterministic link between ontological grounding and political action and the self-imposed need to distinguish both as essentially nonmodern on the one hand endow ontological Anthropocene theory with a false sense of safety: the safety that a 'better', nonmodern ontology would necessarily ground better, non-violent, non-extractive politics. The Indigenous critiques assembled both here and in the third chapter powerfully disrupt this safety, revealing how the Anthropocene reconfiguration of Western ontology, in its engagement with Indigeneity but also in its own presumptions, parameters and goal posts, does not necessarily fair better than its modern-liberal counterpart.

For these critiques, Anthropocene theory is certainly still thoroughly modern – but not in a way that any further ontological reconfiguration could resolve because what marks its modernity is its situatedness in epistemic and political structures that still (almost) exclusively, benefit the Global North. The former has very little to offer for changing these power structures in practice because 'urgent historical and political questions about power and knowledge' (Day 2021: 126) are here displaced 'in favour of metaphysical speculations on human nature and the abstract threat of death' (Day 2021: 126). The lesson for the Western Anthropocene that the critical mirror reveals is a hard one. Becoming ontologically nonmodern by engaging with decolonial scholarship, Indigenous thought or black ontologies might be worthwhile in many ways to undo liberalism's ontopolitical hubris and force engagement with the deep historical wounds it has caused. It does not, however, guarantee that the political action it grounds will automatically do a better job at safeguarding and advancing human and nonhuman life on earth. Only a better politics for the humans and nonhumans of the Anthropocene, can produce better political outcomes. As for the aforementioned cases of Indigenous agency, a particular – relationally entangled – ontological grounding might help to inform the former, but neither can relationality be identified as its sole and necessary ground, nor does it necessary follow from a relational ontology.

On the other hand, the critical mirror of Indigenous ecology reveals that the forms and expressions of political agency deemed permissible within or compatible with a relational ontology are overly limited. Against the Anthropocene reading of Indigenous politics as radically other to those of liberal modernity, Benson Taylor calls for understanding Indigenous agency in a manner that is 'attuned both to ethnographic specificity and to the vicissitudes of humanity' (2021: 12), remains vigilant against 'the illusion of internal homogeneity' (2021: 13) and ceases to portray Indigenous agency as 'incommensurable [or], exceptional' (2021: 13) in its relationship to liberal modernity (see also Lemenager 2021: 135–6). The flat folding of nature into society that is characteristic of Anthropocene ontology leaves no room for human agency to play out in 'disordered and often contradictory relations' (Day 2021: 127) that require the flexible use of radically diverse political tools.

Indigenous agency is grounded in histories woven through dominant structures in complex webs of relation, through migration, assimilation, 'hardship and violence. Love and theft' (Lemenager 2021: 106). It is ontologically grounded, put practically targeted first so that ontological grounding is here mobilized towards (and informs) practical political action that, as Chapter 2 has shown, is goal-oriented, involves rational planning by individuals and collectives and often necessitates long-term steering and management that requires specific interventions from and responsibilities for the humans involved to produce and maintain success. While, as Watts suggests, ecological relationality 'is not intended, at the outset, as a political strategy (though it works as one)' (2013: 30) but 'rather [. . .] is something that we all hold as sacred. Spirit is contained within all elements of nature' (2013: 30). She argues that Indigenous 'humans know [their] actions are intrinsically and inseparably tied to land's intentionality – quite a counter position from notions of diluted formulations of agency' (2013: 30). At the same time, the aforementioned examples of Indigenous agency from the practice of Indigenous fatherhood to the Moloka'i's plan for an Indigenous tourism industry not only transgress the modern/nonmodern binary of the ontological Anthropocene because they contain elements of directed, intentional action that the former marks as intrinsically Western-modern but also because they engage with the values, cultural products and economic structures of liberal modernity in a dynamically flexible manner.

Supported by the examples of Indigenous environmental activism discussed in Chapters 3 and 4, Indigenous agency neither diametrically opposes the structures and institutions of settler states to exhaust itself in a reactive resistance nor is it simply co-opted and subjugated by the former. On the contrary, Indigenous activism draws from the full arsenal of political weapons available to further particular political causes, both of the liberal-modern and of the nonmodern kind. To be clear, this is not to mean that we identify hybridity as a way forward for Indigenous agency. We simply highlight that contrary to what Anthropocene ontology posits, relational ontology does not preclude the former as a register for political action.[4] What Indigenous agency importantly never compromises on is the radical political aim of transforming lived reality beyond the settler-colonial status quo, even if the chances of success seem as slim as ever. This stands in sharp contrast to, and thus challenges the unquestioned necessity of, the politics of an Anthropocene ontology that has to find an answer to the question of 'what to do after having done' (Dillet 2018: 249), to reconfigure action in a radically nonmodern way, before it can take place, or even to relinquish all hope of achieving change and improving lives for the time being in the spirit of Latour's 'getting out of getting out'.

What would the Anthropocene equivalent for the Indigenous mobilization of all political tools available for an environmental politics that manages to let go of its obsession with the 'right' kind of ontological grounding look like? This is indeed the question and scholarly challenge that this book aims to leave Anthropocene theory with. The answer will not be as straightforward as a flexible movement between modern and nonmodern frameworks which mirrors that of Indigenous agency, or in merging modernity with a supposed nonmodern counterpart. The political tools and pathways available to Western Anthropocene societies are, like those of Indigenous communities, highly particular to their historical, political and economic situatedness and thus not readily comparable to those that can be used for Indigenous activism. The answer, in other word, has to be sought on the inside of the wound of liberal modernity that Western Anthropocene societies cannot (and maybe should not expect to) easily repair. The critical mirror of Indigenous ecology however opens up the possibility that this inside, like its counterpart of Indigenous alterity, might be fractured, diverse and creative beyond its totalizing Anthropocene frame.

Epilogue

Anthropocene afterlives

This book started its life from a feeling of discomfort. It began with the authors' profound uneasiness with the way Anthropocene scholarship and the social sciences in the West more generally were turning to 'the Indigenous'. In part, this discomfort was easy to locate. It stemmed from what both Indigenous and non-Indigenous scholars have illuminated as the alignment of this Indigenous turn with colonial mechanisms of exploitation and extraction that uproot and expropriate Indigenous knowledge to the exclusive benefit of those in the West, who require new epistemic resources to better understand and respond to modernity's Anthropocene fallout. However, what seemed to be absent from the range of existing critical interventions was scholarship that interrogated the lessons drawn from nonmodern ecologies of both the Western (posthuman) and the non-Western kind. Critics have rightly problematized whether White modernity should, and ethically could, learn from Indigenous knowledges at all. But what about these lessons themselves – does the Anthropocene failure of liberal modernity really provide us with a clearly contoured nonmodern way forward?

Interrogating Anthropocene theory's lessons for life after the end of the modern world in the critical mirror of Indigenous ecology, we neither claim that Indigenous ecology is, definitively and substantially, different from what its Anthropocene theory readers make it out to be, nor do we suggest that we understand Indigenous ecologies better than the former. On the contrary, the foundational argument of this book is simply that the stories of Indigenous ecology can be told in a way that is not only different from that of Anthropocene scholars, but also, more importantly, challenges some of the Anthropocene literature's foundational ontopolitical presumptions regarding how we should think, interact with and govern nature to escape the fallacies of liberal modernity. Where Anthropocene theory situates rational, goal-oriented planning, large-scale management and emphasis on the special capacities and responsibilities of human actors firmly within the modern-liberal ontology that climate change challenges us to discard, we have shown that the aforementioned are not absent from or diametrically opposed to nonmodern Indigenous thought and Indigenous environmental action. The critical mirror of Indigenous ecology complicates and re-opens the nonmodern future sketched out by those Anthropocene theorists who demand a radical ontological reconfiguration of the human condition. It does so by revealing that the ontological space that can be understood as nonmodern is substantially larger, and more open, than what Anthropocene ontology lets us believe, and has a complicated relationship to liberal modernity that is not exhausted in complete detachment and diametric opposition. Rupturing the certainty that this future will necessarily be one without a special place for human reason, progress and collective action, we have shown how the critical mirror of Indigenous ecology creates room for the possibility of thinking and living the aforementioned outside of modern liberalism.

But this book's critical mirror of Indigenous ecology has done more than complicate Anthropocene ontology – it also interrogates its relationship to politics. The previous chapters have shown how Western Anthropocene environmentalism, both in theory and in practice, has been able to fulfil some of the goals inherent in highlighting the powerful forces of nonhuman agents in the Anthropocene. However, this achievement came at the cost of relinquishing a power-conscious, differentiated and practically oriented theory of political action. The result, we have argued, is an ecological critique that remains primarily targeted at the ontological level. Anthropocene environmentalism demands us to understand ourselves and our planetary position differently, to become posthuman, to tell the truth about the climate extinction and to devise legal instruments not grounded in possessive liberalism before we can act on climate change. In doing so, it universalizes a particular, politically disconnected vision of the Anthropocene afterlife as the necessary ground for ecological politics. This not only subverts political efforts that might alleviate manifest struggles and issues in the face of climate change if these are grounded in 'the wrong', modern ontological principles. It also reproduces the modern certainty that the right ontological grounding will produce the right practical results. The more Anthropocene environmentalism insists, with certainty, that a clear cut with liberal modernity must take place before a meaningful Anthropocene ecology can emerge, the more it remains entangled in modernity's ontological and epistemological networks.

At this point, the reader – as sympathetic to this critique as they might be – may be formulating in their mind a question that has long haunted critical perspectives in the social sciences, especially those of a post-foundationalist bend: then what is next? If a 'better' less modernist, more relational, less Western ontology cannot necessarily deliver on the promise of better environmental politics, than what is the way forward for understanding the human condition, and human responsibilities, in the face of climate change? The answer to this question is, predictably, not a straightforward one. As a grand narrative upheld by the clear binary between a liberal modernity to be discarded and a diametrically opposed, unconnected, nonmodern future to be rung in, the Anthropocene is, for the authors of this book, certainly allowed to wither away. But this is not to say that the complex multiplicity of Western and non-Western ecological stories it holds together, albeit in a way that currently conceals their tensions and contradictions, offers nothing productive, nothing of value to move forward at all. As authors of this book, we would be guilty of our own critical charge, that of refuting totalizing statements, were we to conclude that all Anthropocene theory has to be discarded, *necessarily and as a whole*. We will end this book by retracing some of the intersecting ecological storylines opened up in the afterlife of the Anthropocene as a singular, totalizing and depoliticizing narrative. These are avenues that we suggest, emerge from deep conceptual explorations and as such are theoretically ripe, but also practical-politically oriented and thus do not merely reside at the level of abstract thought.

Hope, love and kin

A main tenet that holds together existing critical interventions in Anthropocene scholarship is the foregrounding of anti-colonial, anti-capitalist critique within the theoretical mapping of the Anthropocene past and present (Gibson-Graham 2020). Across the social sciences, this insight is used to highlight both continuing structural violence that marks the Anthropocene present and renders it radically fractured and spaces for productive resistance (Wakefield, Chandler and Grove 2022; Gibson-Graham 2020). But what does it really mean to make space for productive resistance? Gibson-Graham suggests that this implies 'appreciating' a great variety of practices alternative to extractive, capitalist modes of governance (Gibson-Graham 2020: 16). Others distance such making space first and foremost from caricatures of other(ed) cosmologies situated, somehow, in a distant, utopian, pre-contact Holocene past (see Whyte 2018a). Here, making space for productive resistance – which is different from a merely reactive understanding of resistant action interrogated in Chapter 5 and works towards practical, and radical, transformation – requires both contextual grounding and target-specificity. On the level of academic scholarship, we argue that such making space works precisely against the Anthropocene's production of new ontological certainties. Instead of formulating ontological propositions, it generates opportunities for 'moments of ontological slippage [. . .] where performative modes of creative practice offer alterior experiences' (Randerson and Yates 2017: 40).

This book has attempted to foster such ontological slippages in the stories that Anthropocene scholarship tells of Indigenous ecologies. But the task of allowing for ontological slippages can be understood more broadly as what is at stake in calls to set up an affirmative politics for the Anthropocene. David Chandler (2019), for instance, interrogates the notion of hope to understand the limits (and possibilities) of affirmative politics. Rejecting the temptation to either dismiss hope itself as incurably modernist or offer a clear-cut, nonmodern alternative, Chandler stays with the concept of hope, and within the murky modern/nonmodern conceptual threshold. Acknowledging that hope continues to be understood within a framework that centres on achieving harmony and conciliation, and is thus rejected by critical projects of affirmative action that seek to break with its modern telos, he yet insists that the concept itself can offer theoretical and political potentiality. Reclaiming the notion, conceptually, can help to disentangle and pluralise theoretical and political projects that – while not necessarily nonmodern, pre-modern or even post-modern – represent ever enfolding, overlapping, 'sedimented', realities.

Making space for different hopes in the Anthropocene means opening environmental discourses and politics to a multiplicity of worlds that are being hoped for. For some, the desired future must be a product of turning away, once again, from the universalizing tendencies of posthumanism and its flat entanglements and towards a horizon of distinctly Black and anti-colonial theories of action (Chipato and Chandler 2022). Others suggest reclaiming the possibilities of 'emancipatory trajectories' inherent in struggles 'of liberation from domination' (Wakefield, Chandler and Grove 2022: 399). In the threshold between an ontologically and politically 'sticky' modern-liberal past and a nonmodern future yet to be defined, a common ground of these anthropocenic hopes is the prominence of Anthropos as their author and recipient. While it may be tempting to allow the dissolution of the binary between humans and nature to 'dissolve human agency' altogether, such dissolution, many of our Anthropocene hopers recognize, also erases struggles to fight and resist dispossession and structural violence. For this reason, coupled with a call to unpack and explore the notion of hope, there is an implicit call for the return of the human in entangled relations that might be ontologically flat but which, more importantly, are politically radically uneven. Rather than getting lost in the question of whether and when acknowledging this unevenness means a return to modernism, what is required is a return to the specificity of entanglements enacted in collaborative projects of existence (Davison 2015). Insisting on hope in the Anthropocene offers a meaningful rebuttal to those parts of the scholarship that identify the passive acceptance of learning how to live in the drawn-out end of times as the only way forward.

But the legacy of modernity has a strong pull. One can easily envision how staying with hope in the Anthropocene could bring us back to this book's core problem: the insidiousness of the modern/nonmodern binary as the ghost in modernity's theoretical machine, demarcating suitably anthropocenic hopes from their unsustainable modern counterparts. To deflect the danger of a potentially looping critique, one way forward might be to ensure that ontological slippages are multiple, local and situated. Multiple registers can not only tell us about the specificities of how ecological changes are produced and experienced, but also help to ensure that they matter to and resonate with those affected by the former. This sets any reconceptualization to be achieved apart from the 'nebulous, distributed geographies' (Garlick and King 2022: 2) of the Anthropocene's universally shared catastrophe.

If any attempt to escape modernity's binary logic must produce the opposite effect, an alternative avenue might be to turn away from its ontological heights and towards the ground of complex lived experience, in the face of which all systems of clear-cut categorization collapse. Still, it is difficult to see how such fragments of 'ordinary Anthropocenes', where practices of hope, love and kinship manifest real political change (Garlick and King 2022; Clarke 2018), can take shape without romanticizing encounters through the slippages of worlds as inherently different and other-than-modern, or without mapping forces, actors or effects into distinct categories. After all, it is exactly this slipping back into modernist practices of theorizing that took place with the Anthropocene scholarship's engagement with Indigenous viewpoints, as the CIS critiques assembled in Chapters 2 and 5 powerfully reveal.

Indigenous science fiction, creativity and unlearning

Against this background, a further step back might be necessary. We may need to move beyond the threshold of temporal linearity to dispel the tendency to enclose the other within a fixed system of categories. The potentiality of time, unleashed from its modern confinement without being concealed again by a singular, universalized Anthropocene alternative, offers to shift attention away from relationality understood as conclusively closing the ontological gap between human and nonhuman entities and towards a complex set of performative and affective processes where the boundaries of actions and agents are perpetually blurred. To CIS scholars, Indigenous artists and writers working in the context of Indigenous resurgence and futurities, Indigenous science fiction is a way to envision time working in service of open-ended, unconfined transformation. Some of these perspectives are open – if extremely cautious – to allyship and non-Indigenous efforts to engage with Indigenous world views. However, they are decisively not dependent on framing agency against or in relation to a modern alternative to operationalize theories of change and frameworks of governance in the face of environmental degradation (Whyte 2018a).

Indigenous science fiction conceives of decolonial projects that centre and mobilize 'Indigenous epistemologies and ontologies' (Bouich 2021: 160) not as separate, other-than-modernity, but as complexly enmeshed and enfolding 'alongside elements pertaining to mainstream' (Bouich 2021: 160) – modern – social ideas, concepts and values. In doing so, Indigenous science fiction portray transformative potentialities that unfold from lived realities marked by Indigenous and settler-colonial relations to enable Indigenous communities and individuals to act and affect change. What emerges is a vibrant form of agency that is often bracketed in narratives that primarily see Indigenous communities as 'gradually deteriorating to the point that today's climate and environmental crises of the Anthropocene threaten to kill them off permanently' (Whyte 2018a: 236). Exploring agency in a fluctuating, dynamic, non-binary way means looking at the creative forces through which agency is expressed. These do not necessarily need to be defined as human, nonhuman or more-than-human, because what matters is not their essential quality but rather their particular, situated productivity and its effects – how relational networks sustain, disrupt or change human communities.

Markedly different from the underlying tendency of Anthropocene theory, what matters here is not ontological essence but political shaping power in practice. This allows for decentring environmental politics away from the parameters of the crisis set in the ontological and epistemic registers of the Global North. Creative agency in the Anthropocene, understood in this sense, does not amount to a sanitized search for free expression, harmony or cohesion. On the contrary, it is an exercise in repoliticization. Here, 'deeming something as creative, is [. . .] a political choice – to give credence and attention to that which is ascribed as being "creative"' (Henriksen, Creel and Mehta 2022: 466). Some suggest that mapping creative forces may be a way to harness such creativity towards alternative ways of thinking and making in the Anthropocene. However, again, it is hard to see how such 'marshalling [of] information' (Gibson-Graham 2020: 17) about alterity, and through it, would not leave the threshold space between modernity and nonmodernity and move uncomfortably close to the pure, modernist push to know, measure and control actions and actors. Conversely, anti-colonial, and particularly Indigenous and Black frameworks existing at the intersection of activism, academia and everyday practice, highlight that engagement with creativity concerns not only, or even not primarily, the nature of agency, but also our location, objectives and intentions of engagement.

If the foregrounding of ontology that marks Anthropocene theory's turn to materiality, ecology and relationality is rendered problematic by its universalizing, abstracting and therefore depoliticizing tendencies, then maybe a way forward for critical scholarship lies in the return to an 'old', and recently somewhat neglected, battleground: that of epistemology. In other words, maybe it is time to bring the ontological turn and its Anthropocene ideas about the planet and about the agency that shapes it into the light of 'epistemico-political' interrogation.

The politicization of ideas, knowledges and truths opened up by engagements with Indigenous realities is not unrelated to, but of a slightly different quality than the genealogical mapping of epistemic opponents and battle lines performed by post-structuralist scholarship. A post-colonial (re-) turn to epistemology must be practically specific and politically applied. It does not leave us with theoretical vertigo in the face of deconstruction's groundless grounds, because the situatedness of ideas and concepts, and their immediate intertwinement with power relations and violent struggles does not take away from, but is always-already recognized as being part of, their validity. In this sense, a way forward for making sense of the Anthropocene world is not overcoming liberal modernity towards a new certainty, even if the former is masked behind a façade of plurality and diversity. The challenge is rather to stay with liberal modernity precisely because we are acutely aware of its ontological stickiness and its ongoing, and as it stands still very much possessive and extractive, political operativity.

What emerges in the afterlife of the Anthropocene meta-narrative is hence a radical openness and analytical sensitivity to both ontological plurality and epistemological-political tensions and conflicts. This pathway for thinking in and beyond the Anthropocene might render visible a distant goalpost where alterity and situatedness are the very conditions of knowing and conceptualizing for all and where meaning and value are decided locally and continuously. This does not mean that conceptual frameworks can never be used beyond of their context of origin. But this can neither be presumed as readily possible nor rejected as per se illegitimate, because either is always the subject of a political decision to be made and to be justified with a view to its practical conditions and effects. It is in this spirit that the authors have read the Indigenous scholarship, cosmologies and stories of activism that informed this book's critical intervention, and it is in this spirit that we hope that our ideas will have meaning and value to some readers, in their specific contexts and for their particular causes.

Notes

Introduction

1 Available online: https://twitter.com/fridays4future/status/1580029716672618496 (accessed 17 November 2023).
2 In line with other critical social science scholarship that has recently engaged with Indigenous thought and scholarship, this book will use the term cosmology to describe the ontological framework of a particular Indigenous community or people. Distinct from the ancient and modern idea of ontology, cosmologies are 'integrated worldviews' (Krupp 2020: 1659) that are highly context specific. 'Rooted in observation and interaction with nature, these cosmologies portray the primary components of the environment, including the sky, the ground, the subterranean realm, the waters, atmospheric processes, plants, animals, and more, as an integrated system energized and managed by the power of spirits and gods' (Krupp 2020: 1659).

Chapter 1

1 To be clear, both the catastrophic and the ontological strand of Anthropocene scholarship are in themselves vastly diverse and contain approaches that stand in strong tension to each other. For instance, we place both Chakrabarty's insistence on the Anthropocene as humanity's shared catastrophe (2012) and Malm and Hornborg's (2014) rejection of such Anthropocene holism in favour of an economy-centred assessment that focuses on the responsibility of capitalist industrialized nations on the side of the Anthropocene catastrophe. Similarly, the ontological strand contains both scholarship that views Anthropocene posthumanism as a way to bridge the (ontological) gap to non-Western cosmologies and societies (Colebrook 2014; 2017a) and scholars who identify the failure to do so as the Anthropocene's great flaw (Yusoff 2019; Povinelli 2021).

Not all of the authors brought together in the following even subscribe to the idea of the Anthropocene – some, like Malm and Hornborg, or Moore, place their arguments in explicit opposition to Anthropocene scholarship.

2   The theoretical mapping that this chapter performs certainly cannot claim completeness in terms of the authors, arguments and ideas included. This book's selectivity is driven by our interest in the Anthropocene: the role of the ecological catastrophe that humanity faces, and the way we think the human condition as a consequence. The authors included in the theoretical map to follow offer distinct but in many cases nuanced assessments of the relationship between Anthropocene politics and Anthropocene ontology, often engaging thoughtfully, sometimes even generously, with positions they ultimately distance themselves from. In this sense, the opposition we draw between a catastrophic and an ontological approach to the Anthropocene here is not to be understood as a clear binary. It is instead designed to highlight two in themselves rich and complex strands of Anthropocene theory in their achievements and blind spots in order to counter the prevailing narrative of a smoothly progressing thought on the Anthropocene.

3   Colebrook is careful in theorizing an Anthropocene posthumanism that does not fall back into a modern mode of reasoning. Seeking to avoid fetishizing the posthuman as a new and improved form of subjectivity, she emphasizes the nihilistic quality of Anthropocene posthumanism – what must be affirmed is a planetary force that exceeds human control and understanding, and whose effects on humanity's survival cannot be predicted but only uncovered gradually as they already unfold. The Anthropocene must remain complex and marked by deterritorialized difference; it must resist tendencies to impose order by linearizing or universalizing the Anthropocene that are latently present in the concept (Colebrook 2017a: 1020).

Chapter 2

1   Although the ontological perspectives' desire to reject modernity and its anthropocentrism have pushed it to frame alternatives for action as necessarily standing outside of or fighting the bounds of the current modern system (see Stengers 2013a), Indigenous planning exhibits a much more complex relationship with the system of modern governance. As Kim Tallbear's (2016; 2018) work shows, Indigenous governance does not outrightly reject the possibility of

employing and even exploiting the tools of techno-science offered by modernity if they can be made to serve the aim of promoting Indigenous self-governance and planning: 'contemporary Indigenous peoples use Wester techno-science to govern. To miss that is to miss a key opportunity to expand Indigenous sovereignty' (Tallbear 2016: 76).

Chapter 3

1 Available online: https://www.youtube.com/watch?v=uAH3AkuNCO8
2 Available online: https://twitter.com/NadineElEnany/status/1182599976175755266 (accessed 17 November 2023).
3 Available online: https://www.redpepper.org.uk/environment-climate/climate-change/open-letter-to-extinction-rebellion/ (accessed 17 November 2023).
4 Available online: https://m.facebook.com/ExtinctionRebellion/posts/indigenous-peoples-have-been-the-custodians-of-earth-for-millennia-but-now-at-a-/422220895060691/?_se_imp=2mrfWLIYuR3ric6wz
5 Available online: https://www.goldmanprize.org/recipient/berta-caceres/#recipient-bio (accessed 17 November 2023).
6 Available online: https://m.facebook.com/ExtinctionRebellion/posts/its-a-threat-to-national-security-its-a-threat-to-the-economy-its-a-threat-to-yo/338395490109899/?locale=zh_CN (accessed 17 November 2023).

Chapter 4

1 Available online: https://www.stopecocide.Earth/new-breaking-news-summary/spain-legal-rights-for-mar-menor-ecosystem-in-european-first (accessed 17 November 2023).
2 Available online: https://insideclimatenews.org/news/03122021/ecuador-rights-of-nature/ (accessed 17 November 2023).
3 The Tūhoe, which were at the time not in contact with European settlers, did not sign the 1840 Treaty of Waitangi between the British Crown and about 500 Māori chiefs, which established British sovereignty over New Zealand's Northern Island. The British settlers occupied their lands regardless, which the Tūhoe have been fighting against since their first contact with the settlers in the 1860s (Kauffman 2020: 7).

Chapter 5

1   Critical Indigenous perspectives acknowledge that the English translation of 'land' is inadequate in capturing the totality of the environment as it is conceptualized by the Indigenous communities of the Pacific Islands (see Konai Helu Thaman quoted in Long 2018: 64).

2   Indigenous scholars have pointed to the many ways in which activism equates to radical political action, for example, in urban protest movements such as the Māori group Nga Tamatoa, which is dedicated to asserting their *rangatiratanga* (roughly translated as self-determination) and challenges the state on education, development, land, healthcare, sexim, racism and other pervasive social issues (Waitere and Allen 2011). Here, agency becomes embedded in the fundamental belief that better conditions, improvement, healing, is possible – a horizon that is often rendered inaccessible by critical Anthropocene literature and often associated with the teleological attitudes of modernity.

3   Simpson's critique also suggests that reproducing or promoting the centrality of Western, White and settler conceptions of political action may lead understandings of agency and resistance towards the question of 'what settlers can do' (Simpson 2016: 30), expecting the settler-state to be held accountable, where this may actually be beyond the capabilities of what remains an essentially exploitative apparatus (Simpson 2016: 31).

4   To be sure, this does also not take away from the fact that some Indigenous communities and cosmologies have expressed a clear commitment to practices rooted in other-than-modernity (see Whyte, Caldwell and Schefer 2017).

References

Acosta, A. (2002), *Buen vivir y Sumak kawsay. Una oportunidad para imaginar otros mundos*, Quito: Abya-Yala.

Adams St. Pierre, E. (2017), 'Deleuze and Guattari's Language for New Empirical Inquiry', *Educational Philosophy and Theory*, 49 (11): 1080–9.

Agrawal, A. (1995), 'Dismantling the Divide between Indigenous and Scientific Knowledge', *Development and Change*, 26 (3): 413–39.

Aikau, H., N. Goodyear-Kaʻopua and N. Silva (2016), 'The Practice of Kuleana: Reflections on Critical Indigenous Studies through Trans-indigenous Exchange', in A. Moreton-Robinson (ed.), *Critical Indigenous Studies*, 157–75, Tucson, AZ: University of Arizona Press.

Aitchinson, M., J. Bucks and P. Henn (2020), 'The Middle-Class Eco Rabble Who Want to Kill Off Free Speech: Extinction Rebellion Activists Moan Their Climate Change Doomsday Message Isn't Being Printed on Newspaper Front Pages EVERY DAY . . . as They Block Access to National Presses', *Daily Mail*, 5 September. Available online: https://www.dailymail.co.uk/news/article-8701643/The-middle-class-rabble-want-kill-free-speech-Actress-leads-Extinction-Rebellion-activists.html (accessed 17 November 2023).

Akec, A. (2019), 'When I Look at Extinction Rebellion, All I see Is White Faces That Has to Change', *The Guardian*, 19 October. Available online: https://www.theguardian.com/commentisfree/2019/oct/19/extinction-rebellion-white-faces-diversity (accessed 17 November 2023).

Alaimo, S. (2008), 'Trans-corporeal Feminisms and the Ethical Space of Nature', in S. Alaimo and S. Hekman (eds), *Material Feminisms*, 237–64, Bloomington, IN: Indiana University Press.

Alfred, T. (1999), *Peace, Power, Righteousness: An Indigenous Manifesto*, Don Mills, CA: Oxford University Press.

Allen, C. (2012), *Trans-Indigenous Methodologies for Global Native Literary Studies*, Minneapolis, MN: University of Minnesota Press.

Altmann, P. (2014), 'Good Life as a Social Movement Proposal for Natural Resource Use: The Indigenous Movement in Ecuador', *Consilience: The Journal of Sustainable Development*, 12 (1): 82–94.

Andersen, C. (2009), 'Critical Indigenous Studies: From Difference to Density', *Cultural Studies Review* 15 (2): 80–100.

Andersen, C. (2016), 'Critical Indigenous Studies: Intellectual Predilections and Institutional Realities', in A. Moreton-Robinson (ed.), *Critical Indigenous Studies: Engagement in First World Locations*, 49–68, Tucson, AZ: The University of Arizona Press.

Anderson, E. G. (2021), 'Big Indigeneity', *PMLA: Publications of the Modern Language Association*, 136 (1): 146–53.

Arendt, H. (1958), *The Human Condition*, Chicago, IL: University of Chicago Press.

Axelsson-Linkowski, W., A. M. Fjellström, C. Sandström, A. Westin, L. Östlund and J. Moen (2020), 'Shifting Strategies between Generations in Sami Reindeer Husbandry: The Challenges of Maintaining Traditions while Adapting to a Changing Context', *Human Ecology*, 48: 481–90.

Baker, M. T. (2011), 'Resisting Neoliberal Capitalism: Sustainable Self-determination on Moloka'i, Hawai'i', *International Journal of Critical Indigenous Studies*, 4 (1): 12–20.

Baldwin, A. and B. Erickson (2020), 'Introduction: Whiteness, Coloniality, and the Anthropocene', *Environment and Planning D: Society and Space*, 38 (1): 3–11.

Barker, A. J. (2015), '"A Direct Act of Resurgence, a Direct Act of Sovereignty": Reflections on Idle No More, Indigenous Activism, and Canadian Settler Colonialism', *Globalizations*, 12 (1): 46–65.

BBC (2019), 'Extinction Rebellion: Police Move in on London Protesters', 20 April. Available online: https://www.bbc.co.uk/news/uk-england-london-47987891 (accessed 30 November 2023).

Beitl, C. M. (2016), 'The Changing Legal and Institutional Context for Recognizing Nature's Rights in Ecuador: Mangroves, Fisheries, Farmed Shrimp, and Coastal Management since 1980', *Journal of International Wildlife Law & Policy*, 19 (4): 317–32.

Bendell, J. (2019), 'Doom and Bloom: Adapting to Collapse', in *This is Not a Drill. An Extinction Rebellion Handbook*, 117–28.

Benson Taylor, M. (2021), 'Indigenous Interruptions in the Anthropocene', *PMLA: Publications of the Modern Language Association*, 136 (1): 9–16.

Bonneuil, C. and J.-B. Fressoz (2013), *The Shock of the Anthropocene: The Earth, History and Us*, London: Verso.

Bouich, A. (2021), 'Beyond the End: Indigenous Futurisms' Interventions in the Anthropocene', *SFRA Review*, 51 (4): 160–71.

Brígido-Corachán, A. (2017), 'Material Nature, Visual Sovereignty, and Water Rights: Unpacking the Standing Rock Movement', *Studies in the Literary Imagination*, 50 (1): 69–90.

Burdon, P. D. (2020), 'Obligations in the Anthropocene', *Law and Critique*, 31 (3): 309–28.

Burns, D. and C. Reiman (2019), 'Movement Building', in *This Is Not a Drill. An Extinction Rebellion Handbook*, 161–5.

Byrd, J. (2011), *The Transit of Empire: Indigenous Critiques of Colonialism*, Minneapolis, MN: University of Minnesota Press.

Carter, P. (2018), *Decolonising Governance: Archipelagic Thinking*, London: Routledge.

Césaire, A. (1972), *Discourse on Colonialism*, trans. Joan Pinkham, New York and London: Monthly Review Press.

Chakrabarty, D. (2009), 'The Climate of History: Four Theses on Climate Change', *Critical Inquiry*, 35 (2): 197–222.

Chakrabarty, D. (2012), 'Postcolonial Studies and the Challenge of Climate Change', *New Literary History*, 43 (1): 1–18.

Chakrabarty, D. (2017), 'The Politics of Climate Change Is More Than the Politics of Capitalism', *Theory, Culture & Society*, 34 (2–3): 25–37.

Chakrabarty, D. (2021), *The Climate of History in a Planetary Age*, Chicago, IL: University of Chicago Press.

Champagne, D. (2007a), 'In Search of Theory and Method in American Indian Studies', *American Indian Quarterly* 31 (3): 353–72.

Champagne, D. (2007b), 'The Rise and Fall of Native American Studies in the United States', in G. Horse Capture, D. Champagne and C. Jackson (eds), *American Indian Nations: Yesterday, Today and Tomorrow*, 129–47, New York: Alta Mira Press.

Chandler, D. (2013), *Resilience. The Governance of Complexity*, London: Routledge.

Chandler, D. (2018), *Ontopolitics in the Anthropocene. An Introduction to Mapping, Sensing and Hacking*, London: Routledge.

Chandler, D. (2019), 'The Death of Hope? Affirmation in the Anthropocene', *Globalizations*, 16 (5): 695–706.

Chandler, D. and J. Reid (2018), '"Being in Being": Contesting the Ontopolitics of Indigeneity', *The European Legacy*, 23 (3): 251–68.

Chandler, D. and J. Reid (2019), *Becoming Indigenous. Governing Imaginaries in the Anthropocene*, London: Rowman & Littlefield International.

Chipato, F. and D. Chandler (2022), 'The Black Horizon: Alterity and Ontology in the Anthropocene', *Global Society*, 37 (2): 157–75.

Clark, T., R. De Costa and S. Maddison (2016), 'Non-Indigenous People and the Limits of Settler Colonial Reconciliation', in S. Maddison, T. Clark and R. De Costa (eds), *The Limits of Settler Colonial Reconciliation: Non-indigenous People and the Responsibility to Engage*, 1–14, Singapore: Springer.

Clarke, A. E. (2018), 'Introducing Making Kin Not Population', in A. E. Clarke and D. Haraway (eds), *Making Kin Not Population*, 1–40, Chicago: Prickly Paradigm Press.

Clearinghouse Civil Rights Litigation (2016), 'Complaint for Declaratory and Injunctive Relief. Case 1:16-cv01534 Document 1', 27 July, 1–48. Available online at: https://clearinghouse.net/doc/97866/ (accessed 17 November 2023).

Colebrook, C. (2014), *Death of the PostHuman: Essays on Extinction*, vol. 1, London: Open Humanities Press.

Colebrook, C. (2017a), 'The Time of Planetary Memory', *Textual Practice*, 31 (5): 1017–24.

Colebrook, C. (2017b), 'We Have Always been Post-anthropocene: The Anthropocene Counterfactual', in R. Grusin (ed.), *Anthropocene Feminism*, 1–20, Minneapolis: University of Minnesota Press.

Colebrook, C. (2019), 'The Future in the Anthropocene: Extinction and the Imagination', in A. Johns-Putra (ed.), *Climate and Literature*, 263–80, Cambridge: Cambridge University Press.

CONAIE (2007), 'Propuesta de la CONAIE frente a la Asamblea Constituyente. Principios y lineamientos para la nueva constitución del Ecuador. Por un Estado Plurinacional, Unitario, Soberano, Incluyente, Equitativo y Laico', Quito: CONAIE. Available online: https://biblio.flacsoandes.edu.ec/libros/109339-opac (accessed 17 November 2023).

CONAIE (2010), 'Declaration at the Foot of Taita Imbabura and Mama Cotacachi of the Indigenous Peoples and Nationalities of Ecuador. For a true Continental Summit of the Nations and Peoples of Abya-Yala', Available online: https://www.biodiversidadla.org/Noticias/Ecuador_declaracion_de_la_CONAIE_frente_a_la_X_Cumbre_de_los_Presidentes_del_Alba-TCP_con_Autoridades_Indigenas_y_Afrodescendientes (accessed 17 November 2023).

Connolly, W. E. (2004), 'Method, Problem, Faith', in I. Shapiro, R. M. Smith and T. E. Masoud (eds), *Problems and Methods in the Study of Politics*, 332–49. Cambridge: Cambridge University Press.

Constitution of Ecuador 2008 (rev. 2021). Available online: https://pdba.georgetown.edu/Constitutions/Ecuador/english08.html#:~:text=Article%201.,governed%20using%20a%20decentralized%20approach (accessed 17 November 2023).

Corntassel, J. (2003), 'Who Is Indigenous? "Peoplehood" and Ethnonationalist Approaches to Rearticulating Indigenous Identity', *Nationalism and Ethnic Politics*, 9 (1): 75–100.

Cook, K. (2018), 'Women Are the First Environment: An Interview with Mohawk Elder Katsi Cook,' *Medium*. Available online: https://moonmagazineeditor.medium.com/women-are-the-first-environment-an-interview-with-mohawk-elder-katsi-cook-40ae4151c3c0 (accessed 17 November 2023).

Corntassel, J. (2012), 'Re-envisioning Resurgence', *Decolonization: Indigeneity, Education & Society*, 1 (1): 86–101.

Corntassel, J. and M. Scow (2017), 'Everyday Acts of Resurgence: Indigenous Approaches to Everydayness in Fatherhood', *New Diversities*, 19 (2): 55–68.

Coulthard, G. S. (2007), 'Subjects of Empire: Indigenous Peoples and the "Politics of Recognition" in Canada', *Contemporary Political Theory*, 6 (4): 437–60.

Coulthard, G. S. (2014), *Red Skins, White Masks: Rejecting the Colonial Politics of Recognition*, Minneapolis, MN: University of Minnesota Press.

Cragoe, N. G. (2017), 'Following the Green Path: Honor the Earth and Presentations of Anishinaabe Indigeneity', *Wicazo Sa Review*, 32 (2): 46–70.

Crutzen, P. (2002), 'Geology of Mankind', *Nature*, 415: 23.

Cuestas-Caza, J. (2018), 'Sumak Kawsay Is Not Buen Vivir', *Alternautas*, 5 (1): 51–66.

Cullinan, C. (2011), 'A History of Wild Law', in P. Burdon (ed.), *Exploring Wild Law: The Philosophy of Earth Jurisprudence*, 12–23, Kent Town: Wakefield Press.

Danowski, D. and E. Viveiros de Castro (2017), *The Ends of the World*, Cambridge: Polity.

Da Silva, D. F. (2022), *Unpayable Debt*, Boston, MA: MIT Press.

Davies, H. and Z. Todd (2017), 'On the Importance of a Date, or, Decolonizing the Anthropocene', *ACME: An International Journal for Critical Geographies*, 16 (4): 761–80.

Davies, J. (2018), *The Birth of the Anthropocene*, Oakland, CA: University of California Press.

Davison, A. (2015), 'Beyond the Mirrored Horizon: Modern Ontology and Amodern Possibilities in the Anthropocene', *Geographical Research*, 53 (3): 298–305.

Dawson, A. (2016), *Extinction: A Radical History*. New York and London: OR Books.

Day, I. (2021), 'Ruin Porn and the Colonial Imaginary', *PMLA: Publications of the Modern Language Association*, 136 (1): 125–31.

Deem, A. (2019), 'Mediated Intersections of Environmental and Decolonial Politics in the North Dakota Access Pipeline Movement', *Theory, Culture & Society*, 36 (5): 113–31.

Deleuze, G. and F. Guattari (1987), *A Thousand Plateaus. Capitalism and Schizophrenia*, Minneapolis, MN and London: University of Minnesota Press.

Deloria Jr., V. (1995), *Red Earth, White Lies: Native Americans and the Myth of Scientific Fact*, New York: Scribner.

Deloughrey, E. (2019), *Allegories of the Anthropocene*, Durham, NC: Duke University Press.

Dhillon, J. and N. Estes (2016), 'Introduction: Standing Rock, #NoDAPL, and Mni Wiconi', *Hot Spots, Cultural Anthropology*, 22 December. Available online: culanth .org/fieldsights/1007-introduction-standing-rock-nodapl-and-mni-wiconi

Di Chiro, G. (1992), 'Defining Environmental Justice: Women's Voices and Grassroots Politics', *Socialist Review*, 22 (4): 93–130.

Domínguez, R., S. Caria and M. León (2017), 'Buen Vivir: Praise, Instrumentalization and Reproductive Pathways of Good Living in Ecuador', *Latin American and Caribbean Ethnic Studies*, 12 (2): 133–54.

Dillet, B. (2018), 'Suffocation and the Logic of Immunopolitics', H. Richter (ed.), *Biopolitical Governance: Race, Gender, Economy*, 235–54, London: Rowman & Littlefield.

Draxler, B. (2021), 'How the Women of Standing Rock Inspired the World', *Yes! Solutions Journalism*, 26 July. Available online: https://www.yesmagazine.org/ social-justice/2021/07/26/women-of-standing-rock (accessed 17 November 2023).

Ecoffey, B. (2019), 'OST Taking Steps to Grow Hemp', *Lakota Times*, 18 April. Available online: https://www.lakotatimes.com/articles/ost-taking-steps-to-grow-hemp/ (accessed 17 November 2023).

Elliott, M. (2018), 'Indigenous Resurgence: The Drive for Renewed Engagement and Reciprocity in the Turn Away from the State', *Canadian Journal of Political Science*, 51 (1): 61–81.

Ellis, E. (2019), 'Centering Sovereignty: How Standing Rock Changed the Conversation', in N. Ested and J. Dillon (eds), *Standing with Standing Rock. Voices from the #NoDAPL Movement*, 172–87, Minneapolis, MN: University of Minnesota Press.

Ephraim, L. (2022), 'Everyone Poops: Consumer Virtues and Excretory Anxieties in Locke's Theory of Property', *Political Theory*, 50 (5): 673–99.

Epstein, S. (2022), 'Rights of Nature, Human Species, Identity, and Political thought in the Anthropocene', *The Anthropocene Review*, 10 (2): 1–19.

Erickson, B. (2020), 'Anthropocene Futures: Linking Colonialism and Environmentalism in an Age of Crisis', *Environment and Planning D: Society and Space*, 38 (1): 111–28.

Esmeir, S. (2006), 'On Making Dehumanization Possible', *Modern Language Association*, 121 (5): 1544–51.

Estes, N. (2018), 'Review. Awake: A Dream from Standing Rock. Directed by Myron Dewey, Josh Fox, and James Spione. International WOW, 2017. 84 Minutes', *Environmental History*, 23: 383–6.

Eudaily, S. P. (2004), *The Present Politics of the Past: Indigenous Legal Activism and Resistance to (Neo) Liberal Governmentality*, New York: Routledge.

Evans, B. and J. Reid (2013), 'Dangerously Exposed: The Life and Death of the Resilient Subject', *Resilience*, 1 (2): 83–98.

Evans, B. and J. Reid (2014), *Resilient Life. The Art of Living Dangerously*, Cambridge: Polity Press.

Extinction Rebellion (2019), 'Declaration of Rebellion', in *This Is Not a Drill. An Extinction Rebellion Handbook*, 15–9.

Extinction Rebellion (2022), 'Join the Rebellion'. Available online: https://extinctionrebellion.uk/ (accessed 17 November 2023).

Fisher, M. (2019), *Capitalist Realism: Is There No Alternative?*, London: Zero Books.

Foucault, M. (1978), *The History of Sexuality Volume I*, New York: Pantheon Books.

Friedman, L. (2020), 'Standing Rock Sioux Tribe Wins a Victory in Dakota Access Pipeline Case', *The New York Times*, 25 March. Available online: https://www.nytimes.com/2020/03/25/climate/dakota-access-pipeline-sioux.html (accessed 17 November 2023).

Fritze, J. (2022), 'Dakota Access Pipeline: Supreme Court Turns away Challenge over tougher Environmental Review', *USA Today*, 22 February. Available online: https://www.usatoday.com/story/news/politics/2022/02/22/supreme-court

-allows-environmental-review-dakota-access-pipeline/6840436001/ (accessed 17 November 2023).

Garlick, B. and L. King (2022), 'A Geography beyond the Anthropocene: Ursula Le Guin's Always Coming Home as Topophilia for Survival', *Cultural Geographies*, 0 (0): 1–20. Available online: https://doi.org/10.1177/14744740221126984 (accessed 17 November 2023).

GARN (2010), 'Universal Declaration of Rights of Mother Earth'. Available online: https://www.garn.org/universal-declaration-for-the-rights-of-mother-earth/ (accessed 17 November 2023).

GARN (2011), 'The First Successful Case of the Rights of Nature Implementation in Ecuador'. Available online: https://www.garn.org/first-ron-case-ecuador/ (accessed 17 November 2023).

Graham, J. K. (2020), 'Reading for Difference in the Archives of Tropical Geography: Imagining An(Other) Economic Geography for Beyond the Anthropocene', *Antipode*, 52 (1): 12–35.

Glyn, M. and C. Farrell (2019), 'Arts Factory', in *This Is Not a Drill. An Extinction Rebellion Handbook*, 185–93.

Gibson Graham, J. K. and G. Roelvnik (2009), 'An Economic Ethics for the Anthropocene', *Antipode*, 41 (1): 320–46.

Griffiths, J. (2019), 'Courting Arrest', in C. Farrell, A. Green, S. Knights and W. Skeaping (eds), *This is Not a Drill: An Extinction Rebellion Handbook*, 143–49, Milton Keynes: Penguin Random House.

Grignon, J. and R. W. Kimmerer (2017), 'Listening to the Forest', in G. Van Horn and J. Hausdoerffer (eds), *Wildness: Relations of People & Place*, 67–74, Chicago, IL: University of Chicago Press.

Gross, L. (2014), *Anishinaabe Ways of Knowing and Being*, Farnham: Ashgate.

Grosz, E., K. Yusoff and N. Clark (2017), 'An Interview with Elizabeth Grosz: Geopower, Inhumanism and the Biopolitical', *Theory, Culture & Society*, 34 (2–3): 129–46.

Gudynas, E. (2011), 'Buen Vivir: Today's Tomorrow', *Development*, 54: 441–7.

Gushiken, P. (2019), '"Know Where You Stand": 'Ōiwi Refusals of Settler Futurities and Carceral Violence', *Abolition Journal*, December. Available online: https://abolitionjournal.org/know-where-you-stand-%CA%BBoiwi-refusals-of-settler-futurities-and-carceral-violence-%EF%BB%BF/ (accessed 17 November 2023).

Hallam, R. (2019), 'The Civil Resistance Method', in *This is Not a Drill. An Extinction Rebellion Handbook*, 151–7.

Hamilton, C. (2013), *Earthmasters. The Dawn of the Age of Climate Engineering*, New Haven and London: Yale University Press.

Hamilton, C. (2017), *Defiant Earth. The Fate of Humans in the Anthropocene*, Sydney: Allen & Unwin.

Haque, M. (2019), 'Feeding the Rebellion', in *This Is Not a Drill. An Extinction Rebellion Handbook*, 173–7.

Haraway, D. (1991), *Simians, Cyborgs, and Women: The Reinvention of Nature*, New York: Routledge.

Haraway, D. (2015), 'Anthropocene, Capitalocene, Plantationocene, Chthulucene: Making Kin', *Environmental Humanities*, 6: 159–65.

Haraway, D. (2016), 'Staying with the Trouble. Anthropocene, Capitalocene, Chthulucene', in J. W. Moore (ed.), *Anthropocene or Capitalocene? Nature, History, and the Crisis of Capitalism*, 34–76, Oakland, CA: Kairos.

Haraway, D. (2018), 'Making Kin in the Chthulucene: Reproducing Multispecies Justice', in A. E. Clarke and D. Haraway (eds), *Making Kin Not Population*, 67–100, Chicago: Prickly Paradigm Press.

Harkin, N. (2020), 'Intimate Encounters: Aboriginal Labour Stories and the Violence of the Colonial Archive', in B. Hokowhitu, A. Moreton-Robinson, L. T. Smith, C. Andersen and S. Larkin (eds), *Routledge Handbook of Critical Indigenous Studies*, 147–61, London and New York: Routledge.

Harrington, C. (2016), 'The Ends of the World: International Relations and the Anthropocene', *Millennium – Journal of International Studies*, 44 (3): 478–98.

Hausdoerffer, J. (2017), 'The Akiing Ethic: Seeking Ancestral Wildness beyond Aldo Leopold's Wilderness', in G. Van Horn and J. Hausdoerffer (eds), *Wildness: Relations of People & Place*, 195–204, Chicago, IL: University of Chicago Press.

Hemming, S., D. Rigney and S. Berg (2011), 'Ngarrindjeri Futures: Negotiation, Governance and Environmental Management', in S. Maddison and M. Brigg (eds), *Unsettling the Settler State: Creativity and Resistance in Indigenous Settler-State Governance*, 98–113, Sydney: The Federation Press.

Henriksen, D., E. Creely and R. Mehta (2022), 'Rethinking the Politics of Creativity: Posthumanism, Indigeneity, and Creativity Beyond the Western Anthropocene', *Qualitative Inquiry*, 28 (5): 465–75.

Heringman, N. (2014), 'Deep Time at the Dawn of the Anthropocene', *Representations*, 129 (1): 56–85.

Hess, M., S. R. Flores and U. Geiser (2017), 'Between Grassroots Expectations, Political Visions, and the Contemporary Local State: The Everyday Challenges of Indigenous/Peasant Organizations in the Bolivian Andes', *Journal of Latin American Geography*, 16 (3): 135–58.

Hird, M. J. (2017), 'Proliferation, Extinction, and an Anthropocene Aesthetic', in J. Weinstein and C. Colebrook (eds), *Posthumous Life: Theorizing Beyond the Posthuman*, 251–70, New York and Chichester: Columbia University Press.

Hokowhitu, B. (2009), 'Indigenous Existentialism and the Immediacy of the Indigenous Body', *Cultural Studies Review*, 15 (2): 101–18.

Hokowhitu, B. (2016), 'Monster: Post-Indigenous Studies', in A. Moreton-Robinson (ed.), *Critical Indigenous Studies: Engagement in First World Locations*, 83–101, Tucson, AZ: The University of Arizona Press.

Hokowhitu, B. (2020), 'The Emperor's "New" Materialisms: Indigenous Materialisms and Disciplinary Colonialism', in A. Moreton-Robinson, L. T. Smith, C. Andersen and S. Larkin (eds), *Routledge Handbook of Critical Indigenous Studies*, 131–46, London and New York: Routledge.

Hopper, F. (2018), 'The Ripple Effect: How Standing Rock Violence Inspired Demonstrations Around the World', *ICT*, 13 September. Available online: https://ictnews.org/archive/the-ripple-effect-how-standing-rock-violence-inspired-demonstrations-around-the-world (accessed 17 November 2023).

Horton, J. L. (2017), 'Indigenous Artists against the Anthropocene', *Art Journal*, 76 (2): 48–69.

Ibrahim, H. O. (2019), 'Indigenous Peoples and the Fight for Survival', in *This is Not a Drill. An Extinction Rebellion Handbook*, 87–92.

James, S. P. (2020), 'Legal Rights and Nature's Contributions to People: Is There a Connection?' *Biological Conservation*, 241. Available online: https://doi.org/10.1016/j.biocon.2019.108325 (accessed 17 November 2023).

James and Ruby (2019), 'Cultural Roadblocks', in *This Is Not a Drill. An Extinction Rebellion Handbook*, 179–84.

Jewett, C. and M. Garavan (2019), 'Water Is Life – An Indigenous Perspective from a Standing Rock Water Protector', *Community Development Journal*, 54 (1): 42–58.

Johnson, E. and H. Morehouse (2014), 'After the Anthropocene: Politics and Geographic Inquiry for a New Epoch', *Progress in Human Geography*, 38 (3): 1–18.

Johnson, H. (2017), '#noDAPL: Social Media, Empowerment, and Civic Participation at Standing Rock', *Library Trends*, 66 (2): 155–75.

Johnson, J. T. and B. Murton (2007), 'Re/placing Native Science: Indigenous Voices in Contemporary Constructions of Nature', *Geographical Research*, 45 (2): 121–9.

Jojola, T. (2008), 'Indigenous Planning – An Emerging Context', *Canadian Journal of Urban Research*, 17 (1): 37–47.

Jones, C. (2016), *New Treaty, New Tradition: Reconciling New Zealand and Māori Law*, Vancouver: UBC Press.

Justice, D. H. (2016), 'A Better World Becoming: Placing Critical Indigenous Studies', in A. Moreton-Robinson (ed.), *Critical Indigenous Studies: Engagement in First World Locations*, 19–32, Tucson, AZ: The University of Arizona Press.

Kauffman, C. M. (2020), 'Managing People for the Benefit of the Land: Practicing Earth Jurisprudence in Te Urewera, New Zealand', *ISLE: Interdisciplinary Studies in Literature and Environment*, 27 (3): 578–59.

Kauffman, C. M. and C. L. Martin (2014), 'Scaling up Buen Vivir: Globalizing Local Environmental Governance from Ecuador', *Global Environmental Politics*, 14 (1): 40–58.

Kauffman, C. M. and C. L. Martin (2017), 'Can Rights of Nature Make Development More Sustainable? Why Some Ecuadorian Lawsuits Succeed and Others Fail', *World Development*, 92: 130–42.

Kawsak Sacha (2015), 'The Living Forest: An Indigenous Proposal for Confronting Climate Change. Presented by the Amazonian Kichwa People of Sarayaku', COP 21, Paris, 30 November–11 December. Available online: https://sarayaku.org/wp-content/uploads/2015/11/Kawsak-Sacha-English-1.pdf (accessed 17 November 2023).

Kidd, D. (2020), 'Standing Rock and the Indigenous Commons', *Popular Communication*, 18 (3): 233–47.

Kleinherenbrink, A. (2015), 'Territory and Ritornello: Deleuze and Guattari on Thinking Living Beings', *Deleuze Studies*, 9 (2): 208–30.

Knights, S. (2019), 'Introduction: The Story So Far', in *This Is Not a Drill. An Extinction Rebellion Handbook*, 27–35.

Kotzé, L. and P. Villavicencio Calzadilla (2017), 'Somewhere between Rhetoric and Reality: Environmental Constitutionalism and the Rights of Nature in Ecuador', *Transnational Environmental Law*, 6 (3): 401–33.

Krupp, E. C. (2020), 'Native American Cosmology and Other Worlds', in M. Gargaud, W. M. Irvine, R. Amils, H. J. Cleaves, D. L. Pinti, J. Cernicharo Quintanilla, D. Rouan, T. Spohn, S. Tirard and M. Viso (eds.), *Encyclopedia of Astrobiology*, 1659–67, Berlin and Heidelberg: Springer.

Kuwada, B. K. and A. Yamashiro (2016), 'Rooted in Wonder: Tales of Indigenous Activism and Community Organizing', *Marvels & Tales*, 30 (1): 17–21.

LaDuke, W. (1994a), 'The Indigenous Perspective on Feminism, Militarism and the Environment', *Race, Poverty & the Environment*, 4/5 (4/1): 1–4.

LaDuke, W. (1994b), 'Traditional Ecological Knowledge and Environmental Futures', *Colorado Journal of International Environmental Law and Policy*, 5 (127): 127–48.

LaDuke, W. (1996), 'Nomination Speech for Nader'. Available online: https://www.youtube.com/watch?v=yMiNRCQsFSk&t=335s (accessed 17 November 2023).

LaDuke, W. (2006), 'Indigenous Power: A New Energy Economy', *Race, Poverty & the Environment*, 13 (1): 6–10.

LaDuke, W. (2015), *All Our Relations. Native Struggles for Land and Life*, Chicago, IL: Haymarket Books.

Laing, L. F. (2015), 'Resource Sovereignties in Bolivia: Re-Conceptualising the Relationship between Indigenous Identities and the Environment during the TIPNIS Conflict', *Bulletin of Latin American Research*, 34 (2): 149–66.

Lalit Miglani v State of Uttarakhand & others (2017), 'WPPIL 140/2015 (High Court of Uttarakhand)'. Available online: https://indiankanoon.org/doc/92201770/ (accessed 17 November 2023).

Langton, M. (1997), 'Grandmothers' Law, Company Business and Succession in Changing Aboriginal Land Tenure Systems', in G. Yunupingu (ed.), *Our Land Is Our Life: Land Rights – Past, Present and Future*, 84–116, Brisbane: University of Queensland Press.

Latour, B. (1993), *We Have Never Been Modern*, Cambridge, MA: Harvard University Press.

Latour, B. (2004), 'Why Has Critique Run out of Steam? From Matters of Fact to Matters of Concern', *Critical Inquiry*, 30: 225–4.

Latour, B. (2017), *Facing Gaia: Eight Lectures on the New Climatic Regime*, Cambridge: Polity.

Latour, B. (2018), *Down to Earth. Politics in the New Climatic Regime*, Cambridge: Polity.

Latour, B. (2021), *After Lockdown: A Metamorphosis*, Cambridge: Polity.

Legal Team (2019), 'Police, Arrest and Support', in *This Is Not a Drill. An Extinction Rebellion Handbook*, 211–13.

Lemenager, S. (2021), 'Love and Theft; or, Provincializing the Anthropocene', *PMLA: Publications of the Modern Language Association*, 136 (1): 102–9.

Lewis, A. (2019), 'Too White, Too Middle Class and Lacking in Empathy, Extinction Rebellion has a Race Problem, Critics Say', *CNN*, 24 November. Available online: https://edition.cnn.com/2019/11/24/uk/extinction-rebellion-environment -diversity-gbr-intl/index.html (accessed 17 November 2023).

Liddle, R. (2019), 'Extinction Rebellion should Pack Up Their Plastic Tents and Virtue-Signalling Hysterics and Get Back to Work', *The Sun*, 10 October. Available online: https://www.thesun.co.uk/news/10103451/extinction-rebellion-get-back-to-work/ (accessed 17 November 2023).

Locke, J. (2005), *Two Treatises of Government*, Project Gutenberg e-book. Available online: https://www.gutenberg.org/cache/epub/7370/pg7370-images.html

Long, M. (2018), 'Vanua in the Anthropocene: Relationality and Sea Level Rise in Fiji', *Symplokē*, 26 (1–2): 51–70.

Malm, A. (2020), *Corona, Climate, Chronic Emergency. War Communism in the Twenty-First Century*, London: Verso.

Malm, A. and A. Hornborg (2014), 'The Geology of Mankind? A Critique of the Anthropocene Narrative', *The Anthropocene Review*, 1 (1): 62–9.

Mankiller, W. (2004), *Every Day Is a Good Day: Reflections by Contemporary Indigenous Women*, Golden, CO: Fulcrum Publishing.

Mankiller, W. and M. Wallis (1993), *Mankiller. A Chief and Her People*, New York and London: MacMillen.

Marshall, V. (2019), 'Removing the Veil from the "Rights of Nature": The Dichotomy between First Nations Customary Rights and Environmental Legal Personhood', *Australian Feminist Law Journal*, 45 (2): 233–48.

Matamua, R. (2021), 'Matariki and the Decolonisation of Time', in B. Hokowhitu, A. Moreton-Robinson, L. T. Smith, C. Andersen and S. Larkin (eds), *Routledge Handbook of Critical Indigenous Studies*, 65–77, London and New York: Routledge.

McGregor, D. (2012), 'Traditional Knowledge: Considerations for Protecting Water in Ontario', *International Indigenous Policy Journal*, 3 (3): 1–21.

McGregor, D. (2020), 'Mother Earth', in P. Tortell (ed.), *Earth 2020. An Insider's Guide to a Rapidly Changing Planet*, 134–9, Cambridge: Open Book Publishers.

McKinnon, C. (2021), 'Striking Back: The 1980s Aboriginal Art Movement and the Performativity of Sovereignty', in B. Hokowhitu, A. Moreton-Robinson, L. T. Smith, C. Andersen and S. Larkin (eds), *Routledge Handbook of Critical Indigenous Studies*, 324–226, London and New York: Routledge.

McNern, R. (2019), 'One by One: A Media Strategy', in *This is Not a Drill. An Extinction Rebellion Handbook*, 197–204.

Mitchell, A. (2017), '"Posthuman Security": Reflections from an Open-ended Conversation', in C. Eroukhmanoff and M. Harker (eds), *In Reflections on the Posthuman in International Relations: The Anthropocene, Security and Ecology*, 10–18, Bristol: E-International Relations Publishing.

Moore, J. W. (2016a), 'Anthropocene or Capitalocene? Nature, History, and the Crisis of Capitalism', in J. W. Moore (ed.), *Anthropocene or Capitalocene? Nature, History, and the Crisis of Capitalism*, 1–13, Oakland, CA: Kairos.

Moore, J. W. (2016b), 'The Rise of Cheap Nature', in J. W. Moore (ed.), *Anthropocene or Capitalocene? Nature, History, and the Crisis of Capitalism*, 78–115, Oakland, CA: Kairos.

Moreton-Robinson, A. (2015), *The White Possessive: Property, Power and Indigenous Sovereignty*, Minneapolis, MN: The University of Minnesota Press.

Moreton-Robinson, A. (2016), 'Introduction: Locations of Engagement in the First World', in A. Moreton-Robinson (ed.), *Critical Indigenous Studies*, 3–18, Tucson, AZ: The University of Arizona Press.

Morton, T. (2013), *Hyperobjects*, Minneapolis, MN: University of Minnesota Press.

Muller, S., S. Hemming and D. Rigney (2019), 'Indigenous Sovereignties: Relational Ontologies and Environmental Management', *Geographical Research*, 57: 399–410.

Nail, T. (2017), 'What is an Assemblage?' *SubStance*, 46 (1): 21–37.

Nieves, K. (2019), 'Vegan Activism and Anti-indigeneity: Violating Indigenous Food Sovereignty', *Terra Incognita*, 3 March. Available online: https://www.terraincognitamedia.com/features/vegan-activism-and-anti-indigenity-violating-Indigenous-food-sovereignty2019

O'Brien, S. (2017), 'Resilience Stories. Narratives of Adaptation, Refusal, and Compromise', *Resilience*, 4 (2–3): 43–65.

O'Donnell, E. L. (2018), 'At the Intersection of the Sacred and the Legal: Rights for Nature in Uttarakhand, India', *Journal of Environmental Law*, 30 (1): 135–44.

Oksanen, A.-A. (2020), 'The Rise of Indigenous (Pluri-)Nationalism: The Case of the Sámi People', *Sociology*, 54 (6): 1141–58.

Pain, N. and R. Pepper (2021), 'Can Personhood Protect the Environment? Affording Legal Rights to Nature', *Fordham International Law Journal*, 45: 315–77.

Paine, R. (2004), 'Saami Reindeer Pastoralism: Quo Vadis?', *Journal of Anthropology*, 69 (1): 23–42.

Peña, D. G. (2017), 'The Hummingbird and the Redcap', in G. Van Horn and J. Hausdoerffer (eds), *Wildness: Relations of People & Place*, 89–99, Chicago, IL: University of Chicago Press.

Piper, L. (2019), 'Alternatives: Environmental and Indigenous Activism in the 1970s', in J. Clapperton and L. Piper (eds), *Environmental Activism on the Ground. Small Green and Indigenous Organizing*, 153–70, Calgary: University of Calgary Press.

Povinelli, E. (2016), *Geontologies. A Requiem to Late Liberalism*, Durham, NC: Duke University Press.

Povinelli, E. (2017), 'The Ends of Humans: Anthropocene, Autonomism, Antagonism, and the Illusions of our Epoch', *South Atlantic Quarterly*, 116 (2): 293–310.

Povinelli, E. (2021), *Between Gaia and Ground: Four Axioms of Existence and the Ancestral Catastrophe of Late Liberalism*, Durham, NC: Duke University Press.

Porter, L., H. Matunga, L. Viswanathan, L. Patrick, R. Walker, L. Sandercock, D. Moraes, J. Frantz, M. Thompson-Fawcett, C. Riddle and T. Jojola (2017), 'Indigenous Planning : from Principles to Practice / A Revolutionary Pedagogy of / for Indigenous Planning / Settler-Indigenous Relationships as Liminal Spaces in Planning Education and Practice / Indigenist Planning / What is the Work of Non- Indigenous People in the Service of a Decolonizing Agenda?/ Supporting Indigenous Planning in the City/Film as a Catalyst for Indigenous Community Development/Being Ourselves and Seeing Ourselves in the City: Enabling the Conceptual Space for Indigenous Urban Planning/Universities Can Empower the Next Generation of Architects, Planners, and Landscape Architects in Indigenous Design and Planning', *Planning Theory & Practice*, 18 (4): 639–66.

Prindeville, D.-M. (2004), *On the Streets and in the State House. American Indian and Hispanic Women and Environmental Policymaking in New Mexico*, London and New York: Routledge.

Quick, J. and J. T. Spartz (2018), 'On the Pursuit of Good Living in Highland Ecuador: Critical Indigenous Discourses of Sumak Kawsay', *Latin American Research Review*, 53 (4): 757–69.

Rafaeli, J. S. and N. Woods (2019), 'Fighting the Wrong War', in *This Is Not a Drill. An Extinction Rebellion Handbook*, 73–81.

Raffnsøe, S. (2016), *Philosophy of the Anthropocene*, London: Palgrave Pivot.

Randerson, J. and A. Yates (2017), 'Negotiating the Ontological Gap: Place, Performance, and Media Art Practices in Aotearoa/New Zealand', in S. Monani and J. Adamson (eds), *Ecocriticism and Indigenous Studies: Conversations from Earth to Cosmos*, 23–43, New York: Routledge.

Raworth, K. (2019), 'A New Economics', in *This Is Not a Drill. An Extinction Rebellion Handbook*, 229–44.

Rawson, A. and M. Mansfield (2018), 'Producing Juridical Knowledge: "Rights of Nature" or the Naturalization of Rights?', *Environment and Planning E: Nature and Space*, 1 (1–2): 99–119.

Rea, N. (2020), 'Activists Staged a Dramatic Protest in Front of London's National Gallery to Protest the Loss of Indigenous Lives in Brazil', *Artworld*, 12 August. Available online: https://news.artnet.com/art-world/extinction-rebellion -Indigenous-protests-london-1901410 (accessed 17 November 2023).

Recollet, K. (2016), 'Gesturing Indigenous Futurities through the Remix', *Dance Research Journal*, 48 (1): 91–105.

Reo, N. J., K. Whyte, D. Ranco, J. Brandt, E.Blackmer and B. Elliott (2017), 'Invasive Species, Indigenous Stewards, and Vulnerability Discourse', *American Indian Quarterly*, 41 (3): 201–23.

Reynolds, G. (2003), 'A Native American Water Ethic', *Transactions*, 90: 143–61.

Rickard, J. (2011), 'Visualizing Sovereignty in the Time of Biometric Sensors', *South Atlantic Quarterly*, 110 (2): 465–86.

Ripple, W. J. and N. R. Houtman (2019), 'Scientists' Warnings have been Ignored', in *This is Not a Drill. An Extinction Rebellion Handbook*, 53–7.

Russ, G. (2022), 'The Extinction Rebellion Is Brazenly Dishonest When It Comes to Indigenous People', *National Post*, 14 January. Available online: https:// nationalpost.com/opinion/geoff-russ-the-extinction-rebellion-is-brazenly -dishonest-when-it-comes-to-Indigenous-people (accessed 17 November 2023).

Rival, L.(2009),'The Resilience of Indigenous Intelligence', inK. Hastrup (ed.),*The Question of Resilience: Social Responses to Climate Change*,293–313,Copenhagen:The Royal Danish Academy of Sciences and Letters.

Rowe, S., E. Baldry and W. Earles (2015), 'Decolonising Social Work Research: Learning from Critical Indigenous Approaches', *Australian Social Work*, 68 (3): 296–308.

Sales, D. and K. Feehan (2021), 'Self-confessed "Privileged, White Middle Class" XR Protester, 60, Who Lives in a £900,000 Farmhouse Says she was "exercising Her Human Rights" while Blocking Roads Outside Parliament, Court Hears', *Daily Mail*, 9 September. Available online: https://www.dailymail.co.uk/news/article-9973761/ Privileged-white-middle-class-XR-activist-60-tells-court-human-right-protest.html (accessed 17 November 2023).

Salick, J. and N. Ross (2009), 'Traditional Peoples and Climate Change', *Global Environmental Change*, 19 (2): 137–9.

Sánchez Parga, J. (2011), 'Discursos retrovolucionarios: Sumak Kawsay, dere-chos de la naturaleza y otros pachamamismos', *Ecuador Debate*, 84: 31–50.

Sangster, J. (2012), 'Aboriginal Women and Work across the 49th Parallel: Historical Antecedents and New Challenges', in C. Williams (ed.), *Indigenous Women and Work: from Labor to Activism*, 27–45, Urbana, Chicago and Springfield, IL: University of Illinois Press.

Sarayaku (2003), 'Sarayaku propone un acuerdo integral sobre autodeterminacion y mnejo de sus territories'. Available online: http://www.latautonomy.com/sarayaku .pdf (accessed 17 November 2023).

Satgar, V. (2022), 'The Coloniality of the Scientific Anthropocene', *International Studies*. Available online: https://doi.org/10.1093/acrefore/9780190846626.013.614

Saunders C., B. Doherty and G. Hayes (2020), 'A New Climate Movement? Extinction Rebellion's Activists in Profile', *CUSP Working Paper*, no. 25, Guildford: Centre for the Understanding of Sustainable Prosperity.

Scott, C. (2016), '(Indigenous) Place and Time as FORMAL Strategy: Healing Immanent Crisis in the Dystopias of Eden Robinson and Richard Van Camp', *Extrapolation*, 57 (1–2): 73–93.

SENPLADES (2009), 'National Plan for Good Living 2009–2013' (English version). Available online: https://www.planificacion.gob.ec/wp-content/uploads/ downloads/2016/03/Plan-Nacional-Buen-Vivir-2009-2013-Ingles.pdf (accessed 17 November 2023).

Shiva, V. (2019), 'Foreword', in *This Is Not a Drill. An Extinction Rebellion Handbook*, 21–35.

Shrinkhal, R. (2021), '"Indigenous Sovereignty" and Right to Self-determination in International Law: A Critical Appraisal', *AlterNative*, 17 (1):71–82.

Simmons, K. (2019), 'Reorientations; or, An Indigenous Feminist Reflection on the Anthropocene', *JCMS: Journal of Cinema and Media Studies*, 58 (2): 174–9.

Simpson, L. B. (1999), 'The Construction of Traditional Ecological Knowledge. Issues, Implications and Insights', PhD diss., University of Manitoba, Winnipeg. Available online: https://mspace.lib.umanitoba.ca/handle/1993/2210 (accessed 17 November 2023).

Simpson, L. B. (2011), *Dancing on Our Turtle's Back. Stories of Nishnaabeg Re-creation, Resurgence and a New Emergence*, Winnipeg: Arbeiter Ring Publishing.

Simpson, L. B. (2016), 'Indigenous Resurgence and Co-Resistance', *Critical Ethnic Studies*, 2 (2): 19–34.

Small, G. (1994), 'The Search for Environmental Justice in Indian Country', *The Amicus Journal*, 16 (1): 38–41.

Smith, L. T. (1999), *Decolonizing Methodologies: Research and Indigenous Peoples*, London: Zed Books.

Smithers, G. D (2015), 'Beyond the "Ecological Indian": Environmental Politics and Traditional Ecological Knowledge in Modern North America', *Environmental History*, 20 (1): 83–111.

Steffen, W., Å. Person, L. Deutch, J. Zalasiewicz, M. Williams, K. Richardson, C.Crumley, P. Crutzen, C. Folke, L. Gordon, M. Molina, V. Ramanathan, J.Rockström, M. Scheffer, H. J. Schellnhuber and U. Svedin (2011), 'The Anthropocene: From Global Change to Planetary Stewardship', *AMBIO*, 40: 739–61.

Stengers, I. (2013a), *Another Science Is Possible*, Cambridge: Polity Press.

Stengers, I. (2013b), 'Matters of Cosmopolitics: Isabelle Stengers in Conversation with Heather Davis and Etienne Turpin on the Provocations of Gaia', in E. Turpin (ed.), *Architecture in the Anthropocene: Encounters among Design, Deep Time, Science, and Philosophy*, 171–82, Ann Arbor, MI: Open Humanities Press.

Stengers, S. (2015), *In Catastrophic Times. Resisting the Coming Barbarism*, London: Open Humanities Press.

Stevenson, M. G. (1998), 'Traditional Knowledge and Environmental Management: From Commodity to Process', prepared for The National Aboriginal Forestry Association Conference 'Celebrating Partnerships', Prince Albert, SK, 14–18 September. Available online: https://era.library.ualberta.ca/items/26253b73-96ed-42bb-a003-82ed9045d574 (accessed 17 November 2023).

Stevenson, M. G. (2006), 'The Possibility of Difference: Rethinking Co-Management', *Human Organization*, 65 (2): 167–80.

Stiegler, B. (2014), *Symbolic Misery, Volume 1. The Hyper-industrial Epoch*, Cambridge: Polity.

Stiegler, B. (2015), 'Ce n'est qu'en projetant un véritable avenir qu'on pourra combattre Daech', *Le Monde*, 19 November. Available online: https://www.lemonde.fr/emploi/article/2015/11/19/bernard-stiegler-ce-n-est-qu-en-projetant-un-veritable-avenir-qu-on-pourra-combattre-daech_4813660_1698637.html

Stiegler, B. (2018), *The Neganthropocene*, London: Open Humanities Press.

Stone, C. D. (1972), 'Should Trees Have Standing? Towards Legal Rights for Natural Objects', *Southern California Law Review*, 45: 450–501.

Swanson, H. A., N. Bubandt and A. Tsing (2015), 'Less Than One But More Than Many: Anthropocene as Science Fiction and Scholarship-in-The-making', *Environment and Society: Advances in Research*, 6 (1): 149–66.

Swyngedouw, E. (2010), 'Apocalypse Forever? Post-political Populism and the Spectre of Climate Change', *Theory, Culture & Society*, 27 (2–3): 213–32.

Swyngedouw, E. (2011), 'Depoliticized Environments: The End of nature, Climate Change and the Post-political Condition', *Royal Institute of Philosophy Supplements*, 69: 253–74.

Swyngedouw, E. and H. Ernstson (2018), 'Interrupting the Anthropo-obScene: Immuno-biopolitics and Depoliticizing Ontologies in the Anthropocene', *Theory Culture & Society*, 35 (6): 3–30.

Tallbear, K. (2000), 'Shepard Krech's The Ecological Indian: One Indian's Perspective', *International Institute for Indigenous Resource Management*, 1–5. Available online: https://www.academia.edu/11421153/Shepard_Krech_s_The_Ecological_Indian_One_Indian_s_Perspective (accessed 17 November 2023).

Tallbear, K. (2016), 'Dear Indigenous Studies, It's Not Me, It's You: Why I Left and What Needs to Change', in A. Moreton-Robinson (ed.), *Critical Indigenous Studies*, 69–82, Tucson: The University of Arizona Press.

Tallbear, K. (2018), 'Making Love and Relations beyond Settler Sex and Family', in A. E. Clarke and D. Haraway (eds), *Making Kin Not Population*, 145–66, Chicago, IL: Prickly Paradigm Press.

Tanasescu, M. (2020), 'Rights of Nature, Legal Personality, and Indigenous Philosophies', *Transnational Environmental Law*, 9 (3): 429–53.

Thompson, P. and M. Duell (2019), 'The Cotswold Conspirators: How Four Key Players in the Extinction Rebellion Eco-mob Plotted Chaos in London from Vegetarian Café in Leafy Market Town', *Daily Mail*, 18 April. Available online: https://www.dailymail.co.uk/news/article-6936093/How-eco-mob-plotted-chaos-London-vegetarian-caf-Stroud.html (accessed 17 November 2023).

Todd, Z. (2015), 'Indigenizing the Anthropocene', in H. Davis and E. Turpin (eds), *Art in the Anthropocene: Encounters Among Aesthetics, Politics, Environments and Epistemologies*, 241–54, London: Open Humanities Press.

Tuck, E. and R. A. Gaztambide-Fernandez (2013), 'Curriculum, Replacement, and Settler Futurity', *Journal of Curriculum Theorizing*, 29 (1): 72–90.

Tuhiwai-Smith, L. (1999), *Decolonizing Methodologies: Research and Indigenous Peoples*, London: Zed Books.

Van Gelder, S. (2016), 'How Standing Rock Has Changed Us', *Yes! Solutions Journalism*, 7 December. Available online: https://www.yesmagazine.org/democracy/2016/12/07/how-standing-rock-has-changed-us (accessed 17 November 2023).

Van Horn, G. (2017), 'Introduction: Into the Wildness', in G. Van Horn and J. Hausdoerffer (eds), *Wildness: Relations of People & Place*, 1–8, Chicago, IL: University of Chicago Press.

Vanhulst, J. and A. E. Beling (2014), 'Buen vivir: Emergent Discourse within or beyond Sustainable Development?' *Ecological Economics*, 101: 54–63.

Veber, H. (1998), 'The Salt of the Montaña : Interpreting Indigenous Activism in the Rain Forest', 13 (3): 382–413.

Viane, L. (2022), 'Can Rights of Nature Save Us from the Anthropocene Catastrophe? Some Critical Reflections from the Field', *Asian Journal of Law and Society*, 9 (2): 187–206.

Viteri, C. (2002), 'Visión indígena del desarrollo en la Amazonía', *Polis, Revista de la Universidad Bolivariana*, 1 (3): 1–6.

Viola Recasens, A. (2014), 'Discursos "Pachamamistas" Versus políticas desarrollistas: el debate sobre el sumak kawsay en los Andes', *Íconos. Revista de Ciencias Sociales*, 48: 55–72.

Waitere, H. and E. Allen (2011), 'Beyond Indigenous Civilities: Indigenous Matters', in S.Venkateswar and E. Hughes (eds), *The Politics of Indigeneity: Dialogues and Reflections on Indigenous Activism*, 45–76, London and New York: Zed Books.

Wakefield, S. (2018), 'Inhabiting the Anthropocene Back Loop', *Resilience*, 6 (2): 77–94.

Wakefield S. and B. Braun (2018), 'Oystertecture: Infrastructure, Profanation and the Sacred Figure of the Human', in K. Hetherington (ed.), *Infrastructure, Environment, and Life in the Anthropocene*, 193–215, Durham, NC: Duke University Press.

Wakefield, S., D. Chandler and K. Grove (2022), 'The Asymmetrical Anthropocene: Resilience and the Limits of Posthumanism', *Cultural Geographies*, 29 (3): 389–404.

Wakefield, S., J. Grove and D. Chandler (2020), 'Introduction. The Power of Life', in Wakefield, S., J. Grove and D. Chandler (eds), *Resilience in the Anthropocene. Governance and Politics at the End of the World*, 1–21, London and New York: Routledge.

Walker, J. and M. Cooper (2011), 'Genealogies of Resilience: From Systems Ecology to the Political Economy of Crisis Adaptation', *Security Dialogue*, 42: 143–60.

Walsh, C. (2010), 'Development as Buen Vivir: Institutional Arrangements and (de) Colonial Entanglements', *Development*, 53 (1): 15–21.

Waters, C. N., J. Zalasiewicz, C. P. Summerhayes and A. Barnosky (2016), 'The Anthropocene is Functionally and Stratigraphically Distinct from the Holocene', *Science*, 351 (6269): 137–47.

Watson, A. (2013), 'Misunderstanding the "Nature" of Co-management: A Geography of Regulatory Science and Indigenous Knowledges (IK)', *Environmental Management*, 52: 1085–102.

Watts, V. (2013), 'Indigenous Place-thought & Agency Amongst Humans and Non-humans (First Woman and Sky Woman go on a European World Tour!)', *Decolonization: Indigeneity, Education & Society*, 2 (1): 20–34.

Whitten, N. E. and D. S. Whitten (2015), 'Clashing Concepts of the "Good Life": Beauty, Knowledge, and Vision versus National Wealth in Amazonian Ecuador', in F. Santos-Granero (ed.), *Images of Public Wealth or the Anatomy of Well-Being in Indigenous Amazonia*, 191–215, Tucson, AZ: University of Arizona Press.

Whittenmore, M. E. (2011), 'The Problem of Enforcing Nature's Rights under Ecuador's Constitution: Why the 2008 Environmental Amendments Have No Bite', *Pacific Rim Law & Policy Journal*, 20: 659–91.

Whyte, K. P. (2017a) 'Food Sovereignty, Justice and Indigenous Peoples: An Essay on Settler Colonialism and Collective Continuance', in A. Barnhill, T. Doggett and E. Egan (eds), *Oxford Handbook on Food Ethics*, 345–66, Oxford: Oxford University Press.

Whyte, K. P. (2017b), 'Indigenous Climate Change Studies: Indigenizing Futures, Decolonizing the Anthropocene', *English Language Notes*, 55 (1–2): 153–62.

Whyte, K. P. (2018a), 'Indigenous Science (Fiction) for the Anthropocene: Ancestral Dystopias and Fantasies of Climate Change Crises', *Environment and Planning E: Nature and Space*, 1 (2): 224–42.

Whyte, K. P. (2018b), 'What Do Indigenous Knowledges Do for Indigenous Peoples?' in M. K. Nelson and D. Shilling (eds), *Traditional Ecological Knowledge Learning from Indigenous Practices for Environmental Sustainability*, 57–82, Cambridge: Cambridge University Press.

Whyte, K. P., J. P. Brewer and J. T. Johnson (2016), 'Weaving Indigenous Science, Protocols and Sustainability Science', *Sustainability Science*, 11 (1): 25–32.

Whyte, K. P., C. M. Caldwell and M. Schefer (2017), 'Indigenous Lessons about Sustainability Are Not Only for All Humanity', in J. Sze (ed.), *Situating Sustainability and Social Justice*, 149–79, New York: New York University Press.

Williams, C. (2012), 'Introduction', in C. Williams (ed.), *Indigenous Women and Work: from Labor to Activism*, 1–26, Urbana, Chicago and Springfield, IL: University of Illinois Press.

Williams, R. (2019), 'Afterword', in *This Is Not a Drill. An Extinction Rebellion Handbook*, 283–9.

Willow, A. J. (2009), 'Clear-Cutting and Colonialism: The Ethnopolitical Dynamics of Indigenous Environmental Activism in Northwestern Ontario', *Ethnohistory*, 56 (1): 35–67.

Willow, A. J. (2011), 'Activism Conceiving Kakipitatapitmok: The Political Landscape of Anishinaabe Anticlearcutting Activism', *American Anthropologist*, 113 (2): 262–76.

Wood, M. C. (2014), *Nature's Trust: Environmental Law for a New Ecological Age*, Cambridge: Cambridge University Press.

Wood, N. (1984), *John Locke and Agrarian Capitalism*, Berkeley, CA: University of California Press.

Wynter, S. (1979), 'Sambos and Minstrels', *Social Text*, 1 (4): 149–56.

Wynter, S. (2003), 'Unsettling the Coloniality of Being/Power/Truth/Freedom: Towards the Human, After Man, Its Overrepresentation – An Argument', *The New Centennial Review*, 3 (3): 257–37.

Wynter, S. and K. McKittrick (2015), 'Unparalleled Catastrophe for Our Species? Or, to Give Humanness a Different Future: Conversations', in K. McKittrick (ed.), *Sylvia Wynter. On Being Human as Praxis*, 9–89, Durham, NC: Duke University Press.

Yamin, F. (2019), 'Die, Survive or Thrive?' in *This Is Not a Drill. An Extinction Rebellion Handbook*, 41–51.

Yazbeck, J. (2018), 'The Problem with White Veganism', *Medium*, 1 November. Available online: https://julianayaz.medium.com/the-problem-with-white-veganism-f86c0341e2a2 (accessed 17 November 2023).

Yusoff, K. (2019), *A Billion Black Anthropocenes or None*, Minneapolis, MN: University of Minnesota Press.

Zalasiewicz, J. (2015), 'The Geology behind the Anthropocene', *Cosmopolis*. Available online: https://www.cosmopolis-rev.org/pdf/2015-1/Zalasiewicz_Cosmopolis-2015-1.pdf (accessed 17 November 2023).

Zalasiewicz, J., M. Williams, A. Haywood and M. Ellis (2011), 'The Anthropocene: A New Epoch of Geological Time?', *Philosophical Transactions of the Royal Society A*, 369 (1938): 835–41.

Zelle, A. R., G. Wilson, A. Rachelle and H. Greene (2021), *Earth Law: Emerging Ecocentric Law – A Guide for Practitioners*, Boston, MA: Aspen Publishing.

Index